Gender Norms
& Intersectionality

Gender Norms
& Intersectionality

Connecting Race, Class, & Gender

Riki Wilchins

ROWMAN &
LITTLEFIELD
INTERNATIONAL

London • New York

Published by Rowman & Littlefield International, Ltd.
6 Tinworth Street, London, SE11 5AL, UK
www.rowmaninternational.com

Rowman & Littlefield International Ltd. is an affiliate of Rowman & Littlefield
4501 Forbes Boulevard, Suite 200, Lanham, Maryland 20706, USA
With additional offices in Boulder, New York, Toronto (Canada), and Plymouth (UK)
www.rowman.com

British Library Cataloguing in Publication Data
A catalogue record for this book is available from the British Library

ISBN: HB 978-1-78661-083-6
     PB: 978-1-78661-084-3

Library of Congress Cataloging-in-Publication Data Available

ISBN: 978-1-78661-083-6 (cloth : alk. paper)
ISBN: 978-1-78661-084-3 (pbk. : alk. paper)
ISBN: 978-1-78661-085-0 (electronic)

∞™ The paper used in this publication meets the minimum requirements of American
National Standard for Information Sciences—Permanence of Paper for Printed Library
Materials, ANSI/NISO Z39.48-1992.

Printed in the United States of America

*To Gina and Dylan Jade—you are my life. Thank you for tolerating
the long hours devoted to writing this book instead of to you.*

Appreciation

I'd like to express special thanks to Dhara Snowden at Rowman & Littlefield International for being the first among dozens of editors I approached to "see" how a book devoted to gender norms could work, and then for championing this book and making it possible; to Camilla Saly, for her endless edits, ideas for strengthening (and trimming!) my text, and continual funny, funky asides that kept me in stitches during manuscript re-editing (my least favorite thing); and to Kevin McElrath, for his patient proofreading, researching studies, and work on chapter references. I would particularly like to thank TrueChild's present and past board members, especially our current cochairs—Jules de la Cruz and Cynthia Neff—who have stuck with this work through the years and patiently nurtured its growth: thank you for believing in me and the vision. Finally, I'd like to express my personal appreciation to Barbara D., whose support was pivotal in providing the time and space to write this book, something every author needs and so many fail to get—thank you!

Contents

Foreword

Why This Book

About three decades ago, I began searching restlessly for tools that might help me comprehend the immensity of disapproval and hostility that my transitioning from male to female had begun arousing in others. I had a strong emotional reaction to what was happening to me of course, but I wanted ideas—a framework for understanding it as well. Like most of us, I grew up never really questioning the idea of distinct, binary genders. Yet I found myself brought into daily and often harsh conflict with it. But my search was not going well. This was a time when transsexuals ("transgender" had not been coined yet) were still virtually unknown, and widely considered weird and deviant.

What I found were mostly antitransgender diatribes from self-described "radical feminists," or else medical texts describing my psychiatric "disorder." Both were stigmatizing and personally painful, if in very different ways. There were a few early and very earnest autobiographies by transsexual authors, clearly aimed not at helping me understand myself, but rather at a cisgender (that is, nontransgender) audience, clearly hoping to win greater tolerance from a skeptical and hostile world.

I did find many feminist texts critiquing "the patriarchy" that looked promising at first. But they were not critiques of binary genders *per se*, but merely with that system's very unequal distribution of power and privilege. None of them seemed interested in looking "upstream" to question the very idea of binary man/woman—an idea that my body was busy transgressing.

Even transsexual authors took binary genders as a natural, God-given property of bodies. Male/female, man/woman, masculine/feminine—these were the starting points for all discussion, not the basis for dialog and inspection.

None of these books provided much in the way of tools to help me think through the daily crisis I was in, trapped in the fissures and fault lines of a gender system that had no place for my (now) very queer transitioning body that was just beginning the rounds of hormones, electrolysis, and surgery.

A Language I Could Not Hear

As I was complaining about all this, a lesbian friend casually suggested, "Check out Judith Butler."

Knowing nothing about this Butler person, and even less about esoteric academic trends like postmodernism or deconstruction, I bought her seminal book, *Gender Trouble: Feminism and the Subversion of Identity* . . . twice. Both times I threw it away in frustration—the second time literally against my living room wall, unable to decipher prose that seemed crafted to repel human understanding.

Perhaps the average graduate-school professor was familiar with the "self-referential signifying practices of the prevailing phallogocentric economy," with its "inevitable tropes and metaphors of hetero-normativity." But I had no idea what that meant. There is a reason this kind of writing is mockingly dismissed as *pomobabble* (e.g., postmodern newspeak).

I could not yet know that this sometimes maddening book was written for me. Judith Butler was speaking to me, but I couldn't yet hear what she was saying.

It wasn't just the dense, academic phrases; she was speaking a language I could not yet hear. I was simply unprepared for the kind of arguments Butler was making. Yet it's no exaggeration to say that over time, this book would remake my life. So please permit me a brief digression here, before we get to the main (and I promise much less "wonky") part of this book.

"Queer theory," deconstruction, and postmodernism do not tell us what we should think, but rather they are a set of tools for identifying and then dismantling what we do think and why. They are particularly good at taking apart what we might call the modern "self"—that amalgam of beliefs about who we are and what our bodies mean that determines how we experience ourselves in the world. This includes how we think of ourselves as inhabiting our various identities, as Black or White, female or male, gay or straight, normatively gendered or transgendered, and so forth.

These kinds of identities and ways of understanding our bodies seem natural, timeless, even inevitable—which make them very powerful—but they are anything but. All of them are socially constructed. They arise at particular places and times, and fulfill particular cultural needs. We are meaning-making animals. And one of the first meanings we make is for one another's bodies, particularly qualities like gender, and, of course, race.

Queer theory—that offspring of the marriage of feminism and gay theory—is concerned with difference: how certain kinds of bodies are acceptable, while others get silenced and marginalized. Like mine.

The "facts" of binary genders—that little girls are naturally sugar and spice, wear pink, and are everything nice, and that boys are naturally strong, aggressive, and wear black, gray, and blue—are not inevitable aspects of bodies, but rather meanings we invent and agree upon. Such meanings are constructed on our bodies literally from birth. In one famous experiment, when parents were given a crying infant and told it was a girl, they responded, "Awww . . . she's scared," or "She's sad," and began soothing her. When they were told it was a boy, they'd respond, "Oh, he's angry," and began bouncing him. Even with identical size and weight, parents consistently report babies identified as female as softer and more delicate and males as bigger and stronger.

Binary gender is such a widely accepted system that it is only with those bodies that don't fit that one can see its true operation. What Butler was saying was that the taunts I was now getting from total strangers about whether I was *really* male or female, the sniggers, pointing, and ridicule when I went out wearing a dress, the glares and sometimes outright harassment—all these were not just about whether my tall, perpetually lanky body was a woman's, but rather about a failure of meaning. They were about my body's inability to "do" femininity according to the category's rules, and people's instant and surprisingly strong hostility to that failure. They were symptoms of a system striking back, suppressing difference in order to maintain itself.

They were also signs that a system that put itself forward as universal and natural had some pretty big holes in it. The issue wasn't whether transbodies like mine "really" were boy or girl, but rather how the entire system worked to impose rigid boy/girl on everyone, and suppressed any bodies that didn't fit.

It seemed weird that anything apparently so natural and inevitable had to work so hard to maintain itself, and had so many exceptions to deal with.

The Research

What Butler was trying to explain was that the gender system was less about authenticity and what bodies like mine "really" were, and more about power: about who sets the rules, which bodies are elevated as "normal," and which ones are disempowered through ridicule and shame.

I could certainly see this kind of power exercised in real-time. It was apparent whenever I would try to join a women's or lesbian group and was refused entry, or had my presence be voted on by the "real women," or be evicted by them. Sometimes all three. This was a game, a game of meaning, and legitimacy. And it was clearly one I could never win, because the rules were rigged against bodies like mine. The only possible strategy to pursue was to attack the rules, in hopes of playing a different game. This was something for which queer theory was admirably suited. The more I learned, the more I became angry, and then politicized. As I dug into it, I was finally able to make sense of the hostility and rejection my body seemed to arouse. In 1995, I launched the one of the first trans street action groups—"The Transexual Menace" (*sic*). Then, in 1996, with a number of other activists, I helped launch the first national trans political advocacy organization (GenderPAC). Over time, leading the Menace and then GenderPAC made me fairly popular within the trans (and gay) communities.

Moreover, I began to see that the problem of rigid gender norms wasn't limited to only LGBTQ people. I increasingly saw binary gender norms as a system that shaped all of us, offering social rewards to those who conformed to its fixed ideals, while punishing the slightest deviancy, even the smallest sign of masculinity in women or of femininity in men.

Particularly in childhood, when we're most unsure of ourselves and most psychologically vulnerable, gender norms have an immense effect on nearly everything: depression, dieting, body image, substance abuse, course selection at school, color selection in clothing, who we bully on the playground, how we engage in intimacy or sex. Gender norms oppress gender nonconforming trans and gay people, but also 90 percent of people who mostly conform to gender norms. The often harsh and more visible effects on transgender people are only a fraction of much broader and subtler effects on everyone. Transpeople were, to stretch the metaphor, the canary in the gender mineshaft. If the prevailing gender culture brutalizes transkids, what might it be doing to everyone else?

Challenging the system of gender norms and trying to change it seemed an important, even vital thing to attempt. Looking for evidence and hard data to support this idea, I spent five years devouring academic studies and papers. What I found astonished me. Decades of studies had documented the impact of rigid gender norms in areas like health, education, school violence, the arts, and economic empowerment. The effects of gender norms were particularly important among adolescents. Other than some very exciting physical changes, one of the key tasks of puberty is growing into and mastering one's assigned gender role: learning to "do" masculinity in boys and femininity in girls. And as we will explore later, these impacts could often be amplified in low-income communities.

My discoveries in the academic literature were deeply confirming, yet also deeply troubling. Where was the impact of all these studies on public policy, funding priorities, school curricula, and nonprofit programming for young people? As the parent of an energetic, bright, girl-identified child, I wondered where were all the toolkits, websites, and books to help us explore such issues with our children? Where were the tools to teach young people to think critically about rigid, often harmful gender norms?

Yet few if any of the hundreds of articles, chapters, and books devoted to queer theory that I'd consumed seemed to have much (if anything) to say about its practical application in areas like public policy, philanthropy, or programs for youth.

The Response

In large part this is because queer theory is a marvelous theoretical toolkit for taking dialogs apart. But—because it equates structure and organizing with oppressing those who don't fit—is utterly unable to suggest how to build anything or put another together, like an organization, much less a social movement or a public policy.

Hence, in Butler's second book, *Undoing Gender,* she was unable to recommend much more than small, private, individual acts of gender insubordination as a model of resistance. This is admirable, even useful. Individual acts of rebellion (especially if they are widely adopted) can be important in confounding large systems like gender (just look at #MeToo or #BlackLivesMatter).

Indeed, today it is increasingly common to see young people identifying as *boychix, nonbinary, genderqueer, pan, tryke, demigirl, nonbinary, AG, boi,* and so on in addition to many other new identities that their elders have neither heard of nor imagined. Facebook famously now offers over four dozen gender identifications users can select.

But I'm not convinced. Small, disorganized, atomistic acts of insubordination hardly seem equal to the task at hand. Today, we are finally beginning to recognize what might be called "genderism," like we now recognize racism and homophobia. Gender is a systemic oppression; successfully contesting it will likely require a systemic response.

In fact, because the intolerance, oppression, and marginalization caused by the gender system are so pervasive, perhaps we need a new term—"structural genderism"—similar to the way we've learned to speak of "structural racism." Can we develop a movement that can undo structural genderism's effects? And do so in ways that connect gender with other systems of oppression, like race and class? As stated earlier, on this question, all those academic studies and gender theory books are silent.

Perhaps we need a new field, one that, for lack of a better term, might be called "Applied Gender Studies." I hope that this book, *Gender Norms and Intersectionality,* can become a first step in that direction.

I believe that if we can help public agencies, youth-serving nonprofits, funders, schools, and parents to address gender norms, we can raise healthier, better educated, more authentic, happier, and ultimately more mentally resilient young people: ones who do not grow up shoe-horning themselves into boxes labeled STRONG BOY and PRETTY GIRL, who do not bully those who don't fit, or ridicule those of us who are different.

Building Bridges

I hope this book will build an overdue bridge between theory and real-world practice, in ways that will inform those tasked with raising, educating, and protecting young people.

I think this might require our expanding some of our more models for thinking about gender and equality. One of these—Diversity, Equity, and Inclusion (DEI)—is widely used, and has been successfully employed by many organizations. Generally speaking, "Diversity" is about being part of something, "Inclusion" about participating fully in it, and "Equity" refers to addressing structural disparities that prevent some from having a level field for their participation.

As a transperson who often has been left (or pushed) out, I get the importance of diversity, but DEI can also devolve into (not to disparage) a simplified "check-the-box" approach to inclusion. It also depends on identities that are already present and able to pursue their own inclusion (i.e., women's rights, gay rights, etc.). DEI appears to work less well with small, emergent minorities or more complex ones which don't fit our models. Fortunately, queer theory addresses much of the former, and intersectionality the latter.

Intersectionality (about which much more later) attempts to remedy some of the problems that arise with DEI is oversimplified. It asks us to look for those identities which we might not see because they are more complex than our boxes. For instance, someone who is young *and* lesbian *and* Hispanic *and* low-income *and* recently immigrated.

This is certainly a more complex and nuanced approach that holds up those of us who of live at the boundaries of identity, where categories overlap. And there is always overlap. To paraphrase David Eng's wonderful insight from his book, *Racial Castration: Managing Masculinity in Asian America*—racial oppression is always gendered, and gender oppression is always raced.

However, somewhat like DEI, intersectionality appears to depend on identities which are already tied somewhere into our existing frameworks of analysis, and thus have sufficient agency to announce themselves and demand inclusion and equity.

This is where queer theory comes in handy. Queer theory is concerned with profound difference, with those identities so oppressed and marginalized that they have been erased and are off the grid of social intelligibility. Thus, they are unable to speak their own name, or to demand political recognition and inclusion, much less any sort of equality.

Seven decades ago, this would have included *homosexuals*; just four or five decades ago, it would have included *transsexuals* ("transgender" was still rare). Today, those who identify as intersex or nonbinary might be examples.

These three great equity discourses are not yet entirely on speaking terms with one another. But they need to be. Because each describes a different "part of the elephant," a critical aspect of equity. And we will likely need them all if we are to think more effectively about something as complex as gender.

Unfortunately, none of the really has much to say about gender norms yet (although queer theory deals extensively with nonconformity). Perhaps this is because these models, like our social justice politics, tend to conceptualize social problems in terms of identities and equity.

But the impacts of rigid gender norms affect nearly everyone, so there is no single excluded group to raise questions of inclusion or diversity And while it is this very universality which makes addressing rigid gender norms so urgent, it also means there is no comparison group which might give rise to claims of inequality.

One way to think about this is that rigid gender regimes tend to make all of us less equal to what we might otherwise have been. But this idea makes little sense in terms of our current equity frameworks, which don't do well with universalist forms of oppression, or those not tied to a single identity.

A human rights model would certainly help here, but although international groups use this, it has yet to catch on here in the US. So perhaps thinking about more intentionally gender norms will mean changing, combining, and even expanding our current framework.

With that said, this is very much an applied and not a theoretical book. While you will hear echoes of each of these—DEI, intersectionality, queer theory—at various places, my main goal is to provide you, the reader, with a grounding in the basic terms, concepts, and findings around gender norms and offer some concrete suggestions and examples for how you might actually apply them.

Reading This Book

You need have no particular expertise in gender to read this book, just an open mind. I suspect in many parts, you'll realize that you're already familiar with many of the main research findings, even if you hadn't always considered them from an applied standpoint.

The book is divided into three parts. The first part provides a grounding in the basic ideas and terms related to gender. It also surveys the work of international NGOs and funders, who are often years ahead of their American counterparts, and who often have been thought-leaders on gender norms and their effects on social, health, and educational outcomes.

The second part delves into specific problem areas like education, reproductive health, LGBTQ issues and school bullying, and basic health and wellness—all areas where there is longstanding and extensive academic and theoretical evidence for the impact of gender norms. You may find you want to skip some sections but focus in on those which are most relevant or interesting for you.

Where possible, I have also tried to underline where gender norms have not only "bottom up" effects on youth who buy into them, but also "top down" effects on the systems that serve them. Because the systems we have built to serve our young people—schools, courts, churches or temples, foster care, hospitals, juvenile courts—are also deeply gendered and gendering institutions, and the adults who populate them have also internalized and often, consciously or unconsciously, enforced the same rigid, binary genders when it comes to young people in their care.

The third part presents a deeper dive into the impact of rigid gender norms in specific at-risk populations, with an emphasis on connecting with race and class. These chapters are drawn from white paper reports created by my nonprofit True-Child and its strategic partners.

Wherever possible, I've tried to provide specific examples and leaven the text with insights from my personal experience. Most chapters end with examples drawn from actual programs and groups doing leading work on the ground.

Who Should Read This Book

I've tried to make this book as accessible as possible for the nontechnical reader: educators, nonprofit staff, parents, funders, and policy makers. So I've tried to make the basic, core arguments about gender, avoiding dense footnotes, and keeping citations to a minimum. Where I do cite studies, it's often pivotal ones that broke new ground in our thinking about norms, rather than the very newest. Readers who want to dig deeper into newer data will find references following each chapter.

This book is the culmination of a long and seldom straight trip from my first floundering attempts to understand gender back in 1978. I hope you enjoy it.

Riki Wilchins
September 2018

I

UNDERSTANDING GENDER NORMS

1

A Gender Vacuum

Our grantees and staff get race and class; some are even starting to get sexual orientation. What I want to know is—what happened to gender? Where is the gender analysis?

—Vice president, major US foundation

We're starting to relate things that were not related before. Eating disorders in girls, obsession with boys . . . the very few women who are running Jewish communities, and very few Jewish female role models for girls. It's all becoming part of one big story that's actually undermining our girls and our dreams for our girls.

—Jewish mother in Chicago, Illinois

It's not safe to be any kind of Black man in America.

—Micah Gilmer, Frontline Solutions

In 1990, as the AIDS epidemic was beginning its long and deadly detonation in the American population, the Centers for Disease Control and Prevention (CDC) convened forty leading authorities on youth of color and reproductive health for a day-long retreat in El Paso, Texas.

Their task was to review the current state of knowledge and return with concrete recommendations for new steps that the CDC, and indeed the field itself, should take in response. They spent a day and a half in discussion and dialogue.

The speech by Hortensia Amaro that resulted from that meeting was called "Gender and Sexual Risk Reduction: Issues to Consider" (1994). It and the more formal journal paper created from it, "Love, Sex Power: Considering Women's Realities in HIV Prevention" (1995), have since been cited over a thousand times. In fact, it may be one of the most-cited reproductive-health policy statements ever.

Amaro, a leading researcher, pointed out that, despite the investment of hundreds of millions of dollars, HIV rates among youth of color continued to spiral upward, and prevention efforts had largely failed.

Surprisingly, a major reason for this failure was that prevention had focused mainly on providing accurate health information about prevention and consequences to those at risk. Moreover, the prevention models in use were designed as if each young person was an independent, isolated social unit.

Young people are often embedded in dense social networks. Their early sexual encounters can be subject to immense social pressures and expectations from peers, family members, and so on. So knowledge alone, Amaro pointed out, was almost always ineffective in changing behavior, particularly in something that can be as impulsive and emotionally laden as sex.

For young women, having safer sex was inseparable from the inequalities inherent in heterosexual sex, where boys are usually some combination of larger, stronger, older, and more aggressive.

Programs, policies, and funding models took little account of these realities, which can be important to young people engaging in sex for the first time. Operating out of ignorance and a lack of personal experience, their behavior is likely to be defined by attitudes and prejudices they have absorbed from family members, friends, religious institutions, and the media about what girls or boys are supposed to do in sexual encounters. This is true when these beliefs are clearly grounded in outdated gender stereotypes. We think of sex as the most *natural* of acts. Yet in sex it is gender that determines who does what to whom—when, how, and for what reason.

Who is empowered to "make the first move"; who "gets on top"; who is responsible for preventing conception; what positions or acts are obligatory or forbidden, allowed, or abnormal; who brags afterward; and who is gossiped about and what others might say about them—all of this is gender.

In fact, as we will explore in the chapter on sexual and reproductive health, gender norms affect not only actual foreplay and intercourse, but nearly everything connected to them, including condom negotiation, risk-taking, infidelity, body awareness and pleasure, romance, pregnancy and infant or maternal health, sexual coercion or consent, and intimate partner violence (IPV).

"A Gender Vacuum"

The report from the more than forty experts concluded that the field had been operating "in a gender vacuum." The most important thing the CDC and other leading agencies could do was to adopt a strong, specific focus on rigid gender norms and the inequalities they cause—because this was the biggest single factor, which continued to be ignored, in improving reproductive health outcomes. This was a pretty stunning conclusion—perhaps especially so because gender had already been the target of so much social and academic attention.

In fact, by the mid-1990s, the United States and many developed countries had seen nearly three decades of social upheaval around gender issues. Beginning in the 1960s and 1970s, the rise of women's rights and feminism helped instill a new awareness of the distinction between sex and gender in the United States and many other developed countries.

Barely a decade later, the gay rights movement of the early 1970s exploded in the United States, with gay theorists and academics questioning nearly every aspect of heterosexuality and man/woman relationships.

It was Simone de Beauvoir, a French feminist theorist, who famously declared that, "One is not born a woman, but becomes one."

What she meant was that the behaviors, attitudes, appearance, and privilege that went with being a woman were not a result of the biological facts of being born female, but were learned and imposed, and thus socially determined.

In 1971, pioneering researcher Sandra Bem even developed her Sex-Role Inventory to measure how well individuals fit with common gender stereotypes: for example, I am . . . *tender*, *aggressive*, *competitive*, and so on. But it really wasn't until the mid-1990s, with the advent of "queer theory"—the child of the intellectual marriage among feminism, gay rights, and transgender rights—that a full-throated critique and "deconstruction" of gender roles and norms finally took hold.

Academics and researchers began excavating the myriad ways that gendered attitudes and beliefs shaped nearly every aspect of our appearance, feelings, and behavior. This was an important breakthrough, but it also raised an interesting question. Was there any practical, real-world value to such knowledge?

Fortunately, an innovative social science researcher named Joseph Pleck at the University of Illinois had been examining exactly this issue.

Measuring Manhood, Measuring Health

Building on the groundbreaking work of Sandra Bem, an early (and as it turned out prescient) pioneer on gender roles and norms, Pleck developed and refined a survey that measured the strength of men's belief in key facets of traditional masculinity, such as strength, dominance, and aggression. He named this amalgam of beliefs and attitudes Masculinity Ideology, and his new inventory, the Male Role Norms Scale (MRNS).

This alone would have been a huge advance. But what he did next really changed our understanding of gender and helped reinvent the field of gender study.

Pleck wanted to do more than simply measure normative gender beliefs; he wanted to map these beliefs directly onto real-world health outcomes. What he needed was a large, truly random sample of young people on which to test his ideas. But these are difficult to find, and expensive to recruit. Luckily, Pleck had the ideal partner.

Working in close partnership with the Urban Institute, Pleck developed the National Survey of Adolescent Males, a highly randomized sample of two thousand young men. It was used to investigate young men's behavior and attitudes on a wide variety of attitudes and behaviors, including health and sexuality. Beginning in 1988, Pleck decided to test a version of his MRNS on the National Survey sample to see whether it would enable him to relate belief in traditional masculinity with actual sexual and reproductive health and risk-taking. (He has since run this test every ten years, and the original boys are now in their thirties.)

What Pleck found changed—or perhaps more accurately, helped create—the science of gender norms research. Stronger belief in traditional masculinity was linked to a host of key outcomes, including:

- less-intimate sexual relationships;
- more sexual partners;
- more unsafe sex;
- stronger belief in sex as adversarial;
- stronger belief in pregnancy as validating manhood;
- weaker belief in male responsibility to help prevent pregnancy; and
- less likelihood of seeking medical care.

In effect, he found, a checklist for lower reproductive and sexual health outcomes among young, straight males—a list that was not just for revealing for them, but for their female partners as well.

Since then, Pleck's work has been validated and extended many times. And the map of impacts from rigid masculine norms has proven to be surprisingly extensive and robust.

It would not be until 2000 that another leading academic—Deborah Tolman of Hunter College in New York City—would coin the symmetrical term "Femininity Ideology," and begin the work of devising what she termed an Adolescent Femininity Ideology Scale (AFIS) to measure aspects of feminine norms.

Exhaustive Research

Amaro's and Pleck's groundbreaking work is now almost a quarter century old. Since then, a wave of studies, books, and scholarly articles have confirmed their key finding: that when young women and men buy into narrow codes of masculinity or femininity, they have markedly lower life outcomes.

To illustrate, below are studies returned in 2018 from Google Scholar searches on masculinity and:

- HIV   23,500;
- Violence Against Women   20,200;
- Teen Pregnancy   1,920.

And searches on femininity and:

- HIV   13,900;
- Violence Against Women   13,800;
- Teen Pregnancy   1,370.

In each case, over a thousand and, in some cases, tens of thousands of articles are returned. To be fair, this is completely unscientific: Google Scholar is an *extremely* blunt instrument, returning references to studies that only mention a given search term, but may be otherwise be off point.

Despite that, perhaps these numbers provide at least an extremely rough sense of just how broadly ideas of gender have permeated the field of research and been touched upon by researchers. In fact, the field of gender norms study is by now so well-tilled that many of the original researchers consider it settled and have moved on to other subjects where there are still new things to uncover.

Last time I spoke with her, Amaro was studying substance abuse among women of color; and Pleck—even while planning to analyze his fourth decade of Urban Institute data—had moved on to studying fatherhood.

The Disconnect

With more than two decades of research showing gender norms as the original "mother lode" of unaddressed vectors for worse health outcomes, you would expect them to be at the very center of funding and policy making. And to a large degree you would be right—just not so much in the United States. As Loren Harris, surely among the United States' most insightful and deliberate program officers when it comes to racial justice, has noted: "Gender impacts every issue US funders address, but program officers and grantees are seldom challenged to do innovative grantmaking around gender like they are with race and class."

It's a similar story with government agencies and policy makers. For example, in 2012, TrueChild was invited to the White House to deliver a briefing on gender norms for the Office of National AIDS Policy and the Domestic Policy Council.

While I was pleased and honored, I couldn't help but recall that CDC retreat in 1990, and Amaro's oft-cited diagnosis of a "gender vacuum" in HIV policy. Even as I addressed this collection of national-level policy makers, I was painfully aware that nowhere in the Obama White House's sixty-page *National HIV/AIDS Strategy for the United States* were the words "gender norms," "masculinity," or "femininity."

Despite thousands of studies on norms and virtually every aspect of reproductive health—age of first sex, number of partners, sexual risk-taking, condom use, sexual coercion, partner violence, teen pregnancy, and STD transmission—White House policy makers still found it a novel idea that gender norms were a major variable in sexual behavior. So novel, that they invited us to do this briefing. And this was nearly a half-century into the AIDS epidemic.

Gentle reader, this is what a research policy disconnect looks like.

Nor was the problem limited to "pointed-headed" policy makers, deep in the federal government, who are insulated from the real world. Later that same year, a manager at the CDC invited me and a TrueChild director, Beverly Guy-Sheftall, to do a gender training, open to their entire staff.

Beverly is the founder of the Women's Center at Spelman College, and a big part of the reason that many people consider Spelman to be head-and-shoulders ahead of most of the other HBCUs (Historically Black Colleges and Universities) when it comes to women's and LGBTQ issues. Beverly has written and edited books on gender norms in African American communities, and I doubt she spent, or needed, a moment of preparation.

I, on the other hand, was terrified. We were about to march into the CDC—arguably the world's leading health and disease institution—and tell them (in so many words), "Sorry, but, umm . . . you guys missed this incredibly big and really obvious variable that is backed by thousands of studies for which your sister department of Health and Human Services has been paying for decades."

Even worse, I'm not even a PhD, I'm a *civilian*. So I fully I expected a hostile, indignant crowd, gunning for us to get shot down for our sheer hubris. I spent several days beforehand identifying and printing out pivotal papers and studies, so we could pull them out quickly once we were under fire.

But no pushback ever materialized. Instead, what we got was a packed crowd of about two hundred CDC staffers who hosted an hour-long love-in. They kept asking, "This is so important—why aren't we doing more about it?" And I kept answering, "You're the CDC—why *aren't* you doing more about it?"

They didn't even let us go after we were done. Instead, they took Beverly and me around to each department impacted by our arguments: the Division of Violence Prevention, the Division of Adolescent and School Health, the Division of HIV/AIDS Prevention, the Division of STD Prevention, Division of Violence Prevention—where we essentially repeated our presentation, each time with different emphasis, but with virtually the same warm reception.

On a personal level, I was elated. Here we were telling the mighty CDC that it had missed something very big and very important and very obvious, and having it agree. Yet on a purely professional level, it was also shocking.

Put bluntly, this institution had paid for one of the world's most-cited papers on how to more effectively combat a deadly disease, and then largely ignored its findings for two decades during what was arguably one of the worst epidemics the United States has experienced. And this remains largely true of the field as a whole in the United States today.*

A "Revolution of the Obvious"

Our experience with the CDC illustrates how difficult it can be to get people to recognize and address the impact of harmful gender norms in the United States and many other developed nations.

Even worse, all the thousands of studies done on gender norms don't establish a single fact about masculinity or femininity that most of us didn't all suspect from middle school or from having an adolescent at home.

For example, we pretty much already know that the boy who acted tough, smoked and drank to show how adult he was, bragged about his sexual conquests, bullied the gay kids, and got in trouble with teachers (not to mention the occasional cop) was trying too hard to prove his masculinity, and was probably destined for some sort of trouble. This is why I call educating folks about the impact of gender norms a "Revolution of the Obvious." You're mostly telling them what they already know.

In fact, theory and research have firmly linked harmful gender norms to a cluster of related problems, including reproductive and sexual health (such as unplanned pregnancy, condom use, and HIV); partner violence; school violence and LGBTQ bullying; mental health and substance abuse; academic underachievement (including school "pushouts" and science and math underachievement); and problems with basic health and wellness.

This pattern has led some on the international front to begin referring to gender norms as a "gateway belief system," underlining the idea that once young people internalize rigid gender ideals, they have increased vulnerability to worse life outcomes in a cluster of related areas.

Part of the reason this "revolution" is still in its infancy is that academia does a terrible job of incentivizing the use of its own findings. Academics, living in the world of "publish or perish," are mostly rewarded for original research that advances study itself, rather than being rewarded for applying their findings to real-world situations. Thus the "messiness" of implementing community-based programs, changing

---

* In a very encouraging move, in the Spring of 2016, the CDC quietly made its first three large grants to study the effects of gender norms. Interestingly, they were all in partner violence, which is the one area where there are a substantial number of US groups working in the field that really *get* gender norms. The grants were noncompetitive and simply made as awards. I suspect this is because the CDC knew that the usual committees of leading scholars and advocates who judge grant applications might not have sufficient knowledge and comfort with the area of gender norms to do the job, and they might also lack familiarity because there hasn't been as big of a pool of potential grantees doing gender norms work.

funding priorities, or wading into protracted public policy debates must often take a back seat to the next research study.

So while our researchers continue churning out studies, papers, and books, their insights circulate endlessly within academic silos, never emerging to impact the institutions that need and might actually implement their proposed changes.

Sometimes the disconnect between US policy and funding makers and their international peers can be especially jarring. At the 2012 International Conference on AIDS in Washington, DC, I was pleased to see a special session scheduled on "Gender Norms and HIV Prevention."

Alas, the presenters—and audience—turned out to be all the "usual suspects" on the international HIV front—the US Agency for International Development (USAID), the Joint United Nations Programme on HIV/AIDS (UNAIDS), the World Health Organization (WHO), Sonke Gender Justice (South Africa), Promundo (Brazil), and so forth. Other than TrueChild, I didn't meet another domestic-facing organization in the room that night. Yet we were just a stone's throw from some of the biggest US agencies, donor institutions, and policy-making organizations.

The United States Lags Behind

In 2013, I spoke with Douglas Kirby, a giant of the field and the author of *Emerging Answers 2007: Research Findings on Programs to Reduce Teen Pregnancy and Sexually Transmitted Diseases.* It was in many ways the "bible" of US teen-pregnancy-prevention efforts. I asked how he could write more than two hundred pages on teen sexual behavior without once mentioning masculinity or femininity. He replied that they were paid to evaluate programs, and they couldn't find any with a strong focus on gender norms and good data to evaluate. Once again, that's what a real research and policy disconnect looks like.

As it turns out, the word "masculinity" actually does appear in *Emerging Answers*—in footnote #295 in the title of Joe Pleck's landmark paper about Masculinity Ideology. (To be fair, *Emerging Answers* does generically mention "peer norms" in several places.)

Even powerful and well-funded social programs and academic models like Social Determinants of Health and Social and Emotional Learning (SEL) completely ignore gender norms and their effects, although gender norms are integral to both.

For instance, none of the SEL funders in the United States of whom I'm aware address gender norms. Intrigued by this, I contacted two leading SEL researchers. I wanted to better understand why the field did not perceive the gendering of young people as one of the most profound aspects of their socialization, and an integral part to their emotional and psychological health. Both used the same adjective in responding to this idea: "interesting,"—it was simply not something they had considered.

Queer Studies and Gender Studies departments must also bear some of the responsibility here (particularly painful to admit, since it is my own area). Gender theorists have done crucial and long-overdue work deconstructing gender roles and explicating the effects of rigid gender regimes in great detail. But they've focused almost entirely on the *political* effects of queerness and difference, ignoring the more prosaic, everyday effects of the gender system the other 95 percent of people who largely *do* conform to masculine and feminine norms.

A New Kind of Power

I suspect that another factor in many people's difficulty in grasping or thinking about gender norms is that personal characteristics like race, sex, or disability are what I call "perceptual givens"—they are things you can actually see, and tend to be properties of individual human beings. But gender norms aren't like that.

Race is an individual characteristic you can see by looking at one person. But norms of masculinity and femininity, while they may be embodied or enacted by a single individual, are the result of shared, communal interaction. And they are invisible, composed of shared beliefs, practices, and attitudes rather than characteristics.

So gender norms have this "squishy" quality that can be very confusing. Moreover, Western ideas of power, particularly on the progressive Left, are rooted in ideas of resistance to centralized abuses of power. So when a law is passed that depresses Black voting, a corporation supports the termination of gay or transgender workers, or a Hispanic person is beaten by a rogue police officer, we know how to respond. This is power that is concrete, visible, centralized, and institutional. We have decades of progressive theory and practice to help us confront this kind of power.

But gender norms don't operate like this. Norms are more like invisible "guard rails" that shape and narrow people's thinking, behaviors, and opportunities. Norms often show up as a kind of negative power, as absence rather than presence: doors that just didn't open, choices that couldn't be made, opportunities that just seemed out of reach.

For instance, next time you're standing in a crowded downtown elevator, try announcing each floor as the elevator passes it. There's no reason not to do so, and doing it is totally harmless. But you will probably feel uncomfortable; your fellow passengers will stare; some will avert their gazes to avoid eye contact. That's a social norm at work.

It's the same kind power I encountered when I was transitioning, every time I tried to buy a newspaper, take the subway, or enter the Ladies Room. For instance, on one of my first days at kindergarten, I saw a little girl from down the block named Mary Jo swinging on the schoolyard swing, with long shiny hair and wearing a frilly white dress. I had on a dark tee-shirt, what were then called "dungarees," and a crew-cut so short and butch it stuck up in front by itself.

I already knew by age six that I wanted to look like Mary Jo, and that in ways I couldn't ever explain to any adult that I already really *was* her. But I also knew somehow that to act on this thing inside me, to speak it publicly, would land me in a world of pain. Standing invisibly between me and Mary Jo were legions: humiliated and enraged parents; an older brother who would be mortally ashamed of me; confused and aggravated school officials; dozens of taunting, bullying, harassing boys; and possibly several doctors.

I knew what I wanted was not normal for a boy, and would not be tolerated in one. And no one had to tell me any of this. As with so many norms, I had been learning them since birth when they gave me a boy name, dressed me in blue, and began telling me how "big and strong" I was.

This kind of power is omnipresent, even if we scarcely notice it. It is the power that passes back and forth constantly among individuals interacting in a given culture. It is what postmodernists call the "discursive power," which we are only beginning to understand. It is not centralized and concrete, but diffuse, capillary, and informal. Thinking about this kind of power entails a major shift, and it's not easy even for those who want to make it.

Lee Roper-Batker, executive director of the Women's Foundation of Minnesota (WFM), has been a true thought-leader in this area. Lee once explained to me that she was deeply convinced of gender norms as a crucial factor in improving women's and girls' equity. Indeed, she led WFM to become one of the United States' first foundations to integrate gender norms into its mission and logic model, but she said felt like whenever she tried to explain them publicly, it felt "like wearing boxing gloves."

This resonant image is not unlike what I frequently hear from funders, educators, policy makers, and parents. Imagine how challenging it can be for everyone else to begin understanding gender norms, especially since "gender" is such an overloaded term in the English language, and connected to so many different ideas—gender identity, gender role, gender equity, and gender mainstreaming among them. In addition, gender touches on so many aspects of our lives and social interaction— as one frustrated major donor explained to me, "Once you start seeing gender, you can't *stop* seeing it."

US Funders

US social-justice funders, many of whom consider issues of race and class as core concerns, are one last part of the problem. In 2012, TrueChild asked Frontline Solutions, a thought-leading consultancy for foundations, to survey major funders that had a strong, explicit focus on gender norms in their philanthropic priorities. After surveying scores of public and private foundations, Frontline was unable to identify even one.

One outstanding exception has been the field of intimate partner and domestic violence, where cutting-edge organizations like A Call to Men, Futures Without Violence, Men As Peacemakers, Men Can Stop Rape, and Promundo/US—as well as Canada's global White Ribbon Campaign—have brought a strong focus of masculinity to bear and often brought funders along with them. In the related field of youth reproductive and sexual health, groups like Advocates for Youth and SIECUS have promoted a strong focus on gender norms.

Another exception that perhaps proves the rule when it comes to funding was the Ford Foundation's US youth portfolio, led by Loren Harris. Over five years in the early 2000s, he directed sustained funding to an array of groups that addressed issues of masculinity among young Black and Latino men, seeding many of the organizations who do this work today, and even publishing a landmark paper entitled "Why We Can't Wait: A Case for Philanthropic Action: Opportunities for Improving Life Outcomes for African American Males" with Frontline Solutions. Among its many important insights was the following: "Gender roles influence the way men understand and engage educational opportunity, labor force participation and relationships with women and other men . . . rigid gender roles limit conceptions of opportunity and success and expose some men to stigmatization, abuse and violence." Yet under a new CEO, Harris' portfolio was not continued.

As of 2015, there were a half-dozen foundations—many of them women's foundations or women-led—that have explicitly made gender norms part of their mission or vision. And there are a number of funders that have made significant grants with a strong gender focus, although these more often result from individual program officers who "get it" than because of any overall shift in institutional vision.

If gender norms are so difficult for some of us to grasp, and *gender* is such an overloaded term in the English language, next we ought to explore it more deeply, and provide a kind of "gender dictionary." Chapter 2 is devoted to just that.

Stories from the Frontlines:
The Simmons Foundation

In 2017, the Simmons Foundation attended one of our gender-norms trainings, hosted at the Houston Endowment. The Simmons Foundation describes its mission as being: "To partner with organizations that strengthen women, youth and families while building an educated, tolerant and resilient community." It is a woman-led funder with a living female donor, and has an exceptionally deep social and racial justice lens, and a strong commitment to LGBTQ issues.

Unique among the foundations I know, Simmons regularly "punches above its weight." Although it has a small funding staff of just two program officers and a tireless CEO, Simmons constantly strives to be a thought-leader in how to improve life in Harris County, Texas. Its staff regularly participates in local initiatives devoted to improving "best practice." They present workshops at conferences, and generally look for more effective ways to do philanthropy. In many ways, they are an object lesson in how funders can leverage their social capital and visibility, shift the dialogue, and inspire, above and beyond simply making grants. So I was especially interested when they contacted us about the possibility of working together.

Most foundations want TrueChild to help their grantees integrate gender into their work. Simmons wanted this, but first they wanted to make sure they were "walking the walk"; they had us train their staff, then their board, and finally conduct a full Gender Audit of every bit of intellectual collateral from the pages on their website to their site-visit protocol. It was pretty impressive.

For the next phase of the project, they had us gather together as many CEOs from their more than one hundred grantees, and put them through a Gender Norms 101 training, which took a morning. Then a dozen or so of these organizations volunteered to do a "deeper dive," one that would help them really integrate gender norms throughout their work.

The Simmons Foundation funds many of the leading nonprofit institutions in the city, so we were privileged to work with groups like Houston Immigration Legal Services Collaborative, the University of Houston Graduate College of Social Work, and the Thurgood Marshall School of Law.

Most of these organizations wanted similar services: toolkits, staff and volunteer trainings, Gender Audits, briefing papers on gender norms and a cross-section of issues, and model curricula with exercises they could do in small groups with young people and/or their parents. Many wanted online modules they could make part of their training of new staff, either around LGBTQ issues or cultural competence (one organization noted that their clients speak some seventy different languages).

The vision Simmons implemented was to provide in-depth, long-term capacity building and support to help these core grantees become thought-leaders—what I sometimes call the "Gender Jedi"—in implement race-class-gender work, and models for the rest of their grants portfolio, and indeed the rest of the Harris County nonprofit ecosystem.

References & Selected Reading

Akre, C., Chabloz, J. M., Belanger, R. E., Michaud, P. A., and Suris, J. C. 2013. "Unwanted Sexual Experiences Among Adolescents: Shedding Light on the Gray Zone between Consensual and Non-Consensual Sex," *International Journal of Adolescent Medicine and Health* 25 (1): 69–74.

Ali, M. M., and Dwyer, D. S. 2011. "Estimating Peer Effects in Sexual Behavior among Adolescents," *Journal of Adolescence* 34 (1): 183–90.

Amaro, H. 1994. "Gender and Sexual Risk Reduction: Issues to Consider," National Latino HIV/AIDS Research Conference, Los Angeles, CA.

———. 1995. "Love, Sex, and Power: Considering Women's Realities in HIV Prevention," *American Psychologist* 50 (6): 437.

Brown, J. D., and L'Engle, K. L. 2009. "X-rated: Sexual Attitudes and Behaviors Associated with US Early Adolescents' Exposure to Sexually Explicit Media," *Communication Research* 36 (1): 129–51.

Deptula, D. P., Henry, D. B., and Schoeny, M. E. 2010. "How Can Parents Make a Difference? Longitudinal Associations with Adolescent Sexual Behavior," *Journal of Family Psychology* 24 (6): 731.

Eckman, A., Jain, A., Kambou, S. D., Bartel, D., and Crownover, J. 2007. *Exploring Dimensions of Masculinity and Violence*. Washington, DC: CARE International Balkans.

Eyre, S. L., Flythe, M., Hoffman, V., and Fraser, A. E. 2012. "Concepts of Infidelity among African American Emerging Adults: Implications for HIV/STI Prevention," *Journal of Adolescent Research* 27 (2): 231–55.

Eyre, S. L., Hoffman, V., and Millstein, S. G. 1998. "The Gamesmanship of Sex: A Model Based on African American Adolescent Accounts," *Medical Anthropology Quarterly* 12 (4): 467–89.

Galinsky, A. M., and Sonenstein, F. L. 2011. "The Association between Developmental Assets and Sexual Enjoyment among Emerging Adults," *Journal of Adolescent Health* 48 (6): 610–15.

Garnets, L., and Pleck, J. H. 1979. "Sex Role Identity, Androgyny, and Sex Role Transcendence: A Sex Role Strain Analysis," *Psychology of Women Quarterly* 3 (3): 270–83.

Gender Analysis Overview. 2012. http://transition.usaid.gov/our_work/cross-cutting_programs/wid/gender/gender_analysis.html (accessed January 27, 2013).

Gómez, C. A., and Marin, B. V. 1996. "Gender, Culture, and Power: Barriers to HIV-Prevention Strategies for Women," *Journal of Sex Research* 33 (4): 355–62.

Hanson, M. B. 2008. *On the Road to Equality: Statewide Findings and Policy Recommendations*. Minneapolis: Women's Foundation of Minnesota.

International Planned Parenthood Federation. 2010. *Men Are Changing: Case Study Evidence on Work with Men and Boys to Promote Gender Equality and Positive Masculinities*.

Kerrigan, D., Andrinopoulos, K., Johnson, R., Parham, P., Thomas, T., and Ellen, J. M. 2007. "Staying Strong: Gender Ideologies among African American Adolescents and the Implications for HIV/STI Prevention," *Journal of Sex Research* 44 (2): 172–80.

Kirby, D. 2001. *Emerging Answers: Research Findings on Programs to Reduce Teen Pregnancy*. Washington, DC: National Campaign to Prevent Teen Pregnancy.

Landor, A., Simons, L. G., Simons, R. L., Brody, G. H., and Gibbons, F. X. 2011. "The Role of Religiosity in the Relationship between Parents, Peers, and Adolescent Risky Sexual Behavior," *Journal of Youth and Adolescence* 40 (3): 296–309.

Levant, R. F., Hirsch, L. S., Celentano, E., and Cozza, T. M. 1992. "The Male Role: An Investigation of Contemporary Norms," Journal of Mental Health Counseling 14 (3): 325–37.

Levant, R. F., and Richmond, K. 2008. "A Review of Research on Masculinity Ideologies Using the Male Role Norms Inventory," *The Journal of Men's Studies* 15 (2): 130–46.

Littles, M. J., Bowers, R., and Gilmer, M., eds. 2007. *Why We Can't Wait: A Case for Philanthropic Action: Opportunities for Improving Life Outcomes for African American Males*. New York: Ford Foundation.

Mahalik, J. R., Locke, B. D., Ludlow, L. H., Diemer, M. A., Scott, R. P., Gottfried, M., and Freitas, G. 2003. "Development of the Conformity to Masculine Norms Inventory," *Psychology of Men and Masculinity* 4 (1): 3.

Mahalik, J. R., Morray, E. B., Coonerty-Femiano, A., Ludlow, L. H., Slattery, S. M., and Smiler, A. 2005. "Development of the Conformity to Feminine Norms Inventory," *Sex Roles* 52 (7–8): 417–35.

Martyn, K. K., and Hutchinson, S. A. 2001. "Low-Income African American Adolescents Who Avoid Pregnancy: Tough Girls Who Rewrite Negative Scripts," *Qualitative Health Research* 11 (2): 238–56.

Mollborn, S. 2010. "Predictors and Consequences of Adolescents' Norms against Teenage Pregnancy," *The Sociological Quarterly* 51 (2): 303–28.

O'Hara, R. E., Gibbons, F. X., Gerrard, M., Li, Z., and Sargent, J. D. 2012. "Greater Exposure to Sexual Content in Popular Movies Predicts Earlier Sexual Debut and Increased Sexual Risk Taking," *Psychological Science* 23 (9): 984–93.

Pleck, J. H., and Thompson, E. 1987. "The Structure of Male Role Norms," in Michael Kimmel, ed., *Changing Men: New Directions in Research on Men and Masculinity.* Newbury Park, CA: Sage.

Pleck, J. H. 1996. *Individual, Family, and Community Factors Modifying Male Adolescents' Risk Behavior "Trajectory."* Washington, DC: Urban Institute.

Reed, E., Silverman, J. G., Raj, A., Decker, M. R., and Miller, E. 2011. "Male Perpetration of Teen Dating Violence: Associations with Neighborhood Violence Involvement, Gender Attitudes, and Perceived Peer and Neighborhood Norms," *Journal of Urban Health* 88 (2): 226–39.

Sonenstein, F. L., and Pleck, J. H. 1994. "The Male Role in Family Planning: What Do We Know?" Prepared for the Committee on Unintended Pregnancy, Institute of Medicine. Washington, DC: The Urban Institute.

Stephens, D. P., and Phillips, L. D. 2003. "Freaks, Gold Diggers, Divas, and Dykes: The Sociohistorical Development of Adolescent African American Women's Sexual Scripts," *Sexuality and Culture* 7 (1): 3–49.

St Lawrence, J. S., Eldridge, G. D., Reitman, D., Little, C. E., Shelby, M. C., and Brasfield, T. L. 1998. "Factors Influencing Condom Use among African American Women: Implications for Risk Reduction Interventions," *American Journal of Community Psychology* 26 (1): 7–28.

Swiss, L. 2011. "Security Sector Reform and Development Assistance: Explaining the Diffusion of Policy Priorities among Donor Agencies," *Qualitative Sociology* 34 (2): 371–93.

Thompson, E. H., Pleck, J. H., and Ferrera, D. L. 1992. "Men and Masculinities: Scales for Masculinity Ideology and Masculinity-Related Constructs," *Sex Roles* 27 (11–12): 573–607.

The White House. 2010. *National HIV/AIDS Strategy for the United States.* Washington, DC: The White House Office of National AIDS Policy.

Tolman, D. L. 2009. *Dilemmas of Desire: Teenage Girls Talk about Sexuality.* Cambridge, MA: Harvard University Press.

Tolman, D. L., and Porche, M. V. 2000. "The Adolescent Femininity Ideology Scale: Development and Validation of a New Measure for Girls," *Psychology of Women Quarterly* 24 (4): 365–76.

Tschann, J. M., Flores, E., De Groat, C. L., Deardorff, J., and Wibbelsman, C. J. 2010. "Condom Negotiation Strategies and Actual Condom Use among Latino Youth," *Journal of Adolescent Health* 47 (3): 254–62.

Ventura, S. J., Curtin, S. C., Abma, J. C., and Henshaw, S. K. 2012. "Estimated Pregnancy Rates and Rates of Pregnancy Outcomes for the United States, 1990–2008," *National Vital Statistics Reports* 60 (7): 1–21.

Wingood, G. M., and DiClemente, R. J. 1998. "Partner Influences and Gender-Related Factors Associated with Noncondom Use among Young Adult African American Women," *American Journal of Community Psychology* 26 (1): 29–51.

Zurbriggen, E. L., Collins, R. L., Lamb, S., Roberts, T. A., Tolman, D. L., and Ward, L. M. 2007. "APA Task Force on the Sexualization of Girls," American Psychological Association. https://www.apa.org/pi/women/programs/girls/report-full.pdf.

2

About Gender & Gender Norms

Gender equity is going to be a core philanthropic competency for the twenty-first century.

—Damon Hewitt, Executive Director,
Executives' Alliance for Boys and Men of Color

If pressed, most of us could do a pretty good "mother-in-law" explanation of age, race, class, or sex. Yet, when it comes to gender, many of us would probably be at a loss. Sometimes trying to define *gender* is reminiscent of Justice Potter Stewart's (in)famous declaration about *porn*: we may not be able to define it, but we darn well know it when we see it.

Complicating matters, "gender" is often conflated with Woman (since Man is the "unmarked" or default gender). This is so widespread and common and causes so much confusion—or at least message competition—that it's worth pausing to unpack it a bit here.

Funders or policy makers use "having a gender lens" interchangeably with a greater focus on women and girls. For example, a recent publication by one of California's leading policy groups encouraged the state to *use a gender lens* in its health policy. It mentioned "woman and girls" almost 100 times, but never once *masculinity, femininity, gender norms,* or *men and* boys . . . or *race, class,* or *LGBTQ.* So Woman here is not only synonymous with gender, but is also used as an uncomplicated category in which all members presumably have the same or similar health needs, which we know is not the case.

Similarly, one of the most widely-used guides to philanthropy *with a gender lens* fails to mention *masculinity, femininity, LGBTQ,* or *gender norms* anywhere in its twenty-eight pages. It does advise readers not to forget men and boys in a few places, but contains very little about them.

And a very thoughtful and extensive publication on how to adopt a gender lens to achieve grant making *for inclusion* mentions *LGBTQ* only twice in its thirty pages, *men and boys* three times. Perhaps strangely for a document devoted to inclusion, it mentions race early on . . . but then it disappears in the following dozen pages. And *gender norms* are never addressed at all. Yet right up front in large bold type it highlights the need to find "at least one entry point you can use to influence how the foundation engages with women and girls."

(The frequent omission of LGBTQ from such documents is perhaps not surprising, since the gay funders and advocates historically have had no interest in the dialog on gender and completely ignore it, except as it relates to transgender people. This is counterintuitive, since perhaps as much as a third of LGB individuals are in some way visibly gender nonconforming.)

This may sound like a "gotcha" exercise, and no doubt it's easy to find fault with any work on gender—including this one. But I introduce these examples not because they are anomalies, but because these are among the publications widely considered the standard for "best practice" in the field. In fact, in many ways, they're more progressive and forward-thinking than most.

There is similar conflation of *women* with *gender* among the many social justice funders that present themselves as having a "strong gender lens." In practice, I've found this usually means having women in decision-making positions and earmarking substantial support for issues affecting women and girls. Since women remain under-represented in leadership at the larger foundations (and people of color, especially women of color), and only about seven cents of every US philanthropic dollar is earmarked for women, these are both admirable goals, but they do not constitute an analysis of gender or an awareness of gender norms.

Even when philanthropic and policy organizations do dig more deeply into gender, the conflation of *women* and *gender* often means their use of "gender analysis" to look solely at the *structural* inequalities but not the underlying gendered attitudes and beliefs that may be root causes of inequality. An example is the current well-funded work of two high-profile Silicon Valley firms to improve women's equity by addressing the lack of mentors, the absence of female role models, and the need for recruitment initiatives focused on attracting women—while never examining the underlying white-boy jock culture that permeates coding environments and often deters women.

To be fair, sometimes a structural analysis is the only approach possible. An initiative to reduce the "gender gap" among a state's ten million voters will probably have to address structural factors (ease of registration, hours voting is open, ease of absentee voting for parents with dependent children, etc.), rather than underlying group belief systems and dynamics.

Similarly, a campaign to combat environmental racism might note how Flint Michigan's lead pollution disproportionately affected low-income women with dependent children, especially those unable to afford the daily purchase of bottled water. But it would probably ignore the underlying gendered and raced biases of the policy makers at fault, because they are clearly beyond the reach of appeals to reason or decency.

It is possible to do important work improving equity without addressing gender norms. In fact, this kind of "norms blind" work describes most of what we're doing in the US now. One can also design and implement programs, funding priorities, and policies that are "race blind" or "class blind," and they will also do good work and have problem impact. But chances are their efficacy will only be a fraction of what it could be with a deeper analysis and a more intentional effort to take into account root causes. It's the same with gender.

About Language

In addition to the conflation with women and girls, "gender" is an extraordinarily overloaded term in the English language to begin with, used in a bewildering array of overlapping contexts and phrases, including (but not limited to) *gender equity, gender equality, gender roles, gender analysis, gender mainstreaming, gender stereotypes, gender identity, gender expression, transgender, transsexual,* and *gender transformative.*

And this list doesn't even begin to include the expanding vocabulary of newly minted terms connected to gender nonconformity, generated (primarily) by LGBTQ youth, like *transmasculine, nonbinary, transfeminine, cisgender, cisnormative,* and *genderqueer.* All of these new ideas and terms are only beginning to demand the attention and understanding of funders, educators, policy makers, and parents, and will be more so in the years to come, as increasing numbers of youth identify outside of binary male/female and feminine/masculine.

All this complexity, combined with rapid change, can lead to what I call *jerk-a-phobia*: in which people in positions of authority simply avoid talking about gender because they fear "getting it wrong" and looking foolish in front of others.

With our understanding of gender as a moving target that is literally changing yearly, it is especially easy to get it wrong and be publicly called out for doing so, in a world where simple mistakes, or being a little behind the discourse, are misinterpreted as a form of microaggression.

Although gender is something I obviously spend a lot (okay, too much) time thinking about, I confess having gotten stung by this myself. At a presentation to a group of trans advocates, a young, nonbinary-identified activist took great exception to my using the term "transsexual" because it "genitalizes gender," and said that was "very diminishing" to many people like them.

I immediately loved the critique of "genitalizing gender." While I have never liked such a clinical, made-up term as "transsexual," I was also not yet prepared to surrender it, since I have been calling myself that, and been called that, since at least 1978. It was how one explained oneself to others. Yet my continuing use of it struck this person as a form of social aggression, a diminishing of their authenticity, which was surely not what I intended.

Similarly, I am regularly corrected by friends and others for using the word "trannie." I've always liked the term, but it has regrettably fallen into disrepute, and is now considered a slur by many. And I can no longer mention my "sex-change surgery," but must now refer to something called my "gender confirmation surgery" or "gender affirmation surgery"—phrases that, to my ears, are so saccharine I can't bring myself to use them.

Perhaps fortuitously, "queer"—which in my adolescence was considered the worst kind of insult—has largely been resuscitated. While I see adults my age sometimes grimace when they hear it, I also hear both gay and straight young people using it freely without a hint of disapprobation.

No doubt all these terms, and others about gender, will continue to evolve as our understanding grows. And no doubt we will continue to remonstrate with one another when any of us is a beat behind. This does not encourage funders, policy makers, or practitioners to speak freely and openly about gender, or ask questions about it. It might help to bear in mind that when it comes to gender, we're all trying to figure out some very complex things together and it's going to take some time.

About Norms

So what is a "norm?" Isn't a norm like an average? And if someone isn't doing whatever is the "norm," doesn't that mean, by definition, that they are "ab-normal"? That's a term that seems kind of hostile.

Yes, there is a mathematical meaning to the word. It roughly equates to what is average. But social norms are different—they refer to not what is average, but rather what is widely accepted and shared.

As Allison Brown, head of the Communities for Just Schools Fund explains, when youth of color deal with police officers by avoiding direct eye contact, raising their voices, or standing too erect, they are using shared social norms that communicate being nonviolent and nonthreatening.

The clothes we wear are also a reflection of social norms. There's no particular reason males can't wear skirts (Scots do). But a man in a dress walking into a bar in almost any American city (okay, except San Francisco) may find he is taking his life in his hands. That's a social norm being enforced.

Being *abnormal*—that is, not being the norm—technically just means being different. But when gender and sexuality are rigidly enforced, even minor variations are highly politicized, and—since at least the 1950s—are also medicalized and/or pathologized.

So being "sexually abnormal" or having an "abnormal gender" takes on a very ominous meaning: one is *unnatural* or *deviant*. Gay and transgender people were considered so by psychiatry and medicine until very recently. In fact, "diagnosing" and "treating" individuals for totally harmless gender or sexual "abnormalities" is another form of the discursive power mentioned in chapter 1.

Shaming and scaring a male crossdresser into believing he has an "illness" may not be the sort of concrete, visible power of the nightstick or the gun, but it is no less powerful and still retains the capacity to make people do terrible things to themselves.

"What Culture Makes from Sex"

Gender shapes our beliefs and behaviors across the entire plane of contact with society, practically from birth—as does race. "Gender," as theorist Mary Crawford first offered, "is what culture makes out of sex." She meant that although physical sex may be a matter of biology (and thus immutable), what sex *means* and how it is interpreted is a matter of culture, that is, it's "socially constructed."

Are men and women, in fact, really "opposite sexes," with one from Mars and the other Venus? Or are men and women basically the same in almost all their particulars?

The answer to this is found not in science, but in culture. There is no biological basis for most of the things we commonly associate and often rigorously enforce about being male or female:

- men smoke cigars and pipes, but women only cigarettes;
- boys play baseball, but girls play softball;
- women often end both statements as well as questions on an up-note, as if they were asking something; men don't;
- body hair is acceptable on men, but unsightly on women;
- age and strength are attractive in men, unfeminine in women;
- girls can play with dolls, but if boys do so the toys must be called "action figures";
- women tilt their heads to one side in pictures to indicate deference, but men don't;
- men become doctors, women become nurses; and
- women stand with all their weight poised on a single leg (the classic "stork pose") and the other leg bent at the knee, indicating vulnerability, while men stand with their weight equally distributed and both legs planted squarely apart.

The list is practically endless. All of these "differences" that help make up how we understand Man and Woman result from cultural beliefs and practices, not from the biology of the flesh.

And unlike flesh, these notions change over time. For example, at the beginning of the last century, pink was considered an active color associated with blood and reserved for boys; light blue was for girls. Middle-class kids of both sexes wore long hair and wore what, today, we would consider dresses, until they were out of childhood.

These practices and behaviors are part of a system of differences that helps us think of men and women as unalike and opposite. They make up the "norms" for how each sex must "do" masculinity or femininity socially, and they help determine what it means to be a woman or a man.

Sometime in the next twelve months, a major magazine cover or website home page will trumpet another such study of the "obvious differences" between men and women. As a society, we invest millions of dollars each year on such studies to prove and document our differences. The production of these reports is a very different kind of "sex industry." Yet a ten-year-old with a pencil and a ream of paper could easily fill it all with the "obvious similarities" between all of us. So are men and women really more different than alike? Again, that's not a question of science, but of culture.

Imagine that an intelligent, silicon-based, purple lifeform from Andromeda lands its spaceship in Times Square. Upon emerging, the very first thing it sees is a heterosexual couple. It is highly doubtful that its first thought would be, "Wow, they're so different! One looks like it's from Mars, and the other looks like it's from Venus."

A Difference Engine

We might think of gender as a kind of Difference Engine: one that takes the body and sex as its raw material, and then endlessly creates new ways to shape our understanding of them, all binary and opposing in nature.

So the equation is: whatever *is* feminine is *not* masculine, and whatever *is* masculine is *not* feminine; and a quality or thing *is* masculine to the precise degree that it is *not* feminine. The two ideas are at once mutually exclusive, mutually reinforcing, and exhaust all gendered possibilities (e.g., a thing cannot be neither, a combination of the two, or a different sort of gender entirely).

We might want to see gender's relationship to the body and its meanings as similar to that of a cookie cutter to dough. It's not that the cookies aren't real—they are. Rather, it's that their shapes weren't there beforehand, and nothing about the dough requires those particular shapes, except for that particular cookie cutter. Once stamped out and baked, however, the cookies are totally there and completely "real."

The fact that gender norms are *culturally constructed* does not mean that they, too, are any less real, or to trivialize them in any way. On the contrary: it is precisely because gender norms' impacts are so significant that it is important for us to investigate them.

Nor is saying that gender norms are culturally constructed the same as saying that we can change them at will. Since norms are communally generated and held, although a person can defy them, no one individual alone can change them. Norms, in matters of sexuality and gender, tend to be highly entrenched and especially resistant to change, even when they make little sense or are actually harmful. For example, consider female genital mutilation (FGM), the longstanding use of electroshock therapy to "cure" homosexuality, or the decades it's taken the United States to fully integrate women into the military.

If "gender" is such a contested and overloaded term, and used in so many different contexts and phrases, it might be helpful for us to unpack it a bit—to do what my grad school professors pretentiously called "a little disambiguation exercise."

Most of the following definitions are offered to help distinguish the words below from phrases like "gender norms" and "gender equity," which will be the primary topic for the remainder of this book. If you feel you already have a handle on the terms and definitions, feel free to skip ahead.

Sex

Biological sex refers to the physical characteristics of bodies, including primary sex characteristics like chromosomes, genitals, and hormones, and secondary sexual characteristics including bone structure, fat distribution, musculature, and body hair.

We like to think that sexual characteristics are distinct—men have wide shoulders and deep voices, women wide hips and fuller lips. But when it comes to secondary characteristics (the ones that are actually most visible), there tends to be what statisticians call a "bimodal distribution" (visualize a camel with two humps). What this means is there is a lot of overlap, and almost as much variation within sex categories as between them.

Unsurprisingly, experts still cannot agree on a single, definitive marker for sex. This is why Olympic committees continue to struggle with determining which athletes are "really" female, and have mostly thrown in the towel, especially when it comes to intersex athletes.

Almost all primary and secondary characteristics are linked to one of two things: the so-called "sex chromosomes" (XY for boys and XX for girls), and sex hormones (estrogen for girls and testosterone for boys).

Our culture tends to equate genitals with sex. Consider how central genital status is to transgender people's ongoing struggle to be allowed to use the correct bathroom. But consider that in hospital burn units they keep diagrams that chart the areas of injury, and genitals take up just one percent of the Burn Chart. It is striking to recognize the enormous weight that popular culture tends to attach to that one percent. That's the gender system at work.

In fact, both male and female genitalia come from the same tissue. Penis and clitoris, vulva and testes, all come from the same tissue in neonates, and only later differentiate. Nature's rule regarding sex is: *unless otherwise instructed, make a female.*

In other words, without testosterone, either because of estrogen or an insensitivity to testosterone (not all that uncommon), nature makes a female body, regardless of whether the chromosomes are XX *or* XY. (A small but significant number of women, usually very highly feminized, *are* chromosomally XY, but were born testosterone-insensitive.)

Women

If Nature's rule is *female unless instructed otherwise,* society tends to reverse this as "masculine/man unless instructed otherwise." This is why we use expressions like "all of Mankind" to be the "universal" case: Man is inclusive; Woman is specific and gendered. This is one reason why men can throw on almost anything to go out and look masculine. But a woman who does the same thing is seen to look unfeminine (plain blouses and slacks are often marketed as "boyfriend clothes").

Indeed, *being* feminine socially can become a kind of cosmetic accomplishment that takes practice, time, and skill. It can include make-up, hairstyle, clothing, and adornment, and so on.

This fact is why so many adolescent movies (*The Breakfast Club, Grease, Cinderella, Mean Girls, Clueless, Miss Congeniality, She's All That,* etc.) feature the obligatory "nerd makeover" scene, in which the plain, "ugly duckling" female suddenly emerges from her drab shell and blossoms into full and womanly femininity. (There is *never* a scene like this for teenage males.)

Intersex

About one in every two thousand infants is born with genitals that are, in one way or another, "unexpected." These are usually diagnosed as intersex—what used to be called, inaccurately, "hermaphrodite."

I say "inaccurate" because the term *hermaphrodite* comes from the Greek mythology figure, Hermaphroditus, the beautiful son of Aphrodite and Hermes who was transformed into a male with female breasts.

This has *nothing* whatsoever to do with intersex. There is an unrelated condition called "gynecomastia" or "enlarged breasts" in men—a common side effect when taking estrogen to treat conditions like prostate cancer (or for transpeople who transition from male-to-female), but this has nothing to do with *intersex.*

Another widespread misconception is that being intersex means being "born with both sets of genitals," a condition that verges on the anatomically impossible and is therefore so rare as to be virtually nonexistent.

In actuality, *intersex* encompasses over a hundred conditions—one reason that some advocates have suggested the more accurate term "Disorders of Sexual Development" or DSD, which is seen as more descriptive, and less of an identity. However, the name remains controversial, as some advocates feel it medicalizes and/or pathologizes intersexuality.

The sad fact is that a vast majority of those labeled "intersex" are otherwise normal baby female infants whose clitorises have been considered "too large" and thus are medically redefined as a "too-small phallus." The criterion for "too large" is beyond two standard deviations from the mean. In practice, that is about one inch. This is an entirely arbitrary standard that has no clinical or medical significance.

Alas, in much of Western culture, large penises in boys are considered manly and desirable, and big clitorises in girls unfeminine and undesirable (the gender system at work again). So the standard medical practice for such infants in the United States, and many industrialized countries, is traumatic: cutting away parts of their "phallus" so they better resemble "normal" (i.e., small and feminine) clitorises. As activists have testified time and again, this often leads to profound losses of sexual sensation, cosmetic and functional complications, and profound feelings of confusion and shame, as growing children realize something wrong has been done to their body's most intimate places, without their knowledge or consent.

There is no way to avoid the fact that this constitutes a medicalized Western form of FGM—one reason many advocates refer to it as intersex genital mutilation (IGM). The fact that this completely unnecessary, but common, barbarity continues to be inflicted each year on thousands of uncomplaining infants in US hospitals without their consent remains perhaps the most vivid and concrete illustration of the power of gender norms, not only to dictate things like clothing, posture, and hairstyle, but to be inscribed into the very flesh of our bodies. This is true, also, with FGM, and even male circumcision.

The Astraea Fund for Women, as a response, has started one of the first philanthropic funds to support intersex activism, and other funders will surely follow. One can only hope so. IGM is based on the fear that no male will desire a woman with a large clitoris, and that girls who do have large clitorises are more likely to grow up to be "masculinized," that is, lesbians.

A vibrant activism movement, originally launched by advocate Cheryl Chase and the Intersex Society of North America (ISNA), but now being carried forward by many others, has been working hard to turn the tide on this medieval practice for over two decades, with all the glacial success one would expect when taking on entrenched medical interests and hospital systems accountable to virtually no one.

When transgender allies and the protest group *Hermaphrodites With Attitude!* picketed the American Academy of Pediatricians in the mid-1990s (an event now celebrated as worldwide as Intersex Awareness Day), irritated surgeons asked the activists how they thought such children would survive if they weren't operated on. Yet before the 1950s, when IGM became the new standard of care, the bodies of intersex kids were not seen as problematic.

Gender Identity, Transgender, & Transsexual

"Gender identity" refers to an inner sense or conviction of being male or female (or some combination of the two). Most of us never think about our gender identity because we don't need to. Our physical sex and our inner gender identification agree with one another (well, at least *yours* does). This agreement is called being "cisgender" or more simply, "cis"—a word that is still quite new. It derives from Latin prefix *cis*-, meaning "on this side of." It means people who *are* not transgender (e.g., the vast majority of people).

Gender identity is a very useful concept when thinking about transsexual or transgender individuals, many of whom experience a sense of conflict between their outer physical sex and their inner sense of being male or female (or some combination).

"Transgender" is an umbrella term for anyone who is gender nonconforming, including transsexuals, cross-dressers (most whom appear to be male, married, and heterosexual), drag queens (most of who appear to be gay men), and drag kings (most of whom appear to be lesbian women). Originally used mostly in White communities, it has lately crossed over and become both more mainstream and most often used by transpeople of color (many of whom might simply have once said "I'm gay," rather than "I'm trans").

"Transsexual" is a psychiatric term that refers specifically to the subset of transpeople who want or need medical intervention to bring their biological sex into greater agreement with their inner gender identity. Such interventions can include any combination of hormone therapy, breast reduction or enhancement, and gender confirmation surgery (aka "sex reassignment surgery" or more simply SRS) for genitals.

"Transsexual" is beginning to fall out of favor as an identity, especially among a younger generation who are determined to contest the archaic practices of courts, the police, schools, and governmental agencies that demand to know the status of people's genitals before granting people the dignity of living in their proper gender.

Drag Queens (& Kings)

Drag involves using the gender expression of another sex for public entertainment. It is not an identity *per se*. Most drag performers are satisfied with their biological sex and have no desire to change it through hormones or surgery. That is, they are not transsexual, although there are exceptions. Nonetheless, drag is sometimes included under the *transgender* umbrella.

Drag has a long and storied history, from gay drag queens who seek to embody their favorite and often tragic female stars (Judy Garland, Marilyn Monroe, etc.) to more mainstream comedians that have included TV acts like Milton Berle and Flip Wilson and movie stars like Martin Lawrence, Eddie Murphy, and (of course) Tyler Perry.

For instance, in the 1930s, Marlene Dietrich sang and danced in the black and white classic film *Morocco* in a man's tux and tails, scandalously pausing to dip down and kiss a woman on the lips, but, by the end, gamely followed her lover into the desert when his regiment was sent into battle.

Most drag queens are gay men, often choosing puns as names like *Penny Arcade* or *Kitty Litter*, who focus on perfecting lip synching, dance, and style.*

Although less publicized, a very robust and vibrant "drag king" culture has more recently emerged, with shows made up almost entirely of butch-identified lesbian women who dress up and perform typically masculine roles—often to great effect.

Sexual Orientation & Gender Expression

"Sexual orientation" refers to the romantic attraction between members of the same or other sexes. "Gender expression" refers to how each of us communicates our

---

* There is an old tradition in the gay community that your drag name is your first pet plus your mother's maiden name. That would make mine *Black Satin Bernhardt* (!) so apparently it works.

gender identity (i.e., our feelings of being male or female or some combination of the two) through clothing, hairstyle, behavior, and so forth.

Gender expression and sexual orientation can overlap, but are distinct. Sexual orientation tends to be confused with gender expression because one's gender expression is often the public signature for sexual orientation.

For instance, if a man looks or acts femininely, many people will interpret that feminine gender expression as a sign of his sexual orientation, for example, of being gay. So-called "gaydar"—the mythic ability to intuit whether someone is or isn't gay—is really all about gender expression, not sexual orientation. But this interpretation is far from accurate. Many gay men are quite traditionally masculine, and many male ballet dancers who are slender, graceful, and artistic are totally straight.

Perhaps as much as one-fourth of gays, lesbians, and bisexuals are visibly gender nonconforming, and their gender expression does not fit expectations for masculinity in men or femininity in women. For the remaining three-fourths, perhaps the only gender nonconforming thing about them is that they love those of the same sex. Some have argued that this is the most gender nonconforming thing one could possibly do.

As more and more youth (gay *and* straight) continue to joyfully transgress their elders' most deeply held ideas about binary genders, the number of gender nonconforming youth is only set to increase.

A nice graphic for how to think about ideas like sexual orientation, gender identity, and so on is provided by the widely-used Genderbread person graphic in figure 2.1.

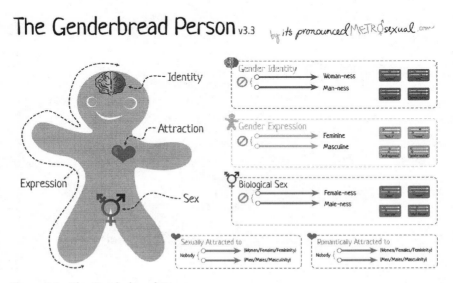

Figure 2.1   The Genderbread Person.
Source: Courtesy of Sam Killermann at www.itspronouncedmetrosexual.com.

LGBTQQI+?

In the 1970s, with the gay rights revolution and the advent of public visibility, the gay community was known simply as . . . the "gay community." And it was good. However, since when mainstream culture heard "gay" it tended to think "male," some worried that "gay" tended to erase lesbians. So, the term was expanded to "gay and lesbian." And all was good.

However, someone soon noticed that "gay and lesbian" obscured an excluded middle: those who were attracted to *both* sexes. So the name was lengthened to "gay, lesbian, and bisexual." And once again, all was good.

While the term was awaiting further expansion, some decided that putting "gay" first implicitly privileged gay men, especially considering that women have been historically disempowered often marginalized. So to keep things moving, "lesbian" was moved first, and the order was changed to "lesbian, gay, and bisexual."

As the transgender political movement emerged in the early 1990s, transactivists began a sustained and often bitter struggle for inclusion. Slowly, the new term, "lesbian, gay, bisexual, and transgender" was adopted. However, this was much too unwieldy to say, so it was shortened to the acronym "LGBT." And once again, all was . . . never mind.

Lately many groups have been adding "questioning" for those individuals—especially among the young—who are still unsure of their gender identity or sexual orientation, and "LGBTQ" is slowly becoming the term of art.

For some (again, especially among young people), the "Q" stands for "queer." While this was pejorative not long ago, it has increasingly been resuscitated as an in-group term of pride. Some folks also use "queer" as shorthand, as a way of avoiding the balkanization implied by saying "LGBTQ." Others explicitly mean both Qs. Some are also adding "I" to call out those who are intersex (LGBTQI). Most recently, young people have added "A" to include those who identify as asexual (LGBTQIA). Finally, "LGBTQ+" is coming into use as well, where the "+" is a stand-in for any unnamed identities that might be left out.

When doing my gender presentation, I usually advise audiences: "Straight people, please don't try to memorize the acronym . . . as soon as you do, we'll add another letter."

Whatever the name, although estimates place the number of LGBTQ Americans between 4 percent and 10 percent, the community receives only about one-tenth of one percent (.01 percent) of US philanthropic dollars. The vast majority of this discouragingly small amount comes from a handful of gay funders. Both are facts the philanthropic community should seek to remedy.

The LGBTQ+ acronym's momentum has not entirely slowed, much less exhausted itself. There are other, even more elaborate acronyms waiting in the wings. I once spoke to a college group reaching for the very apogee of inclusiveness that defined itself as being for "Lesbian, Gay Bisexual, Transgender, Intersex, Straight Sympathetic, Queer, Questioning, and Allied Youth" (LGBTIQQSSAY, for those keeping track).

Although it's easy to indulge in humor at this endless expansion, it also reflects something quite serious. Starting from where we were when "gay" first entered mainstream consciousness and at least replaced psychiatric terms like "inverts" and "homosexuals," we have been on a long process of unpacking a much deeper and more resonant complexity, perhaps, than anyone anticipated. And as that unpacking continues, our terminology, and indeed our understanding, will need to continue to evolve.

These extended acronyms provide a sense of the richness of those gendered and sexual minorities who have been hidden and marginalized, and are only now, at last, emerging and demanding that we speak their name.

As we should. The only really problematic thing about this is that a moving target gaining in complexity tends to shut down discourse, just when I think a rich and open—and even occasionally wrong-headed—dialogue about gender differences may be most important.

Nonbinary & Genderqueer

In 2017, a young, gender nonconforming character appearing for the first time on Showtime's hit series *Billions* introduced themselves to the head of their hedge fund by explaining, "Hello sir, my name is Taylor. My pronouns are 'they, theirs, and them.'"

This was groundbreaking, and yet another step in an arc of public awareness that began for many in April, 2016 when twenty-year-old student Maria Munir came out to (a befuddled) President Obama as nonbinary: "I'm about to do something terrifying, which is I'm coming out to you as a nonbinary person."

In truth, many trans youth today simply identify as "trans" or "genderqueer"— not to mention as "boychik," "demigirl," and other exuberant, nonbinary genders few of us have contemplated, much less adopted. Just as the rest of us are finally mastering things like sexual orientation and gender identity, they are overturning the applecart of binary sexes on which such concepts depend.

For instance, here are two questions: If your partner is nonbinary, what is your sexual orientation? If your child is nonbinary, which locker room(s) at school should they have the right to use?

I was asked to write the foreword for an anthology of nonbinary voices, and one of the first questions I posed was: are nonbinary folks transgender? I certainly tend to think of them as falling under the *trans* umbrella. Yet everything I know about trans is connected to a level of discomfort with one's physical sex or transitioning from one thing to another. Nonbinary people aren't uncomfortable, and most of them aren't going anywhere.

I'm not even sure about the word "genderqueer." I coined the term in the 1990s to refer to those of us who are not only gay or trans, but who don't *pass* as cisgender, who are "visibly queer."

But now I see some nonbinary people claiming genderqueer as a name which I never intended, for the simple reason that in 1990 the idea of nonbinary hadn't been invented.

You can see that all this gets complicated pretty quickly, but is not just a fringe issue. More and more young people are refusing binary genders. Canada and Germany already allow a third sex option on identity papers. Funders, policy makers, educators, nonprofits, and parents need to begin thinking about these new identities now, because they will present new challenges and questions we haven't even anticipated.

Gender Equity & Gender Mainstreaming

Gender equity and *gender equality* are often used interchangeably. *Equity* refers to the equal treatment so that all members of a community have equal access to power, rights, and opportunity, particuarly women. *Equality* goes a step further and refers to actually achieving parity between people. This book will mostly use *gender equity*, which is more common in the United States.

Gender mainstreaming refers to pulling an awareness of gender and gendered power relations throughout all the activities that an organization does, incluing its programs, data collection, recruitment, and strategizing. It becomes part of its organizational DNA, and ceases being something special and external that must be continuously reintroduced into the work. Gender mainstreaming is an important strategy in helping groups better achieve their gender equity goals.

Gender Stereotypes

Gender stereotypes refer to generalizations about the sexes: for example that women are not good with computers or engineering, men can't cook and won't ask for directions, women are emotional but cheer up when they buy new clothes, and men are unemotional but cheer up when they buy new tools (or guns).

The whole "men are from Mars, women are from Venus" meme is a masterpiece of simplistic gender stereotyping. As with any generalization, some gender stereotypes reference underlying truths, while others are simply unfounded and are uninformed bias.

Negative gender stereotypes can negatively impact those in the stereotyped groups in subtle ways if they are in situations where they perceive themselves to be fulfilling the stereotype, even if they don't personally believe in it—an effect known as "stereotype threat." For instance, girls who are given a math test after the teacher casually observes that females aren't good at math consistently score lower than girls who haven't heard the same sexist preface.

Gender stereotypes are also connected to an important concept that will come up later with girls and STEM (science, technology, engineering, and math): implicit bias.

Here's an old riddle. A father and son are out driving and hit a tree, hard. The father is killed instantly, but the son is taken to a nearby hospital with a terrible chest injury. An experienced surgeon is flown in—a thoracic specialist—and the son is hurriedly prepped for an emergency procedure. The surgeon rushes into the surgical room, scrubs and is ready, but just as the young man is about to go under the knife, the surgeon looks at him and takes a step back, declaring, "I can't operate—that boy is my son!" Talk amongst yourselves . . .

Sometimes we act on gender stereotypes, even when we say we don't believe in them. Even feminist teachers who believe strongly in boy–girl equality have been found to unwittingly call on boys more often and/or let them talk longer. This is *implicit bias* at work. Some teachers actually refuse to believe it, until shown tapes of their teaching.

Almost all of us hold such biases that are not conscious and are even the opposite of our professed beliefs. This makes them especially hard to combat. Implicit biases are not limited to gender, but extend to areas like race, class, and disability.

Studies show that adults consistently perceive young Black men as four-and-a-half years older than they actually are. This has a huge impact on their disproportionate rates of suspension by educators, the overpolicing by school safety personnel, and the criminalization of minor schoolyard conflicts (as we will see in the section on school "push-out" policies).

Experts have created a series of tests, such as Harvard's Project Implicit, to measure implicit bias (implicit.harvard.edu/implicit/takeatest.html). However, *implicit* biases do not exhaust our stereotypic notions about gender: many of us hold very conscious and *explicit* beliefs that girls should be quiet and submissive and boys strong and boisterous. This is one reason the programs that TrueChild develops often include gender self-surveys and organizational gender climate surveys: to help people and organizations become more aware of the gender biases and beliefs they already hold.

By the way, the answer to the riddle? The thoracic specialist who was flown in was the boy's mother.

About Masculinity

Traditional masculinity is usually understood as an amalgam of strength, aggression, pride, sexual prowess, social detachment, risk-taking, and emotional toughness.

Academics sometimes refer to this combination as *hegemonic masculinity* (e.g., the dominant version), because it crowds out any other form of being manly. It also helps promote the subordination of women (aka, the patriarchy). We have a much deeper and broader literature of studies and theory on masculinity than we do femininity.

Because it is the dominant term and holds so much social power, masculinity tends to be much more strictly regulated than femininity, and deviations from masculinity are punished much more harshly. For example, a young girl can still climb trees and wear boyish clothes into adolescence without arousing too much open disapproval. But a young boy who is considered *effeminate*, who plays with dolls and goes out wearing his sister's dress, is likely to get a very strong negative response. Thankfully, this is very slowly changing, in many cases due to the advocacy of parents of gender nonconforming and trans children.

About Femininity

Traditional femininity is understood as a combination of the "the three D's": being Deferential, Desirable, and Dependent. It can also encompass qualities like being highly social, emotionally vulnerable, and maternal and nurturing.

Most of these are subordinate characteristics that are linked to women's role in marriage and reproduction: one can be strong alone, but one can only be desirable in relation to an Other.

Pop culture artists like Madonna and others have attempted to create a femininity that valorizes women's sexual prowess and erotic desirability to males to read power back into femininity—what has been called "*Do Me*" feminism—but with distinctly varying degrees of success. (The latest, de-sexed and mommy-friendly version of this is being relentlessly marketed to tween girls as "sassy.")

Human femininity is deeply intertwined with youthfulness, fertility, and what is called "neotony": childish physical traits carried into adulthood. This is why female cartoon characters (particularly in Japanese manga or Disney movies) are usually drawn with enormous eyes and lips but almost no nose, and popular female actresses are often selected for their *adorable* overbites (a trait also common in little children).

In part, because of this, femininity has a complex relationship with power and aging. In many cultures, women are considered to lose their femininity as they age. Although men with power and status are admired, studies consistently find that women with power and authority are disliked by both men *and* women (though less so by women), and are perceived as cold, distant, and . . . unfeminine.

As with masculinity, femininity is complicated by factors like race, class, and ethnicity, so that some experts refer to "femininities" in the plural, emphasizing that there is not just one femininity, but many.

Intersectionality

As mentioned earlier, gender stereotypes are always raced, just as racial stereotypes are always gendered. So factors like gender and race and class are always intertwined.

Film frequently expresses this. Clint Eastwood's slow but deadly *Man with No Name* gunslinger and Curtis Jackson's violent urban gangster *50 Cent* in *Get Rich or Die Tryin'* are both specifically raced and classed representations of masculinity.

One of the artistic shocks of a movie like Tarantino's *Django Unchained* is the pleasant dislocation of combining these two by casting a poor Black man as a deadly Western gunslinger.

Understanding the interplay of factors like age, race, sex, gender, and class is known as "intersectionality." This has recently become a big issue on the right, with some arguing that it means that everything is connected, so, for example, you can't be pro-gay rights and against abortion.

Much of what we know about intersectionality emerged out of the work of the Critical Race theorists, a group of theorists, many of whom were lawyers, who began reevaluating the role of the courts in the wake of *Brown vs. Board of Education*. After *Brown* desegregated schools, the courts had traditionally been seen as a friend to Black civil rights. Yet that view was simplistic. As race-critical theorists pointed out that, *Brown* aside, the courts had more often worked against civil rights, repeatedly redefining what it meant to be "colored" to restrict the rights of Blacks and prop up the White power structure.

Courts also frequently looked for ways to rule against civil rights cases. As theorist Kimberlé Crenshaw (1989, 141) has noted, in the mid-1970s Black women at General Motors sued for workplace discrimination. GM had segregated its workforce by race and by gender. There were positions open to Blacks, but they were all men's jobs. And there were positions open to women, and these were only open to Whites. In effect, Black women were shut out of employment.

Yet a lawsuit brought by Black women was easily turned aside by the courts, which held that they couldn't sue for racial discrimination, because Black men worked at GM. And they couldn't sue for sex discrimination either, because White women did as well. As Crenshaw and others noted, it was only by looking at the *intersection* of identity that the Black women's claims obviously had merit.

In her TED talk on intersectionality, Crenshaw draws on a different example. She asks her audience to stand, and then to sit once they hear her say a name they don't recognize. She starts with the names Freddie Gray, Eric Garner, Mike Brown, and Tamir Rice. Most of her audience are still standing. Then she says the names of Tanisha Anderson, Megan Hockady, Michelle Cusseaux, and Aura Rosser. One or two names in, almost the entire audience is seated.

These are all African Americans killed by the police, but people knew the first set of names, not the second. As Crenshaw notes, this is strange, because the second set touches on two issues that have drawn a lot of attention: police violence against people of color, and violence against women. But the mental "frame" we have for *police violence* tends to be around males who have been killed, not women. As Crenshaw points out, research shows that when data doesn't fit the mental frame, we tend to ignore, forget, or discard it. So many of us know Eric Garner, but not Aura Rosser.

Similarly, when my first organization, GenderPAC, began to research murders of trans-youth, we quickly found scores of them—in fact, the report, originally titled

"50 Under 30" was renamed and reissued just two years alters as "70 Under 30." Yet no one had heard of any of them, and there was little media coverage. I come from a tight-knit Jewish community in Cincinnati; I can't even imagine the outcry by national media and advocacy groups if (god forbid) young Jewish people were being fatally assaulted in anything like similar numbers.

Yet the vast majority of these killings involved individuals who were disenfranchises in every possible way: young, Black, female-identified, from low-income communities, and sometimes even disowned by families. They were simply outside our "frame" for LGBT violence, which tended (to the degree that it existed) to focus on victims Mathew Shepard or Brandon Teena: both of whom were White, male-identified, and rural.

It was a terrible illustration of the profound need for intersectional approaches that are sensitive to more complex identities that fall outside our frame of reference and thus beyond social recognition.

Intersectionality means that people's bodies and lived experience tend to be more complex than the simple categories or frames we use to understand them. Many of us build our homes, and make our lives, at the intersections—not the straightways—of identity. That is where different kinds of oppressions meet and interact.

Intersectionality pushes us to widen our frames to see more people, and to also look for more complex identities that fall outside our frame of reference for an issue. It pushes us toward more nuanced ways of thinking about complex and longstanding social problems—one reason many funders and policy makers are now moving toward more intersectional approaches.

Throughout this book I try to highlight and hold up where gender intersects with factors like race, class, sexual orientation, gender identity, and ethnicity. Even where I fail to do so, however, those intersections are *always* there. Nature is just more complex and subtle than we are.

How Norms Are Learned

In my colleague Micah Gilmer's upcoming book, tentatively titled *The Big Black Man Rules*, we explore how gender norms constitute a kind of hidden curriculum: a set of universal rules, beliefs, and actions that every young person must master to survive, but for which none receives the least bit of formal help or guidance, even in school. This can be particularly true for at-risk youth.

Young people absorb the rules for femininity and masculinity all the time, and from just about everywhere. The earliest source is probably parents' positive: "what a big boy!" and "such a little princess!" as well as negative: "big boys don't cry" and "act like lady!" reinforcement.

They also learn from siblings, extended family members, preschool, and religious institutions. By the time they're exposed to media, they also get gender instruction from children's books, videos, and TV shows, which inevitably feature gender-normative little boys and girls: the boys in short hair, wearing pants, and often being the more active lead characters; the girls with long hair, in dresses, wanting to be models or ballerinas.

Perfect strangers can get into the act, particularly when little children don't toe the line. Recently an angry mother posted a piece that went viral about her two-year-old son wearing a pink headband he wore to Walmart. A male shopper walked over and pulled it off his head, declaring, "One day you'll thank me!"

This is not limited to adults. In childhood, many young children have already learned to join in the social policing of femininity in girls and masculinity in boys.

I recall one girl taunted my daughter when she was barely out of diapers. Dylan had short hair and a gender-neutral name, and this girl kept telling her, "You're Mr. Dylan." Our poor Baby Dyl didn't even get it. She kept replying, "No, I'm just Dylan!" I thought to myself, *Now, this is interesting: here's a four-year-old gender-baiting a three-year-old so young, she doesn't even get the harassment.* And of course the girl's parent stood there and watched the whole interaction and said not a word.

By middle school, this kind of peer gender regulation is in full bloom. Kids tease or ostracize over the least degree of gender nonconformity. Our language has developed a distressingly elaborate vocabulary for stigmatizing the least degree of gender nonconformity: *queer, queen, dork, sissy, lezzie, fag, bitch,* and so on. Children master this dismal lexicon early—any middle-schooler can recite the whole list—and know that having any of these attached to them can result in public humiliation. (Tellingly, there are no positive words in English for gender nonconformity. If words are "instrumental"—tools we create to do things with—clearly we have never felt any need to promote or compliment gender nonconformity.)

By the time they enter adolescence, young people have been exposed to tens of thousands of messages and information from social media, books, songs, TV, advertisements, and movies about how to "do" boy and girl, and what is expected for them as females and males.

Traditional womanhood and manhood are not just learned from individuals' interactions with their peers and parents, they are woven into the very fabric of our cultural institutions: courts, the military, government agencies, and schools.

Schools are highly gendered environments. They sometimes separate requirements and elective courses. Girls and boys can be lined up separately or seated separately for no reason, pitted against one another in competition, and compared for their performance, for example: "Look how nice the girls are behaving today," and complimented differently: boys for being strong, and girls for being pretty and well-behaved.

School sports are often sites for maintaining traditional gender norms: boys and girls play different sports: basketball for boys and jump rope for girls; play the same games but with different rules and equipment: baseball for boys, softball for girls. Coaches often use gendered taunts to regulate behavior: "You men are playing like a bunch of sissies!" and "You throw like a girl!"

Adolescents learn gender not just through external pressures to conform, but also through a complex interplay of pressure, reward, and desire. A young man might feel pressure to "man up" by other boys because he is always a "good boy" and obeys the teachers.

At the same time, external rewards are involved. A boy may be thinking: "The cool guys will hang out with me more if they see me as tough." He may shame himself for not living up to manhood ideals, to wit: "I look like a sissy when I let the teachers intimidate me," as well as reward himself: "I did it, I got punished, but I took it like a Man."

These norms don't simply regulate *public* behavior, they enjoin us to surveil and regulate our own behavior in private, including our own thoughts and feelings. This is that different kind of power again, in a different register than the one in which we're accustomed to thinking.

The Good, the Bad, & the Ugly

Funding and policy are concerned mostly with remediating problems, and thus on causes and interventions. While this book will argue that gender norms are a key, if overlooked, component of many problems, that is not the same as arguing that gender norms are all bad.

Quite the contrary. Even traditional codes for masculinity and femininity have both positive and negative sides.

For example, having a man who is strong and independent and believes in being a breadwinner can be quite helpful if you're a young spouse with a lot of dependent children at home. And for those children, it can be very positive if their primary caregiver is a mother who is sensitive, gentle, and maternal. So I've tried to note in the text a number of places where there's strong research on the positive effects of traditional norms.

However, I also find declarations about the positive impacts of gender norms to be at once both true and disingenuous. Why aren't we teaching girls to be strong and independent breadwinners? Or boys to be sensitive, gentle, and paternal?

Sometimes it seems that young people arrive at even the positive attributes through a process of subtraction. As former Philadelphia Eagles quarterback Don McPherson has pointed out, we don't raise our boys to be men, we raise them not to be women or homosexual.

The point of addressing gender norms is not to stamp them out, but rather to make sure that no young person is forced to conform to them, whether by others or because they've internalized harsh gender ideals. Nor should they be punished and discriminated against for not fitting into them. The only way to prevent that forcing is for people to be aware of those norms and find ways to challenge them, to give young people, who are just learning them and coming under gender pressures, the tools to think critically about them instead of just absorbing them uncritically.

Just to give a sample, a personal example: when the first Barbie doll showed up unbidden in our house as someone's gift to my six-year-old daughter, we didn't take it away from her, although we *were* tempted.

Instead, we started asking her questions, so she would think about it. Why did the Barbies all have long blond hair and blue eyes? Did that look like the girls she knew at our very diverse school? What about her super tiny waist? Did she know anyone who was so incredibly thin-waisted, and where would her stomach go? And why was she forced onto her tip-toes? How would she run or jump or play on the jungle-gym all the girls liked to climb at school?

Gender Transformative Approaches

When I mention stories like these in my presentations, someone inevitably raises their hand and asks, "But don't you think that 'boys will be boys?'" (For some reason, this question is never framed as, "But don't you think 'girls will be girls?'" Apparently, testosterone has some irresistible gonadal power in which estrogen is lacking.)

When we do work that holds up, challenges, and ultimately tries to change rigid masculine and feminine belief systems, we are doing "gender transformative" work. The term was coined by Geeta Rao Gupta, a leading expert in gender, and while it's admittedly a bit of a mouthful, it has caught on as the "term of art" in international circles.

In any case, I suspect that behind such questions about *boys being boys* lurks the fear that gender transformative approaches have an implicit or explicit agenda of making boys more feminine and girls more masculine.

While I do confess to a certain degree of sympathy with just such an agenda, I don't believe it has anything to do with gender transformative work.

First, I believe that young people who can be their full selves grow up to be more complete and well-adapted human beings. They haven't had to suppress interests, skills, or feelings they have simply because they were supposed to belong to those of the other sex. Second, I also believe that young people who learn to embrace their own nonnormative gender impulses are likely to be less homophobic, less transphobic, less sexist in general and less likely to bully people like me. I'm pleased to report that a very small but growing number of studies are now supporting both of these conjectures.

In any case, gender transformative work is not about making people into anything. It's about helping them think critically about the gender norms they embrace and the gendered choices they make. Being masculine can mean keeping a stiff upper lip, serving the regiment, and putting women and children first. It can also mean dominating other men, having lots of sex, and bullying the queers. These are just two of the many definitions of manhood that circulate in different cultures at different times. Gender transformative work aims to give people the tools to become more aware of such varying ideas, to think critically about them, and then to hopefully make more intentional, authentic, and constructive choices about which they chose to embrace.

That is why the second section of this book is devoted to specific issue areas where gender norms have a well-documented and long-understood impact. It is followed by the third and final section, which takes the tools developed in the first two and applies them to thinking through how we might better improve life outcomes among at-risk youth by using an approach that is both gender transformative *and* intersectional.

But first, let's take a brief look at international work: why it sometimes seems like they're far ahead of the United States when it comes to gender transformative approaches, and what they may be missing.

References & Selected Reading

Aboud, F. E. 2005. "The Development of Prejudice in Childhood and Adolescence," in Dovidio, J. F., Glick, P., and Rudman, L. A., eds., *On the Nature of Prejudice: Fifty Years after Allport*, 310–26. Malden: Blackwell Publishing.

Addis, M. E., and Mahalik, J. R. 2003. "Men, Masculinity, and the Contexts of Help Seeking," *American Psychologist* 58 (1): 5.

Arciniega, G. M., Anderson, T. C., Tovar-Blank, Z. G., and Tracey, T. J. 2008. "Toward a Fuller Conception of Machismo: Development of a Traditional Machismo and Caballerismo Scale," *Journal of Counseling Psychology* 55 (1): 19.

Begley, S. 2000. "The Stereotype Trap," *Newsweek*. http://www.newsweek.com/stereotype-trap-157203.

Blackless, M., Charuvastra, A., Derryck, A., FaustoSterling, A., Lauzanne, K., and Lee, E. 2000. "How Sexually Dimorphic Are We? Review and Synthesis," *American Journal of Human Biology* 12 (2): 151–66.

Boudet, A. M. M., Petesch, P., and Turk, C. 2013. *On Norms and Agency: Conversations about Gender Equality with Women and Men in 20 Countries*. Washington, DC: World Bank Publications.

Bowen, A. 2012. *Forty Years of LGBTQ Philanthropy: 1970–2010*. New York: Funders for LGBTQ Issues.

Brush, C. 2014. "The Power of Investing in Women," September 11, 2014. *Forbes*. https://www.forbes.com/sites/babson/2014/09/11/the-power-of-investing-in-women-entrepreneurs/ - 4143842e56f2.

Butler, J. 1999. *Gender Trouble*. New York: Routledge.

———. 2011. *Gender Trouble: Feminism and the Subversion of Identity*. New York: Routledge.

Cain, P. A. 1993. "Litigating for Lesbian and Gay Rights: A Legal History," *Virginia Law Review* 79: 1551–641.

Chodorow, N. J. 2014. *Femininities, Masculinities, Sexualities: Freud and Beyond*. Lexington: University Press of Kentucky.

Coltrane, S., and Messineo, M. 2000. "The Perpetuation of Subtle Prejudice: Race and Gender Imagery in 1990s Television Advertising," *Sex Roles* 42 (5–6): 363–89.

Connell, R. W., and Connell, R. 2005. *Masculinities*. Berkeley: University of California Press.

Courtenay, W. H. 2000. "Constructions of Masculinity and Their Influence on Men's Well-Being: A Theory of Gender and Health," *Social Science & Medicine* 50 (10): 1385–401.

Crawford, M. 1995. *Talking Difference: On Gender and Language* (vol. 7). Thousand Oaks, CA: Sage.

Crenshaw, K. 1989. "Demarginalizing the Intersection of Race and Sex: A Black Feminist Critique of Antidiscrimination Doctrine, Feminist Theory, and Antiracist Politics," *University of Chicago Legal Forum* 1 (8): 139–67.

CWIP. 2008. *ClearSighted: A Guide to Using a Gender Lens*. Chicago.

Fishbein, H. D. 1996. *Peer Prejudice and Discrimination: Evolutionary, Cultural, and Developmental Dynamics*. Boulder, CO: Westview Press.

Francis, L. J., and Wilcox, C. 1996. "Religion and Gender Orientation," *Personality and Individual Differences* 20 (1): 119–21.

Galambos, Nancy L., David M. Almeida, and Anne C. Petersen. 1990. "Masculinity, Femininity, and Sex Role Attitudes in Early Adolescence: Exploring Gender Intensification," *Child Development* 61 (6): 1905–914.

Gauntlett, D. 2008. *Media, Gender and Identity: An Introduction*. New York: Routledge.

Ghaill, M. A. 1994. *The Making of Men: Masculinities, Sexualities and Schooling*. London: McGraw-Hill Education (UK).

Gómez, C. A., and Marin, B. V. 1996. "Gender, Culture, and Power: Barriers to HIV-Prevention Strategies for Women," *Journal of Sex Research* 33 (4): 355–62.

Gottschalk, L. 2003. "Same-Sex Sexuality and Childhood Gender Nonconformity: A Spurious Connection," *Journal of Gender Studies* 12 (1): 35–50.

Gupta, V. 2011. *Breaking the Gender Barrier: Vinita Gupta on Creating More Women Technology Entrepreneurs*. Wharton: University of Pennsylvania.

Gray, J. 1992. *Men Are from Mars, Women Are from Venus: Practical Guide for Improving Communication*. New York: HarperCollins.

Healthy Men. 2011. [Text]. http://patients-consumers/patient-involvement/healthy-men/index.html (accessed March 18, 2018).

Hill, C., Corbett, C., and St. Rose, A. 2010. *Why So Few? Women in Science, Technology, Engineering, and Mathematics*. Washington, DC: American Association of University Women.

Hill, C., and Kearl, H. 2011. *Crossing the Line: Sexual Harassment at School*. Washington, DC: American Association of University Women.

Jewkes, R. 2002. "Intimate Partner Violence: Causes and Prevention," *The Lancet* 359 (9315): 1423–29.

Kaler, A., Kimmel, M. S., and Aronson, A., eds. 2015. *The Gendered Society Reader*. Oxford: Oxford University Press.

Killermann, S. 2013. *The Social Justice Advocate's Handbook: A Guide to Gender*. Austin, TX: Impetus Books.

Klugman, J., Hanmer, L., Twigg, S., Hasan, T., McCleary-Sills, J., and Santamaria, J. 2014. *Voice and Agency: Empowering Women and Girls for Shared Prosperity*. Washington, DC: World Bank Publications.

Laqueur, T. W. 1990. *Making Sex: Body and Gender from the Greeks to Freud*. Cambridge, MA: Harvard University Press.

Levant, R. F., and Richmond, K. 2008. "A Review of Research on Masculinity Ideologies Using the Male Role Norms Inventory," *The Journal of Men's Studies* 15 (2): 130–46.

Lindgren, C. 2010. "Pink Brain Blue Brain: How Small Differences Grow into Troublesome Gaps," *Acta Paediatrica* 99 (7): 1108.

Lipson, J. 2001. *Hostile Hallways: Bullying, Teasing, and Sexual Harassment in School.* Washington, DC: AAUW Educational Foundation.

Lottes, I. L., and Kuriloff, P. J. 1992. "The Effects of Gender, Race, Religion, and Political Orientation on the Sex Role Attitudes of College Freshmen," *Adolescence* 27 (107): 675.

Mahalik, J. R., Morray, E. B., Coonerty-Femiano, A., Ludlow, L. H., Slattery, S. M., and Smiler, A. 2005. "Development of the Conformity to Feminine Norms Inventory," *Sex Roles* 52 (7–8): 417–35.

Martin, E. 2001. *The Woman in the Body: A Cultural Analysis of Reproduction.* Boston: Beacon Press.

Millett, K. 2016. *Sexual Politics.* New York: Columbia University Press.

Moreno, C. L. 2007. "The Relationship between Culture, Gender, Structural Factors, Abuse, Trauma, and HIV/AIDS for Latinas," *Qualitative Health Research* 17 (3): 340–52.

Morgan, M. Y. 1987. "The Impact of Religion on Gender-Role Attitudes," *Psychology of Women Quarterly* 11 (3): 301–10.

O'Connell, H. 2012. *Funding for Inclusion: Women and Girls in the Equation.* New York: GrantCraft. https://library.concordeurope.org/record/796 (accessed March 18, 2018).

Poteat, V. P. 2007. "Peer Group Socialization of Homophobic Attitudes and Behavior during Adolescence," *Child Development* 78 (6): 1830–42.

Pulerwitz, J., Barker, G., Segundo, M., and Nascimento, M. 2006. *Promoting More Gender-Equitable Norms and Behaviors among Young Men as an HIV/AIDS Prevention Strategy.* Washington, DC: Instituto Promundo.

Read, J. N. G. 2003. "The Sources of Gender Role Attitudes among Christian and Muslim Arab-American Women," *Sociology of Religion* 64 (2): 207–22.

Rubin, J. Z., Provenzano, F. J., and Luria, Z. 1974. "The Eye of the Beholder: Parents' Views on Sex of Newborns," *American Journal of Orthopsychiatry* 44 (4): 512.

Rustgi, S. D., Doty, M. M., and Collins, S. R. 2009. *Women at Risk: Why Many Women Are Forgoing Needed Health Care.* New York: Commonwealth Fund.

Spencer, S. J., Steele, C. M., and Quinn, D. M. 1999. "Stereotype Threat and Women's Math Performance," *Journal of Experimental Social Psychology* 35 (1): 4–28.

Thorne, B. 1993. *Gender Play: Girls and Boys in School.* New Brunswick, NJ: Rutgers University Press.

Tolman, D. L., Striepe, M. I., and Harmon, T. 2003. "Gender Matters: Constructing a Model of Adolescent Sexual Health," *Journal of Sex Research* 40 (1): 4–12.

TrueChild. 2014. *Do Internalized Feminine Norms Depress Girls' STEM Attitudes and Participation?* Washington, DC: TrueChild.

Valentine, D., and Wilchins, R. A. 1997. "One Percent on the Burn Chart: Gender, Genitals, and Hermaphrodites with Attitude," *Social Text* (52/53): 215–22.

Varga, C. A. 2003. "How Gender Roles Influence Sexual and Reproductive Health among South African Adolescents," *Studies in Family Planning* 34 (3): 160–72.

Weinraub, M., Clemens, L. P., Sockloff, A., Ethridge, T., Gracely, E., and Myers, B. 1984. "The Development of Sex Role Stereotypes in the Third Year: Relationships to Gender Labeling, Gender Identity, Sex-Types Toy Preference, and Family Characteristics," *Child Development* 55 (4): 1493–503.

Wilchins, R. A., and Taylor, T. 2006. *50 under 30: Masculinity and the War on America's Youth—A Human Rights Report*. Washington, DC: GenderPAC.

Young, R., and Sweeting, H. 2004. "Adolescent Bullying, Relationships, Psychological Well-Being, and Gender-Atypical Behavior: A Gender Diagnosticity Approach," *Sex Roles* 50 (7–8): 525–37.

3

International Institutions & Gender

We're not doing this because it's trendy or politically correct—
after all, we're data-driven economists—
we're doing it because the numbers show it works better.

—Senior Manager, The World Bank

Major international donor institutions like CARE, PEPFAR (the President's Emergency Plan for AIDS Relief), USAID (the US Agency for International Development), UNAIDS (the Joint United Nations Programme on HIV/AIDS) and UNFPA (the United Nations Population Fund), the World Bank, and the World Health Organization (WHO) have all launched initiatives with a strong focus on gender norms.

USAID will no longer fund new initiatives that lack a strong analysis of gender norms and the inequities they cause. PEPFAR has made challenging rigid masculine norms one of its top-three priorities. Interestingly enough, this is not only mandated by legislation passed by the US Congress, but it was strengthened in the revised legislation under which PEPFAR was reauthorized and for which many Republicans voted—although the federal government pretty much ignores the issue of gender norms domestically.

Even the staid World Bank has launched a highly public, multiyear effort costing millions of dollars to pull gender norms through every facet of its work improving equity for women and girls.

Since its founding in 1944, the World Bank has invested hundreds of millions of dollars in credits, loans, and direct aid to improve equity for women and girls. Yet, over time, they found that there was an "invisible ceiling" that prevented further progress—a point of diminishing returns past which greater investment failed to yield greater returns.

No doubt intrigued and concerned, they commissioned a huge study (practically the only kind the World Bank commissions). In the end, they interviewed thousands of people in two hundred communities from dozens of countries.

As reported in its voluminous 160-page report "On Norms and Agency," the World Bank found that while significant advances had been achieved in women's political and economic participation, in things that depended on private agency: education, reproductive health, women's voice, and partner violence, little had changed.

One of the main factors holding women and girls back across many of these was social gender norms. As the report notes, the Bank found that gender norms were actually a "foundation of inequality . . . as important as jobs and opportunity." It concluded that what was needed was a strong, specific focus on challenging rigid cultural codes of femininity and masculinity. This was confirmed in the Bank's 2014 follow-up report, *Voice and Agency* (Klugman et al. 2014).

I had the opportunity to ask one of the Bank's senior managers who could possibly be the intended audience for reports that ran to 160 pages and 226 pages, respectively. Most of us would rather just wait for the movie (which would no doubt star Meryl Streep doing one of those amazing accents). He explained to me that the reports weren't intended for public consumption, but were aimed at their own staff to start a long, internal, education process. The Bank planned to integrate almost every facet of its work with low- and middle-income countries (LMICs).

Then, almost as an afterthought, he said something that really stuck with me, because my own passion for gender norms is animated so much by every abstract theory combined with very painful personal experiences. He said, "We're not doing this because it's trendy or politically correct—after all, we're data-driven economists—we're doing it because the numbers show it works better."

As the World Bank's president, Jim Yong Kim, encouragingly declares in the foreword to *Voice and Agency*: "The good news is that social norms can and do change" (xi).

Nongovernmental organizations (NGOs) like EngenderHealth, International Council on Research for Women (ICRW), International Planned Parenthood, and Population Council have also embraced gender norms, and they've helped lead this effort.

As documented in *Exploring Dimensions of Masculinity and Violence*, CARE and ICRW have partnered to "deconstruct masculinity and determine how gender norms and male socialization lead to inequitable attitudes and behaviors toward women and girls" (Eckman et al. 2007, 9). Declaring that "men are changing," International Planned Parenthood is working with "men and boys to promote gender equality and positive masculinity."

In fact, there has been so much information circulating at the international level that some years ago USAID launched what may be the world's worst-named agency: the "Interagency Gender Working Group" or IGWG, mainly to collate and disseminate information among all the institutions, funders, policy makers, and NGOs doing this work.

As figure 3.1 shows, the IGWG and expert Geeta Rao Gupta have developed a scale to classify gender-aware programs and policies that take transformative approaches. Unfortunately, the work of most US nonprofits and funders today remains gender blind, meaning it does not engage gender norms or dynamics in a meaningful way, like it might race or class.

Programs that are gender aware then fall along a spectrum. Using safer sex as an example, a gender-exploitative program would promote narrow, traditional gender norms to achieve its goals. An example might be a men's condom program with a tagline like, "You're a Real Man: you chose to play safely!" This program might indeed get results, but it does so by promoting hypermasculinity and ideas of male control of sex.

A gender-accommodating program would allow for gender differences without really trying to change them. An example might be a safer sex program that ensures brothel owners enforce condom use on the premises, while doing nothing

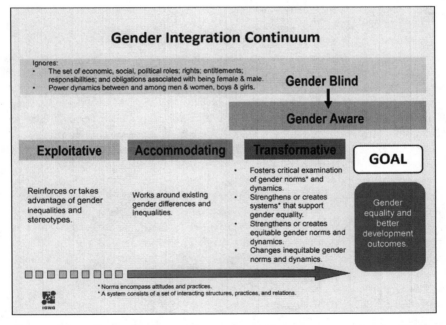

Figure 3.1   Gender Integration Continuum by USAID's Interagency Gender Working and Geeta Rao Gupta. *Source*: Interagency Gender Working Group (IGWG), "Gender Integration Continuum," figure from The Gender Integration Continuum User's Guide, developed with assistance from the United States Agency for International Development's Bureau for Global Health (Washington, DC: IGWG, 2017). Reproduced by permission. All rights reserved.

to empower the women who work there or addressing those who are trafficked or underage.

Gender-transformative programs highlight, challenge, and ultimately try to change rigid gender norms and the inequities they cause. An example might be a program that teaches both girls and boys the facts of safer sex, and then uses that as an entry point to help them explore the power imbalances of sex, the need for young women to have more of an equal say, and the need for boys to take equal responsibility for avoiding unplanned pregnancy.

Such a program would also mine something international experts have begun promoting called "gender synchronization"—which is a ten-dollar term for saying that working with girls *and* boys simultaneously is more effective than doing either alone. What girls think about boys or find attractive in them tends to have tremendous impact on boys' own attitudes and behavior, and vice versa. It's hard to change girls' or boys' gender beliefs or behaviors in isolation, because gender beliefs between the sexes tend to be interdependent and reinforcing. (The same might apply to trying to change gay *and* straight youth's attitudes at once.) In addition, some advocates have begun stressing the importance of "two-generation" or "2Gen" approaches to gender equity, that engage both youth *and* parents.

What Holds Us Back

If all this progress has mostly failed to inform work in the United States, it may be because of a number of interlocking factors. To begin with, when new ideas originate abroad some domestic agencies and foundations seem to combine "American Exceptionalism" with "not invented here." The former assures them that the United States is definitively different from any other country, and the latter that we have little or nothing to learn from other countries, especially those in the Global South.

Also, many international donor organizations have the advantage of employing a human rights model that comprehends issues like age, race, class, gender, disability, and sexual orientation as common aspects of an inviolable personhood that must be addressed simultaneously. This approach encourages them to sidestep the silo-approach that US funders often bemoan (but still use): the one in which each issue and identity gets a separate portfolio: women, racial justice, LGBTQ, economic security, health, and so on.

Unfortunately—again because of "American Exceptionalism"—we have always considered human rights something the US exports to other nations, but never imports from them. Some readers may remember a wheelchair-bound former senator Bob Dole vainly pleading with his Republican Senate colleagues to approve an inoffensive international treaty for the disabled, while they continued warning darkly that passage would leave the United States at the mercy of unnamed foreign forces. Despite its many advantages and widespread application abroad, the human rights model has never caught on here, and is, unfortunately, unlikely to any time soon.

An Empowerment Model

Another, and perhaps deeper reason gender work lags behind in the United States may be the differences in how we think about an individual's ability to make decisions independently and put them into effect—what is termed "agency."

US programs, policies, and funding often approach each young person as a discreet unit endowed with full agency: a rational actor who reaches logical conclusion based on the facts. This assumes the person is fully empowered to take personal action based on this—in other words, like the best possible kind of functional adult. For lack of a better term, we might call this approach the "empowerment model."

It is true that many American youths are relatively empowered compared with their peers in LMICs. Along with generally higher family incomes and better educations, they possess many high-tech toys (smartphones, iPads), easily connect to the Internet, and have a media sophistication once unusual among the young. So perhaps it's no surprise that funders, policies, and nonprofits have tended to focus their attention on offering accurate information, training, and opportunities so that these empowered, logical young people can take the right actions. But as Hortensia Amaro (1994) pointed out in a conference research paper on HIV and reproductive health, most adolescents aren't really anything like that. Sex, money, drinking, and relationships aren't matters of logic and good data. Instead, they are matters of emotion, passion, and social in-group conformity.

Young people are deeply driven by what they fear other kids will think, by what other kids are doing, by the desire to be appear as *cool* as possible and by all means avoid being *uncool*. Even such a "simple" task as a young woman requiring condom use with a first boyfriend will depend on factors like her own sexual knowledge, what her partner wants, his willingness, what she thinks a "woman's role" is in sex, and what she thinks his friends or hers will say about her behavior. These factors and many more will be at play during what will probably be an impulsive, unplanned, and perhaps anxious moment of impulse, and often with a partner who will be some combination of bigger, older, stronger, more psychologically aggressive, and more sexually experienced.

Even with the right information, training, and programs, adolescents don't enjoy anything like the level-headed, logical approach to decisions and complete agency in taking action that an empowerment model would seem to envision or require. These are the challenges mostly young women face.

Boys may face similar obstacles. Consider this story from a researcher who interviewed young men about their sexual history: one of them told her (to paraphrase her words), "I'm thirteen. I shouldn't be having this much sex." So, he's self-aware, which is good. But then he continues, "But if I don't, the other guys will call me a fag, and if I try to settle on one girl, they say I'm her bitch."

I'm sure some school program or community organization has already taught this young man the facts of HIV and pregnancy prevention. They pulled out the banana and did the "how to" demonstration, so he was instructed in proper condom use.

On the counter at his local community health clinic, there was probably a big bowl of free, brightly-colored condoms.

All of these are important. Probably everything possible was provided to help him reach constructive, autonomous decisions . . . except to address the social pressures around manhood and masculinity that were driving his behavior.

In addition, most adolescents lack the social capital to have anything like full agency, and are often still highly dependent upon parents, educators, and other adult gatekeepers. Consider one parent's story from *On the Road to Equality*, a report by the Women's Foundation of Minnesota:

> Our daughter was one of the top welders in her junior-high-school program and would have been very successful in that field, but she wasn't encouraged by us as parents or people in construction. Why not? Because she would have had to struggle for acceptance by men in that field, and they would not be welcoming. So, she's not in that career. Even though they may have the skills, women have to always fight that battle. (2014, 5)

This young woman had training, opportunity, and resources. But all that wasn't enough to move her into the high-paying field for which she was trained and to which her skills entitled her. Deeply held beliefs among those around her were enough to trump programs, training, and the best of adult intentions.

The Clan, the Tribe, & the Village

If international funders and NGOs working in LMICs are better at addressing social gender norms, it may be in part because they operate in patriarchal cultures where young women cannot walk the streets unescorted, own property, select their own spouse, or expect to be his sole mate. In such environments, an empowerment model makes little sense, and advocates are pretty much forced to challenge communal beliefs and practices about manhood and womanhood if they want to improve equity for women and girls. Moreover, smaller towns and villages often operate as virtually "closed" societies: small, highly interconnected social systems in which there is little privacy and often less agency, and young people are seldom out of view of their elders. In such cultures, communal norms, the opinions of others, and the necessity of fitting in all take on enormous power.

As a result, international funders and policy makers have learned to think less of young people as discrete, autonomous, empowered individuals and instead focus on the social systems and norms in which they are embedded and must operate: instead of the individual, the tribe, the village, or the clan is the unit of analysis. This is a lesson in the importance of communal beliefs and practices that Western funders might do well to study and internalize.

When it comes to sex, health, or education, even the most empowered young person is deeply enmeshed in complex social networks of relationships and gendered expectations that help determine their behavior, particularly in low-income communities where social capital and connectedness is crucial to surviving and thriving.

Not Only at the Hands of Men

While international NGOs and institutional funders have generally been ahead of the United States when it comes to gender norms, much of the focus has been devoted to issues of men and masculinity, especially to stopping violence against women. Much of this is done with the stated goal of increasing their economic security. In deeply patriarchal cultures where financial power is mostly held by men and women have little agency and are at risk of physical abuse in their marriages, this kind of triage makes good sense.

Yet in a cluster of important areas for the development of young women and girls—such as child marriage, sex trafficking, genital cutting, ritual fattening, menstrual health, and education deprivation—beliefs and attitudes about femininity among mothers, female elders, and especially aunts (who represent the husband's family) can be even more important to creating lasting change. While a core of place-based NGOs is providing groundbreaking programs that challenge rigid feminine norms, such norms are still rarely discussed. Little of the infrastructure groups like Promundo and others have developed to support the "men and masculinities" work—data collection, regular convenings, online networks, white paper reports—exists for these girl-serving groups.

It is hard to find studies on feminine norms in the Global South. Whenever I see an omission like that, I assume that something important is up. So TrueChild conducted three dozen interviews with funders, researchers, NGOs, advocates, and agencies to develop formative research. From that data, we developed one of the first white papers devoted to this issue: "Feminine Norms: An Overlooked Key to Improving Adolescent Girls' Life Outcomes?" (which we called internally simply "TrueGirl").

The paper was an effort to recenter feminine norms in the global dialogue on women's equity, while also serving as an entry point for the emerging dialogue on gender nonconformity and LGBTQ in the Global South. For those who would like to read more about this, that report forms chapter 11 of this book.

As Abigail Burgesson of the African Women's Development Fund explained in the paper,

> Norms are critical. It all comes down to beliefs and practices. So I am very glad that this issue of gender norms is finally being addressed. What people fail to realize is that it is often also women who impose and perpetuate these harmful traditions and practices . . . out of a desire to preserve beliefs, practices, and norms that come from patriarchy but that they have inherited.
>
> Women believe that if things change for the next generation of girls, that will be taking something away from them or make them incomplete. We often hear, "This was here before our time and it's still the way things must be done today." So we will never change these things as long as we assume women are implementing, and not agents of this system. We need to bring together the women's groups doing this work; we need a high-level network and engagement of donors, advocates, and activists. We need an alliance. Because when we work as a movement, we get results. (TrueChild n.d., 2)

Some Caveats

Now that we've covered the basics terms and concepts, Part II of this book will be devoted to looking more deeply at specific problem areas where research on the impact of rigid gender norms is both broad and well-accepted, and Part III will examine the impact of gender norms in specific populations. Before moving on, a few important caveats are in order.

Cultural Competence

Much of this book addresses the special challenges faced by low-income Black and Latinx youth. However, I write as an outsider, one who has grown up with White privilege, as well as a large degree of class privilege, and who has no personal experience with what it's like to live Black or Latinx or in poverty in America. As in all other sections, whether explicitly stated or not, observations about gender norms and youth of color are based on the available studies, not on personal knowledge.

In addition, while it is stated several times in the text (as in the opening quotes to chapter 1), it bears repeating that where the book addresses the internalizing rigid masculine or feminine norms among youth of color, this should not be read as promoting a return to "respectability politics." The outdated fantasy that if young Black and Latino males would just "hitch up their pants," use "proper" English, and generally act more like middle-class, White suburban youth, the problems of structural racism would disappear has long been discredited.

And while we're on the topic of race and cultural competence, it's also important to note that I hope this book's focus on problem areas will not be read as contributing to the already-extensive "crisis literature" on youth of color and the grim outcomes many of them face in low-income communities. As strong, community-based initiatives like Black Male Engagement (BMe) keep pointing out, youth of color continue to bring immense resources and resilience to the challenges they face, and it's important to focus on their positive contributions to solving the world's problems.

Study Size, Samples, & Rigor

Although the results of academic studies are used throughout this book, it should be also noted that as a rule many studies tend to oversample the young White, middle-class, college-age men (and sometimes women) who are most available for academics for study. This makes the results somewhat less applicable to youth of color and/or low-income youth. This is not to say that youth of color are absent from the samples of many studies, but rather that they may be in such limited numbers that valid conclusions cannot be drawn, or results have not been disaggregated by race.

In any case, we have far too few studies specifically designed to better understand Black and Latinx youth, and particularly how they are affected by issues of gender. In addition, some of the studies cited in this book may have used relatively small sample sizes, not very random samples, or have failed to conduct the kind of long-term follow-up that enables you to be really sure the results reported were permanent.

The widely accepted behavioral science "gold standard" for evaluating curricula and programs is the randomized controlled trial or RCT. These involve recruiting a large, randomized sample, giving them a program, and then comparing their results against another large, randomized sample (the "control group") to see how they differ. RCTs are time-consuming, complicated, and hugely expensive—and beyond the reach of many nonprofits, agencies, academics, and NGOs who are doing important work on the ground on gender. Even recruiting a large group, collecting and analyzing pre-post measures, and then following them up long-term say, a year later, can be difficult and costly.

Partly as a result, few of the studies we have on gender-aware programs rise to the standard of RCTs, or even collect enough pre-post measures with long-term follow-up that we can say with confidence they've been "rigorously evaluated." All of which is to say, the study of gender norms is still very much a work in progress, even more so when we move from academic studies (which usually simply test a single idea), to testing if a complex program with lots of moving parts actually works (which is what practitioners and nonprofits really need).

Correlation

It is also worth noting that the majority of studies about the impact of belief in rigid gender norms are correlational in nature. It has long been established that young women who have stronger beliefs in traditional feminine norms are more likely to develop eating disorders, for example. However, this does not mean that such beliefs *cause* eating disorders. While there certainly is a strong *prima facie* case that such attitudes are implicated, that kind of A-causes-B results are very hard to produce, particularly in areas of human behavior.

To bridge this gap, in most places I've tried to address this by confining claims to stating that an outcome is "more likely" or "tends to develop," or "is strongly linked to," and avoided using the specific language of causation. It is up to each individual reader to decide for themselves how much of this correlation is a marker for actual causation (and hopefully future studies).

The entire premise of this book is that there is an extremely strong argument to be made that attitudes and beliefs around femininity and masculinity *are* deeply implicated in problem behaviors like eating disorders, unplanned pregnancy, or teen bullying, and, more broadly, that gendered beliefs and attitudes *do* drive behavior. But we do not yet always have definitive proof.

Intervening Variables

This book was intended as an accessible introductory text for a lay reader across a wide range of issues—each of which could fill its own book—not a scientific treatment for academics. Given this focus, I have tried to document the main thrust of the available research is each area, without getting lost in complications and counterexamples. It is simply beyond the scope of an introductory text to give each subject anything like the detail they deserve.

However, this approach certainly has shortcomings. The section on school bullying, for example, notes that young men who have a stronger belief in the ideals of aggression and dominance are more likely to engage in bullying. However, this finding is complicated by that fact that such beliefs are *necessary but not sufficient* for violent behavior.

Other studies have found that such bullying is much more likely to happen when young men also believe that using force against others is morally acceptable. If they don't hold that belief, then holding ideals about aggression and dominance do not seem to lead to significant increases in bullying. It's safe to say that in nearly every issue area this book touches on, there are these kinds of intervening variables. And a longer and more technically detailed book would certainly offer this kind of nuance in every issue area.

Silver Bullets

In addition, problems like seeking out care when you're sick (e.g., health-seeking) or educational achievement are complex and multidimensional. There is no single variable, no "silver bullet" for resolving any of them. In none of these problem areas is gender norms the sole variable, or even necessarily the biggest one. Rather, I would suggest that in most of them gender norms are the biggest variable *not being* addressed. If you were a foundation, a public agency, a hospital, school, or nonprofit looking for the next big "drop on the meter" in improving programmatic or policy outcomes, gender norms are definitely something to consider.

Behavior Change Is Hard

Carefully controlled studies about the impact of rigid or harmful gender norms do not always translate into effective programs to teach young people to think critically. Just as we are still at the very beginning of our learning to think about gender norms, we are also at the beginning of learning how to develop programs, for young people and for the systems that serve them. We are going to need a lot of trial and error to get there.

Dr. Kim at the World Bank Group did say that "social norms can and do change"; he might have added, "but it's really, really hard, and we're just learning how." We're nearly at the bottom of a long and steep learning curve.

A respected gender researcher recently wrote me about a large, multiyear RCT study of a new teen reproductive-health curriculum. The curriculum was solidly developed and well-grounded in theory, but did not produce the desired outcomes.

It's not easy, and behavior change—particularly with emotionally laden and sometimes impulsive behaviors like sex. It is not easy. But the good news is we're trying, there are more programs and curricula with a gender focus all the time, and they're only going to improve.

Stories from the Frontlines: Promundo

One of the success stories in this work has doubtless been Promundo, a Brazilian NGO that now has an office in Washington, DC as well. Founded in 1997 and headed by visionary leader Gary Barker Promundo, it began working in low-income communities in Rio de Janeiro, seeking to engage men and boys as allies in combating violence against women. In many ways, it has grown into a model for how to move the discourse on gender norms forward.

For instance, its extensive Program H for men and boys and (more limited) Program M for women and girls have become "gold standard" curricula for working with young people. These are widely used by other groups as well, and my own organization, TrueChild, has used many of their exercises as the basis for our own curricula.

In partnership with ICRW, Promundo has collected and analyzed a global data set from men in a dozen countries. The International Men and Gender Equality Survey (IMAGES) is helping advocates better understand men's attitudes on gender equality. Promundo's MenEngage network connects hundreds of NGOs and individuals in scores of countries working to engage men and boys in women's rights generally, and works toward stopping violence against women, specifically. Promundo has also been fortunate that many of the experts Barker has been able to attract over the years, like researchers Andrew Levack and Lori Rolleri, are both talented and dedicated to promoting a gender norms analysis.

References & Selected Reading

Eckman, A., Jain, A., Kambou, S. D., Bartel, D., and Crownover, J. 2007. "ZExploring Dimensions of Masculinity and Violence (Western Balkan Gender-Based Violence Prevention Initiative)." Washington, DC: CARE International Balkans. https://www.care.org/sites/default/files/documents/Exploring-Dimensions-of-Masculinity-and-Violence.pdf.

Amaro, H. 1994. "Gender and Sexual Risk Reduction: Issues to Consider." Paper presented at the Latino HIV/AIDS Research Conference, "Defining the Path for Future Research," Santa Monica, CA, April 23–24.

Klugman, J., Hanmer, L., STwigg, S., et al. World Bank Group. 2014. *Voice and Agency: Empowering Women and Girls for Shared Prosperity*, report for the World Bank Group. Foreword by Jim Yong Kim. https://openknowledge.worldbank.org/handle/10986/5993.

TrueChild. n.d. "Feminine Norms: An Overlooked Key to Improving Adolescent Girls' Life Outcomes?" TrueChild.org. https://static1.squarespace.com/static/599e3a20be659497eb2490 98/t/59df186a18b27ddf3bb14668/ 1507793016558/__TrueGirl+%5BWMM%5D.pdf.

Women's Foundation of Minnesota. 2014. *On the Road to Equality: Statewide Findings & Policy Recommendations*. A report by the WFM (in partnership with the Institute for Women's Policy Research and supplement to *Status of Girls in Minnesota*.

II

GENDER NORMS & EDUCATION, HEALTH, VIOLENCE

4

Sexual & Reproductive Health

Male peacocks grow enormous—and largely useless feathers—to attract a mate. Male fish grow large tails or multicolor scales to advertise their masculine availability to females (and perhaps the occasional male as well).

As humans we're much less ornamental in our gender displays, and unlike most species, we put the burden mostly on the female. But gender norms communicating femininity and masculinity are still central to human courtship, sex, and reproduction. In fact, it may be the mainspring of courtship and sex, of what kinds of partners we seek and wed.

We have developed social practices that impact almost every aspect of how our bodies move through space and communicate our gender to others, including: hair length, style, and color (blondes may "have more fun," and are almost always associated with greater femininity); nail length and coloring; lip and cheek coloring (fullness or blushing communicates sexual arousal); eye area coloring and eyelash lengthening (the illusion of wide open eyes and pupil dilation communicates arousal); piercings (ears of course, but also eyebrows, lips, and noses); and adornment (earrings, necklaces, bracelets, rings).

Of course dress is heavily gendered for both lower and upper body garments. Various garments can only be worn by men or women (skirts, ties, hose), and certain colors are mainly reserved for one sex or the other.

Footwear is still heavily gendered, particularly formal footwear. Particularly for formal occasions or business, women must still put appliances on their feet which hobble their movement, shorten their stride, accentuate their hip sway, and tighten both their calves and buttocks so the lower back half of their bodies is pushed up and back slightly, as if presented for mating. Other appliances, like push-up bras, Spanx "shapewear," and nylon stockings serve similar functions.

Posture also communicates gender. Men stand with their legs wide apart, and many sit the same way, which is why it is known as "manspreading"—increasingly a public transit problem worldwide. Men also cross their legs with one ankle across the opposite knee. All of these postures show strength, dominance, territoriality, and asserting one's space.

Women, as noted earlier, often stand in the "stork pose," with the legs together and all their weight on one foot, indicating pliancy or weakness, and a lack of territoriality. In formal pictures women will often tilt their heads to show accessibility and avoid directness. In some non-Western societies, women must also look down to avoid direct eye contact, slouch, and remain silent unless spoken to, to communicate deference and submissiveness.

Gestures are heavily gendered. Some women will point with their wrist "broken," rest their hands on their hips with the fingers pointing backward, and examine their nails with the fingers extended and the palm pointing away, and so forth.

Just how much weight we give to small gestures was brought home some years ago when a documentary crew was setting up to interview a group, including myself, on transgender activism. Before they'd really started, I made the mistake of pointing at something off-camera with my wrist "broken." I immediately knew they would use this to communicate, "*Look, this six-foot transperson gestures like a 'real female.'*" Sure enough, that otherwise pointless shot opened the film's final cut.

Body modification is also commonly used by women to communicate femininity and sexual attractiveness. This includes breast augmentation, nose reduction (strong noses signal presence and strength, and tiny, up-turned button noses the opposite), and of course the ever-popular "Brazilian Butt Lift"—which is just what its name implies. Women in many Western cultures are also expected to regularly remove body hair from their upper lips, arms, armpits, legs, and the sides of their pubic area.

Men, of course, modify their bodies to show masculinity, strength, and virility through weightlifting, sports, steroids, and hair transplants.

Even vocal behavior and inflection are harnessed socially to signal masculinity and femininity. Men and boys interrupt more often, make more declarative statements, use a narrower pitch range, and tend to end sentences on a down or even note, which communicates definitiveness. Women and girls make fewer declarative statements, use a much wider pitch range (and giggle, which men *never* do), and end both questions and statements on an up note, as if merely suggesting, asking, or requesting something.

A Continuous Nonverbal Conversation

Almost everything about our bodies is used to signal to others that we want to be seen as feminine or masculine. We continue most of these signals, displays, and behaviors even well past the time or age when we are actually interested in attracting romantic partners. Indeed, they are deeply woven into every facet of how we interact with others and participate in society.

From adolescence onward, each of us is engaged in a continuous nonverbal conversation with society about our gender and how we want others to see it.

The impact of gender norms doesn't end with displays and signals, but continues into courtship and sex itself, which is also deeply gendered. This may sound strange, since sex is supposed to be entirely natural and biologically driven, and is perhaps our most basic instinct. But while the urge for sex and the most basic mechanics may be indeed biological, pretty much everything else about it is cultural and constructed.

Far from being "natural," sex might be one of our most overconstructed social behaviors. Perhaps because of this, reproductive health is one of the first areas that gender researchers investigated, and so it is also one for which we have the most studies.

Nearly everything connected with sexual intimacy—emotional vulnerability, sexual risk-taking, infidelity, specific acts and pleasures, the role of consent, attitudes toward pregnancy prevention, the meaning of promiscuity, responsibility for child and maternal health, and the role, if any, of sexual coercion or partner violence—is deeply connected to what people believe is expected for them as females and males.

For instance, Andrew Levack used a presentation at EngenderHealth that showed some of the reasons youth in one focus group gave for deciding to have sex. The boys' side includes: "For fame," "Something 2 brag on," "To please girls," and "My rep." The girls' side includes items like: "To fit in," "For a boy to like them," "Peer pressure," "To get attention from guys and girls," and "Relationship pressure from guys." Even in this most intimate and consequential of decisions, gendered expectations and gender pressures (and rewards) play an enormous role in behavior.

According to theorists like Butler, it might even be said that we do not simply have intercourse with male and female bodies, but rather with highly gendered bodies. For instance, although kissing is nearly universal in Western cultures, it may seem odd that a minority of the Earth's known cultures engage in this practice. Yet to us, it seems instinctive, and we find it difficult to imagine romantic intimacy without it. Even the division of the female body into so many named zones of eroticism is both learned and socially constructed. The public display of breasts is not risqué or scandalous in much of Western Europe like it is here; while in Japanese culture, the nape of a woman's neck (one of the few exposed body parts other than hands and face) was traditionally considered highly erotic.

It may seem strange to discuss things like pleasure and romance in a chapter devoted to reproductive health. The focus of policy, philanthropic, and often programmatic attention understandably involves a "social problems" approach that focuses more narrowly on issues like unplanned pregnancy, early sex, condom use, and so on.

But for any young person, this might seem like a very cramped model of "health"—one that ignores many aspects of sexual intimacy with which young women in particular must grapple, including desire, sexual self-efficacy, body comfort, and the risks and enjoyments of pleasure.

Healthy and appropriate sexuality is not just the absence of unplanned pregnancy, risky sex, STDs, and other dysfunctions or diseases, as noted femininity researcher Deborah Tolman has repeatedly pointed out. It includes a healthy relationship with one's body and partner, the ability to form and maintain intimate relationships, and knowing what one enjoys and being able to experience that pleasure directly.

Engendering Desire

For many young men, sexual desire for females must seem relatively more straight-forward, at least as compared with young women. As Tolman (1999) notes, this is entirely predictable, because sexuality is constructed within a system of male privilege where masculine pleasures and desires determine most of its terms. In this sense, femininity is a projection of the needs of masculinity.

This may be one reason why traditional feminine norms tend to detach young women from healthy and pleasurable sexuality. Explains Tolman, "holding conventional beliefs regarding femininity is [actually] a barrier to positive sexual health for girls" (139).

For young women and girls, to give sex, to have sex, and to want sex are all socially complex, fraught with mixed messages and double-binds which are nearly impossible to finesse, and with which society—which glorifies traditional submissive and hyperfeminine forms of womanhood—offers no help.

Put bluntly, young men are socially encouraged to want sex and to do so publicly (indeed this is part of manhood); young women are not. Instead, girls are encouraged to "be the objects of boys' sexual desires, without having sexual desires of her own." This is one reason why there is no pejorative comparable term like "slut" to describe sexually active males, and no complimentary term comparable to "stud" to describe a sexually active female.

Feminine norms dictate that girls may like sex, but not too much, and never ever publicly. Certainly, they should never talk about how much they want sex because it is very unfeminine to be too explicitly interested in having actual sex.

Girls should act, look, and be sexy, but not be sexual. As Tolman puts it, "Girls are under systemic pressure not to feel, know, or act on their sexual desire" (2005, 3). Their sexual desires are something society does not want to acknowledge or engage with, and would prefer kept out of sight or discussed openly.

One unfortunate result of this attitude is that many girls' first sexual experience is encapsulated by the sad phrase, "it just happened." In practice, this means "it" happens entirely on the boys' terms and timetable, without the negotiation of—or preparation for—safer sex, without the girl really considering the risks or costs of unplanned pregnancy or contracting HIV, without her having thought through whether she really wanted to have intercourse at all, or what her own desires were, or if she wanted any kind of sex. As with almost every other aspect of women's reproductive health, gender norms that suppress the expression of female desire can have huge effects.

Embodiment & Pleasure

Theorist Judith Butler makes the point that it is gender, not sex, that carves the female body up into so many specific zones of eroticism: the lips, breasts, buttocks, and groin. Each of these is given a specific sexualized meaning (this is the basis for how women are *objectified* as a collection of so many body parts), and the many, many objectifying male names for each (*jugs, melons, hooters, headlights, poon, bootie, bazoombahs, badonkadonk*, etc.).

Not just boys, but girls as well, learn to view these female body parts as erotically charged. Each of these is associated with activities that are important for male pleasure (buttocks, breasts, vagina, first base, second base, etc.).

Perhaps predictably, because the sexual construction of female bodies is devoted to male pleasure, the clitoris and the labia—the body parts most important to most women for arousal and satisfaction—are largely ignored, not particularly eroticized in popular culture, and the subject of relatively few slang names. For the same reason, there are almost no similar erotic zones and slang names for male body parts, except, of course, for the penis.

In practice, this means young women and girls learn to constantly surveil their own bodies, seeking to evaluate, control, and "improve" each "piece," rather than authentically feeling and experiencing *from the inside*. This self-sexualization has been called "internalizing the male gaze"—a way of experiencing one's body as a girl believes the males around her perceive it. The disconnect from an authentic experience of one's own body can make enjoying sexual pleasure—or even knowing precisely what pleasures a young woman might want—difficult.

In addition, sex among young couples is generally centered on male desire, its needs, arousal, and satisfaction. Too often neither partner is particularly concerned with female arousal and satisfaction. The upshot is that girls may join in sex, but more as spectators and accomplices than as full participants.

Given such dynamics, it is unsurprising that rates of climax among young women in early sexual encounters are abysmally low. Male knowledge of female anatomy and sexual response in such encounters is also very low. Distressingly, so is female knowledge. Part of the reason for this is that sexual innocence among girls is highly prized in many American subcultures. Being perceived as a "good girl" is incompatible with accumulating highly detailed sexual knowledge, let alone the kind of extensive sexual experience that might provide it.

In sex, we can see the social scripts of normative femininity clearly: the emphasis on young women as objects of desire, femininity defined as being "possessed" and "taken," the use of the act to satisfy male prerogatives, and the female partner taking pleasure mainly in the passion her body evokes in her partner.

It may not be an exaggeration to say that normative femininity and actual female sexual pleasure are mutually exclusive, with the former substituting for the latter with whatever limited psychological pleasures are to be had from feeling wanted, being desirable, and providing the site of others' sexual satisfaction.

Initiative, Agency, & "Reputation"

Gender norms can also dictate girls' sexual initiative and agency. This agency comes with highly gendered rules of engagement, including rules for promiscuity, virginity, and infidelity (almost exclusively for girls), initiative-taking (boys "make the first move" in courtship or sex), and allowable acts and positions (boys "get on top"). In some subcultures, oral-genital sex with women is gendered, and considered highly unmanly for men.

For girls, there is an enormous and elaborate social machinery for publicly regulating feminine sexual agency, which is managed as a familial and even communal property. Primary among these are "reputation," including what is increasingly known as "slut-shaming." "Reputation" is a communal public awareness of a young woman's sexual agency, experience, and availability, often communicated through gossip, whether in-person or online.

A girl who transgresses proper feminine boundaries is said to have a "bad reputation." She is punished and shamed for this with a series of sex-phobic epithets intended to demean, depersonalize, and sexualize. They include the terms *slut*, *slag*, and *whore/ho*—what is now called "Slut Discourse." For young women in some subcultures, this may also have specific overtones: for instance, young Black women who exhibit sexual agency may be derided as *video vixens* or *gold diggers*.

Sex-shaming and reputation attack are carried out against young women by both young men and young women (sometimes more enthusiastically by the latter). Being a *slut* or *ho* or *having a reputation* dramatically decreases a young woman's social capital, particularly as a prospective partner for courtship, much less marriage. Should a male suitor express romantic attraction to a woman with a *bad reputation* he risks becoming the object of community ridicule and shame himself.

A young woman's family, and especially her school-age siblings, may be targeted for ridicule because of her perceived behavior. This blanket spreading of harm to prospective partners and family members amplifies the costs of defying traditional feminine mores, and increases the punishment's effectiveness.

The investment of social energy and attention, shaming the reputation of girls and women, exerts a strong pressure to limit female sexual agency and it is often highly effective in deterring or at least inhibiting it, particularly in small towns that function virtually as closed social systems where girls have little privacy. This is similar to some Islamic and African cultures where a young woman's sexuality or "honor" becomes a matter for her entire family or village.

A young man may be allowed many transgressions as he learns to navigate his sexuality, and still regain good social standing; a young woman makes only a single transgression—"mistake"—and it clouds her reputation of purity permanently.

Studies have shown that young women tend to be highly aware of these regulatory boundaries, and are anxious about them, even when they completely disagree with them, and will go to great pains to avoid transgressing them.

Unfortunately, the boundaries between being a "good girl," and a "bad girl" or "slut" are complex, malleable, and differ widely among communities, and even in different parts of the same community. Moreover, they are always changing with time and social expectations.

The boundaries can be much narrower in more traditional subcultures that expect young women to remain virginal until marriage. In some Hispanic subcultures, being a virgin can be an important signifier of womanly virtue, religious piety, and innocence—all important attributes as well as public evidence that a family has raised a "good girl."

Young women in some subcultures report that once they've had sex, other boys consider them open targets, and try to have sex with them at will. This may be true even when the initial sex was the result of coercion.

A young woman who shows ownership of her desire and damages her *reputation* opens herself up to sexual harassment and ridicule, and a young woman who damages her *reputation* just opens herself up to even greater sexual harassment and ridicule. But studies show young women are sexually harassed whether they show sexual agency or not. This often arises as a means for boys to express male anxiety about female sexuality, and to display their dominance.

To be sure, masculine norms may also rob young men of sexual agency, such as when they feel compelled to be sexually active lest they be ridiculed as homosexual. But while virginity in young women is often deeply prized, in young men it is generally considered shameful, which only increases with age.

There is no comparable communal management of male sexual agency, which may actually *increase* a young man's social capital. While social rules for adolescent female virginity are culturally common, similar rules for male virginity are almost unknown among the world's many cultures—none of whom *even have a word* to name male virginity.

On Romance (& Its Absence)

Romance is a key aspect of and motivation for sex. Yet traditional gender norms can complicate romantic intimacy for both girls and boys.

Manhood demands that young men be emotionally tough, impervious to pain, aggressive, self-reliant, and independent. Romantic intimacy requires that they be emotionally vulnerable, accessible, social, responsive, connected, and caring—all deeply "feminine" traits. In fact, strong emotional relationships themselves can create a kind of vulnerability that is itself deeply unmanly.

It has become common among doing work around *healthy masculinity* to note that traditional manhood also includes positive relationship virtues, like protectiveness and breadwinning. While there is, doubtless, truth to this, to me it seems to beg the question, since many of the values are still mainly the product of being dominant. Perhaps we need to start reframing qualities like vulnerability as scary—it is, requiring great courage—and therefore revealing it as integral to manliness.

Sometimes it seems that traditional masculinity promotes beliefs and attitudes that make real, romantic intimacy nearly impossible. The equation of sexual prowess with manliness is completely opposed to monogamy that grounds most deep, long-term marriages. If traditional femininity and female pleasure are mutually exclusive, so are traditional masculinity and male emotional intimacy.

This is clearly illustrated by any action movie that puts traditional hypermasculinity on display: Tom Cruise, Clint Eastwood, Bruce Lee, Shaft, James Bond, Vin Diesel, or Jason Bourne—pick your period or genre. The proto-male hero is always aggressive, independent, and violent. He may occasionally be sexual, but is seldom caring or romantic. He interacts with the world mainly through the pursuit of violent conquest. He goes his own way, forms few attachments, and is always ready to ride off.

He never, ever has children, lives with family members, or provides any sort of (feminine) caretaking that might demonstrate responsibility for others. He needs no one and no one needs him. While he may show kindness, even gentleness at times, he is a tough, hardened alpha-male, standing alone on the field of combat.

Teen Pregnancy, Condom Use, & HIV

Traditional manhood and male heroism are also inextricably connected to risk-taking behavior, whether with drugs, alcohol, guns, fast cars, or sex. This demonstrates emotional toughness through disdain for disease or pain—even death. So it is unsurprising that studies show young men with stronger beliefs in traditional manhood also report lower rates of condom use and higher rates of STIs, including HIV. Virility is a big part of manliness, and condom use can impair it. A young man must stop sex at the appropriate moment (not too soon but not too late), open the wrapper, and put the condom on correctly. Doing this takes time, and the diversion of concentration to the task at hand risks causing a loss of erection. Such men are also more likely to view impregnation as a sign of manliness, sexual relationships as adversarial, and pregnancy prevention as the woman's problem, not theirs.

Studies show that condom use can be used as a proxy for proof of relational intimacy and caring. So young women will require condom use with new or casual partners, but in regular relationships, they no longer do so. Sometimes their male partner will protest his love and declare that he is monogamous, using a woman's insistence on continued condom use as evidence that she must not really love him because she doesn't trust him, or is even *cheating*, herself.

This rhetorical move can put a young woman in a difficult bind: choosing between prioritizing her health and hurting her partner's feelings, perhaps offending his masculine pride, and losing him, or provoking him to anger or even violence.

It only hints at the extraordinarily complex dynamics many young, heterosexual women just learning about sex must negotiate with partners.

Hortensia Amaro (1994) places these dynamics firmly in a gender context, noting that when she asked women about their frustrations with male partners and condom use, they repeatedly cited feelings of powerlessness, low self-esteem, and inability to affect their male partner's decisions.

She noted that part of this is rooted in women's permanent social inequality. From birth, many of them are encouraged to develop psychological characteristics that are pleasing to the dominant group. This includes submissiveness, pliability, the inability to decide and take action, and deference to male prerogatives. Traditional femininity bred low self-efficacy combined with sexual submissiveness. Safer sex negotiation requires women to act in ways that are unfeminine and in conflict with their traditional socialization as the subordinate partner.

Tolman echoes this observation in *Dilemmas of Desire: Teenage Girls Talk about Sexuality* (2005), noting that girls are taught from an early age to be as attractive as possible to boys, to prioritize other's needs ahead of their own, to suppress anger, and at all costs project gentleness and vulnerability.

Simply put, girls are taught the importance of conflict avoidance and being "nice." Postponing intercourse or having safer sex with a stubborn, demanding male partner requires social competencies and psychological strengths (assertiveness, persistence, courage) that many girls have been discouraged from developing from birth. Girls must bring them to bear at a moment of intense emotion, extreme intimacy, and physical vulnerability.

In addition, as they age through puberty girls may face increasing pressure to find a man, get married, and become pregnant. In many more traditionally minded American subcultures, a woman's primary role is being a wife and mother, not necessarily completing her education. She may be pressured to forgo a career and creating an independent life for herself (things we often *do* expect of young men) in favor of raising a family. Yet US schools and extracurricular programs provide girls with few opportunities to think critically about such pressures or tools to better understand what they really want.

In 2011, with support from the California Endowment, TrueChild developed a model teen pregnancy curriculum to help young Latinas think critically about traditional Hispanic femininity. It was adapted from Promundo's Program M, which had been developed in Spanish-speaking countries like Brazil, Guatemala, and Mexico. The curriculum was piloted by the YWCA of Watsonville, California and its dedicated executive director, Leticia Mendoza. We were fortunate that she had two rock-star program coordinators, both of whom had studied gender theory in college and, even before we conducted any gender norms trainings, were already knowledgeable and enthusiastic.

The Y's program focused on young, high-risk Latinas in seventh and eighth grade, some of whom had had gang involvement, and many of whom knew at least one older teen who had had an unplanned pregnancy. So we were unsure how our curriculum would be received. But the Y's program coordinators directors reported having these very intense conversations with the women, many of whom were eager to discuss the diverse and conflicting pressures they felt, and how to think them through.

Men Who Have Sex with Men (MSM)

One might think that gay men would be likely to reject heterosexual masculinist ideals, since homosexuality is often seen as incompatible with "real" masculinity, associated with weakness, femininity, and shame, and the basis for taunting, rejection, and ridicule. And indeed, some gay men do reject them. But many young gay men do buy into traditional masculine heterosexual norms, not only internalizing but amplifying them in the process, including in matters of sex.

Rafael Diaz points out, in *Latino Gay Men and HIV: Culture, Sexuality, and Risk Behavior* (1998), that homosexuality is popularly seen as the height of unmanliness. Young gay men often grow up tormented and unsure of their masculinity, leading some to repeatedly try to prove their manhood. This is particularly true if they do have any traditionally feminine characteristics.

Studies show that young gay men who associate masculinity with risk-taking, strength, sexual prowess, and invulnerability are more likely to avoid condoms and engage in "bare-backing," and to view attracting and having sex with a wide range of partners as proof of manhood. They are also likely to view penetration of partners as the "gold standard" for manly sex, avoiding less risky and more emotionally vulnerable forms of nonpenetrative intimacy, such as touching, hugging, or kissing. They are also more unlikely to discuss having less-risky sex with partners, because "real men" are 100 percent strong and fit, and have no need to explore one another's health, vulnerabilities, and desires for intimacy.

During intimacy they may also avoid putting on condoms out of fear that doing so might result in the loss of an erection, as with straight males. They are less likely to report or seek health advice about receptive anal sex because they think taking the "feminine" position is unmanly. Because of this the data we have on receptive anal sex among young MSMs is likely to be dramatically understated.

In an experiment I repeated many times when doing workshops with gay men, I would ask how many of them were gay. Everyone's hand would go up without hesitation. Then I would ask how many of them were "bottoms." Everyone's hand would go right down, very quickly. Apparently there are no self-identified "bottoms" anywhere in the gay male community—they are all "tops."

I can think of few better illustrations of masculinity and the power of internalized gender shame: even in a time of gay rights, even in a closed group of their peers, it was still deeply shameful for gay men to admit that they might prefer being "catchers" to "pitchers." And this shame and stigma associated with anal sex can engender health risks. Men who are deeply ashamed about wanting anal sex are unlikely to carry condoms. When intimate encounters occur, they are unlikely to have thought through which acts they want to avoid. Whatever sex happens is likely to be impulsive, unpremeditated, unnegotiated . . . and unprotected.

They may also engage in substance abuse beforehand, because getting drunk or high depresses feelings of shame and lowers inhibitions. It also provides a ready excuse the next morning, when a sexual encounter can be written off because he was "blotto" and conveniently remembers nothing.

Transgender, Intersex, & Nonbinary

Nonbinary

Few studies have addressed the effects of gender norms on reproductive health among those who are gender nonconforming, including individuals who are transgender, intersex, and nonbinary. Nonbinary in particular is so new, as a term and a concept—although nonbinary people themselves have always been with us—that little is known about it.

Intersex

The effects of IGM on sexual health often are devastating. As Cheryl Chase, the founder of the modern intersex rights movement, has explained, the perpetual shame and secrecy surrounding an intersex person's wounded genitals makes a healthy relationship with their own bodies and their femininity difficult, if not impossible.

Many intersex people grow up highly aware that something sexually debilitating was done to their bodies. Yet all the adults they look up to in their lives—parents, extended family members, pediatricians—continue lying to them. This only increases the very shame and confusion it was intended to avoid.

Clitoral reduction leaves many with scar tissue as well as damaged erotic sensation. In Chery's case, which is far from uncommon, IGM left her with a lifelong inability to reach orgasm. This not only inhibited her sexual pleasure directly, but the anger and frustration she felt further diminished her ability to experience pleasure, and complicated her romantic relationships (something about which she has been bravely public and frank about).

Many other IGM survivors have reported similar experiences, including radically diminished erotic sensation and/or confusion and pain regarding sex. Much more research is needed, particularly by researchers and clinicians who do not have a vested interest in maintaining or justifying IGM.

Transgender

Although there have been few studies, there is anecdotal evidence, including my own experience, that some transgender people can feel their bodies and/or genitals are deficient or not properly feminine or masculine. While some transpeople are content with their nontransitioned or pretransitioned bodies, others may experience profound feelings of being insufficiently feminine or masculine, particularly those who feel that they are (in the outdated and clichéd phrase) "trapped in the wrong body." Naturally, this can and does present challenges for them, both in romantic intimacy and healthy sexuality.

Moreover, medical intervention does not necessarily change this. The penis is an extraordinarily laden masculine signifier, particularly in American culture. Transmen, many of whom elect not to have complete "bottom surgery" to create a phallus, may worry that their manhood will be impaired. They may also worry that a prospective partner who is cisgender may hesitate when it comes to sex, or even reject them, whether that partner is female or a gay male.

Transwomen who elect not to have bottom surgery—and even those who do—may experience similar anxieties for similar reasons.

This is complicated by a cisgender society that still discriminates against and often rejects transgender people. Battles over pronouns, bathrooms, and so on leave many transgender people still feeling like their bodies are unacceptable, even despised.

In general, transbodies are not judged for how they are, but rather against preexisting cisgender standards of femininity and masculinity. Potential romantic partners might see transwomen or transmen not so much as embodying a desirable masculinity or femininity, but as performing or approximating a cisgender person—as *copies*, if you will, instead of *originals*. This complicates romance and sex.

For some transpeople, the prospect of intimacy immediately brings up a host of questions: *Should I tell them? What do I say? When is the right time? What if they already know?* All of these can make both pleasure and desire more challenging.

Even with a loving and accepting partner, some dialogue might be required about what kinds of sexuality is wanted and/or possible. On the other hand, some partners are, fortunately, attracted to transpeople specifically *because* they find the gender fluidity and/or gender incongruity attractive and desirable.

Stories from the Frontlines:
Engender Health's *Gender Matters*

As Lori Rolleri notes in her excellent series, "Gender and Sexual Health" (2014), few reproductive and sexual health curricula developed in the United States will have a strong gender norms focus *and* have been rigorously evaluated. One exception is SIHLE (Sisters Informing, Healing, Living, and Empowering), developed by Emery University researchers for young Black women, which has shown to increase condom use and reduce unplanned pregnancies. Three other promising programs are Wise Guys 2013, Streetwise to Sexwise, and Gender Matters.

In 2011, EngenderHealth launched a five-year project funded by the US Department of Health and Human Services Office of Adolescent Health. Called *Gender Matters*, or simply *Gen.M*, it tested an innovative approach for youth, ages fourteen to eighteen, in Travis County, Texas, where teen pregnancy rates are the highest in the state. The program's goals are to delay age of first sex, increase the use of effective contraceptive methods, and specifically increase condom use for sexually active youth.

The Gender Matters program is twenty hours, paired with social media posts and text messages designed to reinforce the core curriculum messages related to gender norms and healthy sexual behavior.

Gen.M remains one of the few sexual-health education programs available that integrates a strong and specific focus on challenging rigid gender norms that are closely linked to negative sexual health outcomes. The curriculum is available, along with support guides for implementation and adaptation, through EngenderHealth, with a supplemental guide for native youth populations.

References & Selected Reading

Altman, L. 2008. "HIV Study Finds Rate 40% Higher Than Estimated," *New York Times*, August 3.

Amaro, H. 1994. "Gender and Sexual Risk Reduction: Issues to Consider." Paper presented at the Latino HIV/AIDS Research Conference, "Defining the Path for Future Research," Santa Monica, CA, April 23–24.

Amaro, H. 1995. "Love, Sex, and Power: Considering Women's Realities in HIV Prevention," *American Psychologist* 50 (6): 437.

Anderson, E. 1989. "Sex Codes and Family Life among Poor Inner-City Youths," *The Annals of the American Academy of Political and Social Science* 501 (1): 59–78.

Atkin, L. 2009. Engaging Men and Boys in Achieving Gender Equality: A Summary Report. Washington, DC: Promundo.

Bond, L., Wheeler, D. P., Millett, G. A., LaPollo, A. B., Carson, L. F., and Liau, A. 2009. "Black Men Who Have Sex with Men and the Association of Down-Low Identity with HIV Risk Behavior," *American Journal of Public Health* 99 (S1): S92–S95.

Bowleg, L. 2004. "Love, Sex, and Masculinity in Sociocultural Context: HIV Concerns and Condom Use among African American Men in Heterosexual Relationships," *Men and Masculinities* 7 (2): 166–86.

Bowleg, L., Teti, M., Massie, J. S., Patel, A., Malebranche, D. J., and Tschann, J. M. 2011. "'What Does It Take to Be a Man? What Is a Real Man?'": Ideologies of Masculinity and HIV Sexual Risk among Black Heterosexual Men," *Culture, Health and Sexuality* 13 (5): 545–59.

Brooks, R. A., Etzel, M. A., Hinojos, E., Henry, C. L., and Perez, M. 2005. *Preventing HIV among Latino and African American Gay and Bisexual Men in a Context of HIV-Related Stigma, Discrimination, and Homophobia: Perspectives of Providers*. National Institute of Health. http://www.ncbi.nlm.nih.gov/pmc/articles/PMC1360177/.

Denizet-Lewis, B. 2003. "Double Lives on the Down Low," *New York Times Magazine*, 3, 28–33.

Denner, J., and Dunbar, N. 2004. "Negotiating Femininity: Power and Strategies of Mexican American Girls," *Sex Roles* 50 (5–6), 301–14.

Diaz, R. 1998. *Latino Gay Men and HIV: Culture, Sexuality, and Risk Behavior*. New York: Routledge.

Fields, E. L., Bogart, L. M., Smith, K. C., Malebranche, D. J., Ellen, J., and Schuster, M. A. 2012. "HIV Risk and Perceptions of Masculinity among Young Black Men Who Have Sex with Men," *Journal of Adolescent Health* 50 (3): 296–303.

Fitzpatrick, K. M., and Boldizar, J. P. 1993. "The Prevalence and Consequences of Exposure to Violence among African American Youth," *Journal of the American Academy of Child and Adolescent Psychiatry* 32 (2): 424–30.

Fullilove, M. T., Fullilove III, R. E., Haynes, K., and Gross, S. 1990. "Black Women and AIDS Prevention: A View Towards Understanding the Gender Rules," *Journal of Sex Research* 27 (1): 47–64.

Fullilove, R. E. 2001. "HIV Prevention in the African American Community: Why Isn't Anybody Talking About the Elephant in the Room?" *AIDScience* 1 (7): 1–7.

Girls Incorporated. 2010. *Findings from the Girls Incorporated Girls Shape the Future Study: Early Predictors of Girls Adolescent Sexual Activity*. New York: Girls Incorporated.

Gómez, C. A., and Marin, B. V. 1996. "Gender, Culture, and Power: Barriers to HIV-Prevention Strategies for Women," *Journal of Sex Research* 33 (4): 355–62.

Goodyear, R. K., Newcomb, M. D., and Allison, R. D. 2000. "Predictors of Latino Men's Paternity in Teen Pregnancy: Test of a Mediational Model of Childhood Experiences, Gender Role Attitudes, and Behaviors," *Journal of Counseling Psychology* 47 (1): 116.

Herbst, J. H., Kay, L. S., Passin, W. F., Lyles, C. M., Crepaz, N., Marín, B. V., and HIV/AIDS Prevention Research Synthesis (PRS) Team. 2007. "A Systematic Review and Meta-analysis of Behavioral Interventions to Reduce HIV Risk Behaviors of Hispanics in the United States and Puerto Rico," *AIDS and Behavior* 11 (1): 25–47.

Impett, E. A., Breines, J. G., and Strachman, A. 2010. "Keeping It Real: Young Adult Women's Authenticity in Relationships and Daily Condom Use," *Personal Relationships* 17 (4): 573–84.

Impett, E. A., Schooler, D., and Tolman, D. L. 2006. "To Be Seen and Not Heard: Femininity Ideology and Adolescent Girls' Sexual Health," *Archives of Sexual Behavior* 35 (2): 129–42.

Korte, J. E., Shain, R. N., Holden, A. E., Piper, J. M., Perdue, S. T., Champion, J. D., and Sterneckert, K. 2004. "Reduction in Sexual Risk Behaviors and Infection Rates among African Americans and Mexican Americans," *Sexually Transmitted Diseases* 31 (3): 166–73.

Lescano, C. M., Brown, L. K., Raffaelli, M., and Lima, L. A. 2009. "Cultural Factors and Family-Based HIV Prevention Intervention for Latino Youth," *Journal of Pediatric Psychology* 34 (10): 1041–52.

Levant, R., Richmond, K., Cook, S., House, A. T., and Aupont, M. 2007. "The Femininity Ideology Scale: Factor Structure, Reliability, Convergent and Discriminant Validity, and Social Contextual Variation," *Sex Roles* 57 (5–6): 373–83.

Mahalik, J. R., Morray, E. B., Coonerty-Femiano, A., Ludlow, L. H., Slattery, S. M., and Smiler, A. 2005. "Development of the Conformity to Feminine Norms Inventory," *Sex Roles* 52 (7–8): 417–35.

Malebranche, D. J. 2008. "Bisexually Active Black Men in the United States and HIV: Acknowledging More Than the 'Down Low,'" *Archives of Sexual Behavior* 37 (5): 810–16.

Marín, B. V., Gómez, C. A., Tschann, J. M., and Gregorich, S. E. 1997. "Condom Use in Unmarried Latino Men: A Test of Cultural Constructs," *Health Psychology* 16 (5): 458.

McKinley, N. M., and Hyde, J. S. 1996. "The Objectified Body Consciousness Scale Development and Validation," *Psychology of Women Quarterly* 20 (2): 181–215.

McNair, L. D., and Prather, C. M. 2004. "African American Women and AIDS: Factors Influencing Risk and Reaction to HIV Disease," *Journal of Black Psychology* 30 (1): 106–23.

Mueller, T. E., Castaneda, C. A., Sainer, S., Martinez, D., Herbst, J. H., Wilkes, A. L., and Villarruel, A. M. 2009. "The Implementation of a Culturally Based HIV Sexual Risk Reduction Program for Latino Youth in a Denver Area High School," *AIDS Education and Prevention* 21 (Supplement B): 164.

Olfman, S., ed. 2009. *The Sexualization of Childhood*. ABC-CLIO.

Paterno, M. T., and Jordan, E. T. 2012. "A Review of Factors Associated with Unprotected Sex among Adult Women in the United States," *Journal of Obstetric, Gynecologic, and Neonatal Nursing* 41 (2): 258–74.

Preventing Teen Pregnancy—Primary Prevention Programs. DC Campaign to Prevent Teen Pregnancy. http://dccampaign.org/.

Rolleri, L. A., 2014. *Gender and Sexual Health*, Parts 1–4. ACT for Youth Center of Excellence (a collaboration of Cornell University, the University of Rochester, and the New York State Center for School Safety).

Shearer, C. L., Hosterman, S. J., Gillen, M. M., and Lefkowitz, E. S. 2005. "Are Traditional Gender Role Attitudes Associated with Risky Sexual Behavior and Condom-Related Beliefs?" *Sex Roles* 52 (5–6): 311–24.

Stephens, D. P., and Phillips, L. D. 2003. "Freaks, Gold Diggers, Divas, and Dykes: The Sociohistorical Development of Adolescent African American Women's Sexual Scripts," *Sexuality and Culture* 7 (1): 3–49.

Tolman, D. L. 1999. "Femininity as a Barrier to Positive Sexual Health for Adolescent Girls," *Journal of the American Medical Women's Association (1972)* 54 (3): 133–38.

Tolman, D. L. 2005. *Dilemmas of Desire: Teenage Girls Talk about Sexuality*. Cambridge, MA: Harvard University Press

Tolman, D. L., Impett, E. A., Tracy, A. J., and Michael, A. 2006. "Looking Good, Sounding Good: Femininity Ideology and Adolescent Girls' Mental Health," *Psychology of Women Quarterly* 30 (1): 85–95.

Tolman, D. L., and Porche, M. V. 2000. "The Adolescent Femininity Ideology Scale: Development and Validation of a New Measure for Girls," *Psychology of Women Quarterly* 24 (4): 365–76.

Tolman, D. L., Striepe, M. I., and Harmon, T. 2003. "Gender Matters: Constructing a Model of Adolescent Sexual Health," *Journal of Sex Research* 40 (1): 4–12.

Villarruel, A. M., Jemmott, L. S., and Jemmott, J. B. 2005. "Designing a Culturally Based Intervention to Reduce HIV Sexual Risk for Latino Adolescents," *Journal of the Association of Nurses in AIDS Care* 16 (2): 23–31.

Villarruel, A. M., Jemmott, L. S., Jemmott, J. B., and Eakin, B. L. 2006. "Recruitment and Retention of Latino Adolescents to a Research Study: Lessons Learned from a Randomized Clinical Trial," *Journal for Specialists in Pediatric Nursing* 11 (4), 244–50.

Villarruel, A. M., Jemmott, J. B., and Jemmott, L. S. 2006. "A Randomized Controlled Trial Testing an HIV Prevention Intervention for Latino Youth," *Archives of Pediatrics and Adolescent Medicine* 160 (8): 772–77.

Wingood, G. M., and DiClemente, R. J. 1998. "Partner Influences and Gender-Related Factors Associated with Noncondom Use among Young Adult African American Women," *American Journal of Community Psychology* 26 (1): 29–51.

Wingood, G. M., and DiClemente, R. J. 2000. "Application of the Theory of Gender and Power to Examine HIV-Related Exposures, Risk Factors, and Effective Interventions for Women," *Health Education and Behavior* 27 (5): 539–65.

Wolfe, W. A. 2003. "Overlooked Role of African American Males' Hypermasculinity in the Epidemic of Unintended Pregnancies and HIV/AIDS Cases with Young African American Women," *Journal of the National Medical Association* 95 (9): 846.

Wood, J. T. 2004. "Monsters and Victims: Male Felons' Accounts of Intimate Partner Violence," *Journal of Social and Personal Relationships* 21 (5): 555–76.

Zavella, P., and Castañeda, X. 2005. "Sexuality and Risks: Gendered Discourses about Virginity and Disease among Young Women of Mexican Origin," *Latino Studies* 3 (2): 226–45.

5

Education

Sandra Romero and Bibiana Vega do their best to shrug off taunts from fellow Latino classmates at Del Mar High School in San Jose. The seventeen-year-old seniors are called "whitewashed." Mataditas—dorks. Cerebritas—brainiacs. They're told they're "losing their culture"—just because Sandra has a 4.0 grade-point average and Bibiana has a 3.5. The put-downs are clear: Smart is not cool. And too many Latinx students are choosing cool over school . . . Harvard University found that White students were more popular when they had higher grade-point averages. But Black students' popularity sharply declined when their GPAs reached a B-plus. For Latinos, the price of good grades was even costlier: popularity peaked at a C-plus, then plunged.

As the San Jose *Mercury News'* 2008 article "Smart vs. Cool: Culture, Race and Ethnicity in Silicon Valley Schools" notes, being a *nerd* and a *brainiac* has long been known to be inimical to peer acceptance in many schools. Excelling in academics and getting top grades is viewed among many adolescents as not only *uncool*, but conflicting with traditional notions of femininity and masculinity. (See Noguchi and Mangaliman 2008.)

This can be particularly true in low-income or more traditional communities, where womanhood and femininity may be closely associated with homemaking and motherhood, and masculinity with *manly* physical blue-collar labor like working on cars or building construction.

And while this is undoubtedly also true for many young White men as well, scholarship in this area has often focused on Black and Latinx youth. In her landmark study "Psychosocial Development and Black Male Masculinity: Implications for Counseling Economically Disadvantaged African American Male Adolescents," researcher Shanette Harris (1995) found that "many academic problems originate from the repudiation of stereotypical feminine qualities. . . . Unlike their European

American counterparts, African American male adolescents are more likely to deny, devalue, and actually forgo intellectual interests to avoid the ridicule and shame that arise from academic success" (281).

As a result, Harris points out that some young men conceal their academic performance by hiding books or avoid revealing grades. Still others perform hyper-masculine roles like drug dealer or gang member that compensate for any suggestion of unmanliness.

Some researchers have noted that such attitudes coincide with Richard Major and Janet Mancini Billson's (1992) well-known theory of the "cool pose," which proposed that the Black male adoption of masculine façades which expressed aloofness, emotionlessness, and detachment were a response to lifelong experiences of racism, discrimination, and oppression in White society.

As the anecdote that opens this chapter suggests, school excellence involves many characteristics and behaviors—being disciplined, displaying politeness, obeying adult authority figures, and following orders—which are not only perceived as conflicting with traditional masculinity, but as being weak, feminine, and gay. Moreover, as researchers Forham and Ogbu (1986), among others, have suggested, being obedient to a dominant culture in the face of longstanding structural racism may expose some young Black, Latino, and Native American men to charges of "acting White."

STEM & Girls

The Leaky Pipeline

The causes of girls' lower participation and interest in STEM (science, technology, engineering, and math) have been long addressed and widely debated. Millions of dollars are invested annually by school systems, state agencies, and foundations hoping to lure more girls (and sometimes boys) into science and technology fields.

This can be especially important for girls in low-income communities, since technology offers one of the few fast-growing areas of the US economy that provides high-paying jobs, and, while it is certainly male-centric, it is new enough to lack the "old boy network" that dominates many older professions.

Researchers, funders, advocates, and educators have investigated and addressed a host of external barriers to girls' STEM participation and achievement. These include a lack of female role models, parental attitudes, and stereotype threat (when a group's aptitude for a task is disparaged so that they internalize it and then underperform at it). Many of these hypotheses engage the effects of feminine norms, if only through the actions adults take, or the gendered attitudes adults hold. But sometimes it can feel like the girls themselves are missing—there only in terms of how they are acted upon by other. The girls' own feelings, thoughts, and efficacy are often vague or simply missing.

This is remarkable, because much of the STEM field itself is deeply feminist in nature, so girls' agency would seem to be a central concern. Yet it sometimes seems as if much of the field operates on that tacit assumption that girls' absence is solely the results of patriarchal barriers, and if each of these could just be identified and addressed, the girls would naturally blossom into STEM.

Yet it's been stubbornly difficult to improve their participation and interest rates. This is despite the fact that girls actually do as well or better than boys right up until grades 5 through 9 (those "gender intensification" years). In fact, interest and achievement starts to fade even among girls who formerly had good STEM grades and who reported liking STEM. By eighth grade, half as many girls are interested in pursuing STEM careers—a decline that increases with age. By the time they matriculate into college, girls score lower than boys on math SAT tests, take fewer AP tests in calculus, physics, and computer science, and are less likely to select college STEM majors.

While some school systems have improved participation rates by making science and math mandatory rather than elective, this mostly just postpones the inevitable: during the last years of high school, when girls can choose many of their courses, STEM is rarely among them.

This process is so well-known that the field even has a name for it: the "leaky pipeline."

Clearly barriers like implicit bias, stereotype threat, and the lack of role models are important factors—but one is forced to ask, why weren't they important factors *before* the onset of adolescence? Clearly there is an age-related trigger right around the time of middle school. Yet how girls begin internalizing feminine norms and how this might affect their academic interests remains most missing from STEM policy and programs, and is only marginally reflected in STEM research.

"Not in Junior High"

To better understand this decline, TrueChild convened focus groups of young women of color through support provided by the Motorola Solutions Foundation, which is the charitable giving arm of Motorola Solutions, Inc. The Foundation has been a long-time thought leader in STEM, specifically on programs for girls and young women.

When we asked them if girls couldn't be both smart *and* feminine, girls answer "Yes." They knew the "right" answer. But they immediately went on to describe a pretty classmate with long hair who "no one sees as a pretty girl . . . because she is so smart. She's like a nerd."

When we asked one group specifically if they couldn't be feminine, smart, and popular with boys, they broke out laughing, explaining, "Yes . . . but not in junior high!" Because as they became more interested in boys, they had to "dumb it down."

When presented with research that around third grade girls stop doing as well in math and science, our participants agreed that one reason was because that's when girls start noticing boys:

- "[This is when] girls start giving up [on math]."
- "It's when they start noticing the boys. [Participants agree.]"
- "Girls focus more on, 'Oh, he wants me to be pretty.'"

Clearly what boys think of girls, or what girls worry boys will think of them, plays a large role. This points to the need for the field to challenge not just girls' attitudes about femininity, but also boys' attitudes toward girls.

There were other important impacts of such feminine norms on academic achievement. Some participants complained that as they got older they had to spend so much time on appearance that it left little time and energy for school-work. Explained one, "I would wake up at four a.m. to get ready for junior high." While her view might have been extreme, she was far from alone. Many participants expressed the belief that late elementary school and middle school was when girls begin "slacking on academics and start worrying about their appearance."

Subjects like math depend heavily on building sequential competency. Girls noted that they loved math in elementary school, but as they focused more on appearance in late elementary school, they began falling behind. And once they fell behind even a little, catching up became nearly impossible. As a result, they lost all interest in math.

Both our limited focus groups and a growing number of studies suggest that as girls enter adolescence they are caught in a double bind in which they must opt out of being feminine or opt out of STEM, and in this largely unequal contest, STEM inevitably loses.

Interestingly, in Japan, where math is just another academic subject everyone is expected to take, girls do as well as boys right through high school. Math is prob-ably the STEM field where the United States is having the most success, but we have a long way to go before we are equal to countries like Japan in degendering math excellence.

Boys suffer some of the same negative impacts from gender norms. Highly physi-cal occupations and activities requiring strength are the *sine qua non* of traditional manhood. Although being a "computer nerd" may be popular in Silicon Valley, in most communities it's boys who are sports jocks that are the cool ones, not the math or science whizzes.

"Getting Root" & Drinking Shots

Researchers and educators are not the only ones concerned with getting more young women and girls into STEM. Technology companies are very inter-ested in diversifying their workforces and in maximizing the supply of potential white-collar employees.

Unfortunately, even the few women who do major in STEM fields often drop out short of a career. Those who do make it into a career have a much higher rate of leaving their jobs than their male colleagues. One of the top reasons cited by women who exit tech jobs is the culture in tech firms. This is interesting because Silicon Valley firms are unique in considering themselves strict meritocracies. Google is famous for its billboards that expose arcane formulas to the public as a recruiting tool, based on the conceit that only those few top intellects who can understand and are *technoid* enough to "get them" will be in on the joke and respond.

The idea is that tech success is raceless and genderless. Silicon Valley, Wall Street, and other hypercompetitive corporate cultures think of themselves as morally innocent environments where only results count, and if you have the technical chops to excel, you win.

But this isn't really true. Consciously or unconsciously, *every* workplace culture promotes and sustains specific assumptions about things like race, class, and, of course, gender. The "pure meritocracies" of the tech industry are often the very ones likely to foster narrow gender cultures, even if they are not aware of doing so.

As of this writing, Facebook serves about a billion people but somehow has not found a single outside woman to be on its board. In one iconic scene from *The Social Network*, a movie about how Facebook hired its first employee, we see this played out:

> Zuckerberg: "They have ten minutes to get root access to a Python web server, expose it's SSL encryption and then intercept all traffic over its secure port . . . Here's the beauty. Every tenth line of code written, they have to drink a shot. And every time the server detects an intrusion, the candidate responsible has to drink a shot. I also have a program running that has a pop-up window appearing simultaneously on all five computers. The last candidate to hit the window has to drink a shot. Plus every three minutes they all have to drink a shot."

Competing to illegally hack into a server before a cheering, half-drunk crowd while downing whiskey shots every few seconds may look like a level, meritocratic playing field. In actuality, it is a hypermasculine jock-nerd idea of a playing field that will only appeal to a certain kind of personality—aggressive, hard-drinking, proud, competitive, risk-taking, boisterous, psychologically tough, and rule-breaking. It is one that many young women—and more than a few level-headed young men—would quickly walk away from.

Granted, this is college, and the dialogue is entirely fictional. But the scene is telling, both in channeling how Silicon Valley, Wall Street, and other hypercompetitive, male-oriented cultures see themselves, and how their masculinist cultures undermine their perception of themselves as the world's last pure meritocracies.

I worked as a consultant on Wall Street trading floors in banking and brokerage firms for two decades, another environment that conceives of itself as a real meritocracy but actually rewards and embraces the same kind of towel-snapping, testosterone-drenched "big swinging dick" manhood that mainly appeals to the young, middle-class, White (and Asian) males who populate them.

A recent *New York Times* op-ed cited a *Harvard Business Review* report that found women leave high-tech jobs at twice the rate of men. Among the most frequently cited reasons women gave for leaving was extreme pressure and a hostile culture.

These kinds of unconscious but conspicuously masculinized approaches to work and workplace environment can be especially important in technology-driven companies, where this jock-nerd atmosphere not only discourages women but also repels professionals of color and those who are LGBTQ, who often seek out progressive, diverse workplaces.

Tech-oriented firms like Google and Intel have led the way in announcing new initiatives with great fanfare and hundreds of millions of dollars in funding designed to attract and keep women through better recruiting, more mentoring, and so on and so forth.

It won't work. Until they also address the masculine norms implicit in their workplace cultures, women—and many minorities—will continue to stay away in droves. And those that do make it in, will continue to either fail to advance or quit, or both.

Masculinity & the Arts

An extraordinary number of funders and nonprofits serving at-risk youth have begun prioritizing the arts—the A in the "STEAM" acronym that is increasingly being used instead of "STEM." They believe that artistic expression helps build young people up and make their voices and presence visible. And that in the end, society changes not because of objective facts but because it learns new and human stories. Certainly, these young people have unique voices and important stories to tell. Yet rigid gender norms shape both the stories that reach us and who tells them.

It is a well-known truism that even though the arts are often dominated by popular male artists at the top-most levels (drama, painting, dance, and singing), young men tend to consider the arts an effeminate pastime suitable mainly for girls and gay men.

In many ways, the arts promote everything that is unmanly: expressiveness and deep feeling; emotional vulnerability; grace, beauty, and refinement; and deep social connection with the audience.

Because the arts are defined by aesthetic refinement, they are disconnected from the harsh, manly work of everyday things. Although artists work with their hands, painting a canvas or composing an aria, they could hardly be seen as being more different from a mechanic fixing an engine block, or a quarterback scrambling to throw a touchdown pass.

The expressive arts are simply not perceived as a manly pastime for males. As Mary Louise Adam's unforgettably named study "Death to the Prancing Prince" notes, arts have always been suspected of being the weak-kneed province of homosexuals, and male dancers have been accused of effeminacy (if not outright homosexuality) at least since the 1800s.

The same thing could be said for drama and choir. As Nicholas McBride (2016) notes in "Singing, Sissies, and Sexual Identity," music teachers have had to counter messages that "singing is for sissies." For instance, in one study of nearly eighty middle-school youth by Charlotte Mizener (1993), two-thirds of boys said they liked to sing, but only half of these (33 percent) said they wanted to sing in a choir. School choirmasters have had to resort to a variety of tactics—enlisting athletes, creating all-male ensembles, and stressing teamwork—in order to recruit boys.

Yet stereotypes of the gay singer/dancer/artist remain widespread, common-place, and difficult to dislodge. While school sports confirm boys' masculinity, participation in the arts tends to leave them open to question. Laments one musician in Phillip Brett's "Musicality, Essentialism, and the Closet in Queering the Pitch" (2006), "All musicians, we must remember, are faggots in the parlance of the male locker room."

The same is true for musical instruments, which are perceived by young people as highly gendered. Percussion and drums, guitar, and larger brass instruments (trombones, tubas, trumpets) are manly; violins, harps, pianos, and flutes are feminine.

As Harrison Scott notes in his voluminous study, *Masculinities and Music: Engaging Men and Boys in Making Music* (2008), researchers have actually developed highly specific scales that measure very precisely the perceived femininity or masculinity of each orchestral instrument in the minds of young people.

Manhood being the more restrictive gender, boys tend to confine themselves to a small number of instruments that are considered manly enough, while girls' interests range more broadly (although drums and electric guitar have long been considered off-limits for girls).

In some ways, all this is so recognized and understood that there is a paucity of recent studies on it. Yet it affects arts programs and funding everywhere. And it will continue to do so until funders and policy makers begin recognizing and addressing masculine norms.

For instance, in scanning one of New York City's most prominent and well-funded foundations for arts among youth of color, one sees many outstanding nonprofit work like Urban Bush Women and Women Make Movies, but almost no groups with names like Urban Bush Men or Men Make Movies. Boys may write, they may do poetry slaps or rap, but beyond that, much of the field is not so much funding arts but girls in the arts.

Much the same is true in many schools. Arts classes and after-school clubs like choir, dance, and theater tend to be dominated by girls. Funders and policy makers continue ignoring the absence of young men, the benefit they could gain from participation, and the important stories they have (and need) to tell us.

Femininity & Sports

If boys have a problem with school arts, girls have a similar problem with school sports. According to the CDC, only a quarter of senior high-school girls engage in regular exercise (the figure is twice that for boys), and most drop out of sports right when they enter adolescence, just when they could benefit the most.

One key reason is feminine norms. Studies show that children know as young as age eight which sports and physical activities are "for boys" and which are "for girls."

Girls' sports tend to feature props (pompoms, jump ropes, etc.), often focus around coordinated group motion, are uncompetitive, and aim for aesthetic results. *Boys' sports* tend to focus on speed, strength, aggressive competition, and overall athleticism.

Strenuous and/or playful exercises that might once have been considered acceptable "tomboy" pursuits at age six—wrestling, climbing trees, skateboarding, and such—are considered unwomanly and even undignified for girls at age twelve (if not before). Strong, sweaty exertion itself is viewed as very unfeminine—note the many items marketed to teenage girls with well-known slogans like "I don't sweat—I glow."

Girls who participate in "boys'" sports or exhibit aggressive and athletic play in competitive activities risk not only being stigmatized as unfeminine, but also being labeled as lesbians (the reverse is also true for boys participating in "girly" sports like jump rope, but boys also have many more sports alternatives).

Schools unintentionally reinforce such attitudes; for instance, in middle school phys. ed. classes where boys are given basketballs and footballs, but girls get hula-hoops and jump ropes. Boys play baseball, girls softball. Up until a few decades ago, if girls were allowed to play basketball, they were only allowed three dribbles before they must pass or shoot. As Rosalind Wiseman (2009) notes in her book, *Queen Bees and Wannabes*, a girl can be athletic and have social status, but only if she has a thin, "feminine" body and avoids musculature or any hint of bulk. (This is echoed in adult sports in many ways. Although male bodybuilders are rewarded for outstanding musculature, women competitors are penalized for it. In basketball, a woman who dunks is still controversial, and many athletes in the WNBA who could aggressively slam-dunk avoid it. In fact, many professional sports like the WNBA still insist that team pictures feature athletes done up in make-up, and carefully promotes them as athletic but feminine—a kind of requirement that Michael Jordan never had to meet.)

Other demands of femininity in adolescence also work to discourage girls from sports and heavy exertion, including make-up and hair. Gym classes seldom allow enough time or have access to the proper cosmetics for girls to repair the damage done to carefully constructed hair and make-up.

This problem can be exacerbated for girls of color, who suffer the greatest declines of physical activity in adolescence. For instance, as researcher Sarah Wilcox (2002) and others have noted, African American girls may have the added challenges of the hairstyles popular in the Black community.

Studies show such girls report avoiding strenuous exercise because they don't want to sweat out their hairstyles, and find the time required to wash, dry, and restyle prohibitive. Maintenance of such styles can also be expensive, and complex hairstyles may be intended to be preserved for days or even weeks

Policy makers and advocates have rightly used Title IX to focus attention on barriers to girls' sports participation posed by inadequate funding, attention, and facilities; they need to expand their focus to internal barriers posed by rigid gender norms and social attitudes as well.

School Pushout Policies

On October 27, 2015, at Columbia, South Carolina's Spring Valley High School, a Black teenage girl was reportedly being disruptive and refusing to leave her classroom. School resource officer Deputy Ben Fields was called in to warn her that she must leave. Before she could respond, Fields wrapped a forearm around her neck, and flipped her and her desk over backward onto the floor. The victim, along with a friend who had recorded the video and verbally challenged Fields, were arrested under the state's nebulous "disturbing schools" law. (The charges were dropped a year later.) Fields was suspended, but faced no charges after a department investigation, eventually being fired by Sheriff Leon Lott, who told media after viewing the video, "I wanted to throw up."

On April 3, 2017 a fourteen-year-old Black teen was questioned in Pittsburgh's Woodland High School's office about a missing cellphone by school safety Officer Steve Shaulis. The student left and Shaulis followed him into the hall, using a gay slur. The boy responded in kind, and Shaulis threw him against the wall, hitting him repeatedly in the head and face, knocking out his front tooth. Principal Kevin Murray watched this happen, but did not intervene. The boy was taken by ambulance to the hospital, where his tooth was sewn back into his mouth. Four more surgeries were needed to repair the damage to his face. The student was suspended and charged with resisting arrest, simple assault, aggravated assault, and making terroristic threats. Neither Shaulis nor Murray were charged. Eventually, more students came forward alleging similar abuse, and even recorded Principal Murray threatening one student that he would "knock his . . . teeth down his throat."

As these disturbing incidents illustrate, it is unsafe to be a student of color in many of America's middle and high schools today. In large part, this is because school systems, responding to what they perceived as an escalating level of violence over past decades, have increasingly embraced new "get tough" policies known by names like *Zero Tolerance* or *Three Strikes*.

Tactics like suspension, expulsion, and arrest—what experts call "exclusionary discipline"—effectively separate "problem" students from their educations, pushing them out onto the streets or into juvenile and criminal justice systems. This expanding movement of students of color from the classroom, through the courts, and into juvenile detention or a jail cell is what advocates increasingly refer to as the "school-to-prison-pipeline" (STPP).

Today there is growing awareness among education funders that school pushouts are an educational emergency hiding in plain sight: a school-based version of what author Michelle Alexander (2012) called "The New Jim Crow": a system of social control functioning as a racial caste system that permanently disempowers, and too often criminalizes, adolescent classroom misbehavior.

The STPP is both a metaphor and shorthand for this expanding convergence of educational and criminal justice systems. As researcher Nancy Heitzeg notes (2009, 2014), minor classroom misbehavior is increasingly criminalized, turning what for decades had been simply school disciplinary issues into grounds for arrest, prosecution, and a criminal record. In effect, many schools are becoming part of a caste system in which White, Asian, and upper-class peers are subject to one disciplinary system, and their low-income Black, Latinx, and Native American peers subjected to another, much tougher one.

Discipline & Boys of Color

For some time, education researchers and youth advocates have been raising alarms about exclusionary policies, and the unequal rates of suspension and expulsion among youth of color. Yet studies confirming this have been scarce. Then in 2010, an Indiana University researcher, Russell Skiba and his partner Daniel J. Losen at the Civil Rights Project at the University of California, published a groundbreaking study that proved definitive.

They painstakingly analyzed four years of Department of Education statistics from the years 2002 to 2006, collected from 9,220 of the United States' sixteen thousand public middle schools, or nearly 60 percent. They found conclusively that youth of color were punished more often, and more harshly, and often for the same infractions as their White or Asian peers. Among their key findings were that young Black men were nearly three times as likely to be suspended as their White peers, young Black women were nearly four times as likely to be suspended, and both Hispanic and Native American students were suspended at higher rates than their White counterparts.

Some findings defied not only expectation, but also explanation. In two middle-school districts in Palm Beach (Florida) and Milwaukee (Wisconsin), over 50 percent of Black middle-school boys had been suspended at least once in the past year. Skiba and Losen found that the percentage of students suspended yearly almost doubled from early 1970s through 2006, when new Zero Tolerance and similar "get tough" policies became popular, and this new caste system was being implemented.

Since then, new studies have found that educators increasingly view low-income youth of color as a permanent underclass, "future felons" deserving of harsh discipline, "difficult" youth who must be proactively separated from school.

These studies have also documented the subtler ways that school disciplinary regimes target youth of color and are intertwined with gender, such as Murphy, Acosta, and Kennedy-Lewis poignantly titled study, "'I'm Not Running Around with My Pants Sagging, So How Am I Not Acting Like a Lady?': Intersections of Race and Gender in the Experiences of Female Middle School Troublemakers" (2013). They note that Black and Latinx youth are much more likely than their White peers to be punished for subjective behavioral infractions, like "being disruptive" or "defiant behavior," rather than actual violations of black-letter rules.

Explains Murphy, "White students are more likely to be referred for objective infractions (e.g., smoking, leaving campus without permission), whereas Black students are punished more for subjective infractions (e.g., disrespect, excessive noise).

Because such subjective infractions are mostly a matter of adult perception, they are highly vulnerable to existing teacher bias about low-income youth of color" (590).

While such violations might at first seem minor, their aggregate takes a toll. As a leading school discipline researcher noted to me in a private conversation, often a student's first or second offense is nothing more than "oppositional attitude" or "defiant behavior," which may translate into a boy trying to look tough by having an attitude, talking back, or otherwise showing the teacher up. Then, when a student does break an actual rule, they have already been labeled a "troublemaker" with two strikes, and are likely to be suspended or expelled, or shunted into juvenile court and the STPP.

Punitive and unfair policies that also enforce rigid ideas of gender take a toll on teachers as well. Recent articles in outlets like the *New York Times* and *The Atlantic* document how educators of color are burning out and leaving teaching. In one *Times* piece, Christopher Emdin (2016) explained that Black male teachers are expected to not only educate, but to dispense masculine role modeling through "tough love" that transforms "difficult" young Black men into passive, compliant students—"tough love" here being code words for harsh punishment, lack of gentleness or patience, and moral inflexibility.

Young Men Just Learning to *Do* Masculinity

Emdin's emphasis on the importance of both toughness and masculinity is telling: while leading authorities have successfully documented the importance of race and class, the central role of gender norms in pushout policies is usually overlooked.

Yet, a school's disciplinary efforts to police masculinity in boys of color—and femininity in girls of color—is integral to any understanding of school pushouts and the criminalization of youths of color. Indeed, it is at the heart of the problem. As boys enter adolescence and come under increasing pressure to "man up." Unfortunately, boys tend to establish social hierarchies through behaviors like physicality and boisterousness, public risk-taking, defying adult authority, and suffering punishment silently which are mostly likely to bring them into conflict with school disciplinary regimes (and juvenile justice systems).

This is exacerbated by studies that show police and educators tend to perceive Black and Latinx boys as about four-and-a-half years older than they actually are, and thus not only less child-like but more threatening. As my colleague Micah Gilmer explains in an anecdote from his upcoming book about the intersection of school sports, race, and manhood:

> The player, Big Rod, had clearly had his feeling hurt by the teacher's over-reaction. "I was just joking with him, Coach." Coach Sapp put his hand on Big Rod's shoulder. It was the first time I heard him articulate The Rules. And instead of trying to make the boy feel better, he just went right at him. "Rod, you got to understand The Big Black Man Rules. You say something like what you said to your teacher to me, and I'm going

to laugh. And if you weren't big and Black you could probably have said that to your teacher. But you say something like that to him, and he thinks you are trying to 'intimidate' him. So you can go through life wondering why everybody is misunderstanding you. Or you can start living according to The Big Black Man Rules."

As Anne Arnett Ferguson noted in *Bad Boys: Public Schools in the Making of Black Masculinity* (2010), boys of color are generally viewed as more challenging and oppositional, students whose behavior, dress, and speech need constant monitoring and punishment. School administrators and safety officers are often too inclined to view disruptive or disobedient behavior from young Black or Latino men through a lens of delinquency or criminality rather than tween-age misbehavior or hijinks.

Suspension, expulsion, and arrest impose maximal penalties for young men just learning to "do" masculinity, providing them with precious little margin for error in navigating the twin shoals of adult manhood and school disciplinary regimes. In effect, masculinity and school discipline form two systems in blind and often disastrous collision: an urban male "gender culture" that demands that adolescent boys master public displays of masculine strength, toughness, and indifference to authority; and school disciplinary systems inclined to view precisely those displays as oppositional and threatening, a cause for increased surveillance and punishment, and signs of emerging criminality.

As Ferguson memorably recalls in the opening words of *Bad Boys*: "An African American man pointed to a Black boy who walked by us. 'That one has a jail-cell with his name on it.' We were looking at [Lamar] a 10-year-old, barely four feet tall, whose frail body was shrouded in baggy pants and a hooded sweatshirt."

Girls: Pushed Out & Overpoliced

While earlier studies of pushout policies focused primarily on boys of color, in recent years studies like Kimberlé Crenshaw's *Black Girls Matter: Pushed Out, Overpoliced, and Underprotected* (2015) and Monique Morris' *Pushout: The Criminalization of Black Girls in Schools* (2016) demonstrate that girls of color are being victimized as well.

While girls also are surveilled and monitored by educators for their dress and deportment, the emphasis for those who are Black, Latina, Native American, or low-income Asian American Pacific Islander can be somewhat different.

Boys of color might be targeted for too uninhibitedly embodying traditional masculine attributes of physicality, independence, and aggression. Girls of color are often targeted because they are perceived as failing to enact middle-class feminine norms of submission, deference, and passivity.

In effect, somewhat like many LGBTQ students, they are picked out because they are perceived as not conforming to gender norms. Morris argues that Black girls are punished more severely and at much higher rates because of stereotypes about Black femininity that leave educators predisposed to view them as unfeminine, unmanageable, and unruly.

Morris (2016) notes that schools tend to view young Black women as "either 'good' girls or 'ghetto' girls who behave in ways that exacerbate stereotypes about Black femininity" (10). "Ghetto," she continues, is "often a euphemism for actions that deviate from social norms tied to a narrow, White middle-class definition of feminity" (10). Black girls' "nonconformity to traditional gender expectations," prompts teachers to perceive them as "'loud, defiant, and precocious' and . . . to be reprimanded for being 'unladylike'" (11).

Similarly, in the 2007 article "'Ladies' or 'Loudies?'" researcher Edward Morris found that "teachers encouraged these girls to exemplify an ideal, docile form of femininity, emblematized in the prescription to act like *ladies*. Teachers viewed the existing femininity of these girls as coarse and overly assertive, leading one teacher to describe them as 'loudies'" (490). Interestingly, Morris found that some of the teachers involved were themselves of color, and were responding to the girls as an "embarrassment" to their racial identity.

In addition, as with boys of color, educators are predisposed to view low-income Black and Latina girls as about three years older than they actually are, and more oppositional. As Murphy, Acosta, and Kennedy-Lewis (2013) explain, this "corresponds with stereotypical views of Black women as 'hypersexualized, angry, and hostile'" (601).

Often this gender regulation is confusing for adolescent girls, who—like boys—are still unsure and learning to master womanhood just when gender norms become the basis for running conflicts with teachers. Complains one girl interviewed by Murphy after being admonished not to be so "loud and unladylike":

> I'm not acting like a dude. I'm not walking around with my pants sagging, so how am I not acting like a lady? Like how a lady supposed to act? I'm walking, I'm talking. So I don't know how they want me to act if I don't act like a lady. I don't understand. (601)

For girls, an unrecognized part of the problem is that many experience regular sexual harassment that goes unaddressed by school systems and is considered "normal." When they resist, it is their behavior rather than the harassment that is punished.

For one potential project, TrueChild reached out to partner with a unique Los Angeles based girl-serving group—Black Women for Wellness (BWW). BWW is led by its dedicated executive director, Janette Robinson Flint, and implements its Get Smart B4U Get Sexy program in the Compton, Pasadena, and Los Angeles public schools. Both organizations were excited at the possibility of working together, prioritizing issues like self-esteem, safer sex, and family planning.

However, the young women had other priorities. Their number one concern was sexual catcalls, lewd propositions, and unwanted sexual touching. They were constantly victimized by this on the way to school, in the hallways, and after class. It was so pervasive that the girls had begun pushing back and defending themselves, sometimes physically. And of course when they did, *they* were the ones caught and suspended. School staff, faculty, and security were all complicit, sometimes in victimizing the girls with their own sexualized comments, and sometimes simply in writing off boys' sexual aggression as hormonal hijinks and ignoring girls' complaints.

This kind of predatory, sexually charged environment is all too common in schools everywhere, including in rural and suburban schools, and across demographics. Studies show it is not only ubiquitous, but it ends up hurting girls academically. As with LGBTQ kids who are bullied, sexually harassed girls are more likely to call in sick, cut classes, stay out of school for months, or simply begin resenting classrooms as another site where they will be unsafe, victimized, and abused.

Pushouts & LGBTQ

This institutional urge to police and regulate gender even when it involves punishing the victim and normalizing the perpetrator extends to LGBTQ youth as well.

Researchers like Stephen Russell, Shannon Snapp, and others have drawn new attention to disciplinary disparities among LGBTQ youth, especially those who are Black or Latinx. They have documented how LGBTQ youth who are bullied or harassed risk being punished for protecting themselves or resisting their own victimization.

In other cases, boys who are perceived as unmasculine or girls as unfeminine are targeted, or because they otherwise fail to fit binary gender stereotypes at all as Snapp et. al. (2015) found in "Messy, Butch, and Queer: LGBTQ Youth and the School-to-Prison Pipeline."

Snapp et al. (2015) also found that LGBTQ youth constitute a significant portion of the STPP, as evidenced by their overrepresentation in juvenile detention facilities: "LGBTQ youth are twice as likely as their heterosexual peers to be detained for non-violent offenses such as running away, prostitution, and truancy" (58).

Schools, like many religious institutions, both act as guardians and regulators of very traditional and rigid binary gender ideals, of what is appropriate or allowable for boys and girls. This can be seen by the separate dress codes, and in some older schools, even separate entrances.

School officials are predisposed to view openly gender nonconformity as "flaunting it" or being deliberately "disruptive" or "inappropriate"—although students are simply trying to express who they are, or even struggling to discover what that truly is.

In addition, like society in general, educators and officials may be predisposed to view dress or behavior that seems gay or transgender, or that embraces femininity in boys or masculinity in girls, as personally offensive, distasteful, and even morally wrong. This of course enhances the probability that they will single out and punish such behavior. Explained one California youth: "In my school, some of my security guards are coaches, so when they do see like a more feminine male, they do kind of tease them and they're like, 'oh, he's a fairy.'"

Because of such prejudices, when students are bullied for being gender nonconforming, educators are reluctant to intervene, sometimes feeling "they brought it on themselves" (Peters 2003). In effect, LGBTQ students are blamed for interactions in which they are the victims.

As Snapp et al. (2015, 59) note, this all leads to a vicious cycle, where unfair discipline and "discriminatory harassment make LGBTQ youth more susceptible to truancy, assault, and disorderly conduct charges [which lead to], disparate rates of suspension or expulsion." Sometimes this leads to a lose-lose proposition, where LGBTQ students are caught between peers and school officials. As one Arizona Latina explained:

> I got bullied, so I, like, started dressing like a boy and got this thug mentality. They looked at me like I was the bad Chola, the Mexican lesbian bitch. So no one messed with me anymore at school, but the administration, they were always watching me. (Snapp et al. 2015, 64)

Systems Change & Implicit Bias

Schools are gendered systems that often act as repositories for the most outdated or stereotypic norms and expectations. Some schools still line up students by sex; seat them by sex, and in classroom exercises, encourage them to compete against each other, and compare them to one another for disciplinary reasons ("Look how good the girls have been today"). Schools often enforce different dress codes and hair rules (even where there is no reason girls couldn't wear pants or boys have long hair). My daughter's elementary school just passed a policy forbidding girls from wearing skirts without leggings, to stop boys from looking up them or being "distracted"—punishing girls for boys' behavior, which is tacitly accepted. And gender nonconformity is still an enormous problem—witness all the news stories about school systems wrestling with which bathroom trans students should be allowed to use simply to relieve themselves.

Gender norms also impact day-to-day teaching in the classroom. Like everyone, teachers also have *implicit* biases that lead them to treat boys and girls in very different, and unequal, ways. Girls tend to be praised for being neat, quiet, and calm, while boys are more likely to be praised for speaking up or being active and independent. Teachers call on boys more often and make more and longer eye contact with them. Even when girls and boys get the same test results, they tend to see boys as mathematically more competent. When girls succeed in a subject, teachers are more likely to attribute it to hard work, while with boys they attribute it to innate ability (there's also evidence that women in the workplace make similar attribution errors about their own successes). Teachers tend to give girls easier problems to solve, and express more dissatisfaction when they get bad grades.

What makes such trends especially challenging is that they hold true even for teachers who are morally opposed to them, and deeply committed to equity. In one study, outraged teachers refused to believe the findings, until they were shown the scored videotapes from their own classroom. And this doesn't count the many teachers who are much less committed, and still hold very *explicit* gender biases, which they've never questioned (including educators in very traditional or conservative religiously based institutions).

The profound gendering of education through implicit biases, dress and deportment rules, school disciplinary practices, the acceptance of sexualized harassment, and hostility toward gender nonconforming and/or LGBTQ students, show that school systems engagement with gender norms needs to be rethought from the top down. In fact, TrueChild has been working with partners like the National Alliance for Partnerships in Equity (NAPE) to create toolkits, gender self-surveys, school gender climate surveys, and gender audits that might help educators and administrators become more aware of the ways that schools model and enforce narrow, binary gender norms and what changes they might want to consider making.

Teaching is a phenomenally difficult job. Thinking through schools' gender assumptions is one way to create the more equitable environments that educators, parents, and students *all* want.

Stories from the Frontlines: FaST Curriculum

With key STEM partners like NAPE and the National Girls Collaborative Project (both of whose exceptional CEOs, Mimi Lufkin and Karen Peterson, were incredibly generous with their experience and expertise)—and support from the Motorola Solutions Foundation—TrueChild developed a pilot curriculum based loosely around Promundo's Program M. Called FaST (Femininity and STem), the curriculum's six exercises aimed to help improve STEM interest, participation, and achievement among young women of color by teaching them to think critically about rigid feminine norms. FaST was piloted with students at SUNY Stony Brook's TechPREP program over two weeks, as part of a larger program within SUNY's Women in Science and Engineering (WISE) program. As the graphic below from the third-party evaluation firm shows, all our target metrics showed substantial improvement. FaST has since been adopted in many other locales: Chicago's South Side, Oakland, San Francisco, and SeaTac. As of this writing, FaST is undergoing its first entirely school-based pilot in select East San Jose public high schools, through support provided by the Applied Materials Foundation and Silicon Valley Community Foundation. This new, ten-exercise, co-ed version of FaST also addresses boys' attitudes, and incorporates exercises specifically focused on gay and trans issues, based on new studies that have found that many of the same masculinist attitudes that can push girls away from STEM, also do so for LGBTQ students, too.

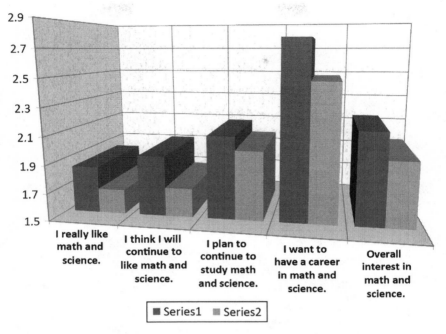

2.9
2.7
2.5
2.3
2.1
1.9
1.7
1.5

I really like math and science.

I think I will continue to like math and science.

I plan to continue to study math and science.

I want to have a career in math and science.

Overall interest in math and science.

■ Series1   ■ Series2

Figure 5.1   Pre-Post Measures from SUNY Stony Brook's TechPREP Pilot of FaST.
Source: Eads 2015, 2.

References & Selected Reading

Adams, M. L. 2005. "'Death to the Prancing Prince': Effeminacy, Sport Discourses and the Salvation of Men's Dancing," *Body and Society* 11 (4): 63–86.

Alexander, M. 2012. *The New Jim Crow: Mass Incarceration in the Age of Colorblindness*. New York: The New Press.

Anderson, M. 2016. "The Black Girl Pushout: Monique Morris Interview," *The Atlantic*. https://www.theatlantic.com/education/archive/2016/03/the-criminalization-of-black-girls-in-schools/473718/.

Armstrong, J. M., and Price, R. A. 1982. "Correlates and Predictors of Women's Mathematics Participation," *Journal for Research in Mathematics Education* 13 (2): 99–109.

Arredondo, M., Gray, C., Russell, S., Skiba. R, and Snapp, S. 2016. *Documenting Disparities for LGBT Students: Expanding the Collection and Reporting of Data on Sexual Orientation and Gender Identity*. Discipline Disparities Series, The Atlantic Philanthropies and the Open Society Foundations.

Badger, K., Craft, R. S., and Jensen, L. 1998. "Age and Gender Differences in Value Orientation among American Adolescents," *Adolescence* 33 (131): 591.

Blake, J. J., Butler, B. R., Lewis, C. W., and Darensbourg, A. 2011. "Unmasking the Inequitable Discipline Experiences of Urban Black Girls: Implications for Urban Educational Stakeholders," *The Urban Review* 43 (1): 90–106.

Bloomfield, E. A. 2015. *Gender Role Stereotyping and Art Interpretation.* Iowa City: University of Iowa Press.

Brett, P. 2006. "Musicality, Essentialism, and the Closet in Queering the Pitch," in Brett, P., Wood, E. and Thomas, G. C., eds., *Queering the Pitch: The New Gay and Lesbian Musicology.* New York: Routledge.

Brown, B. B. 1982. "The Extent and Effects of Peer Pressure among High School Students: A Retrospective Analysis," *Journal of Youth and Adolescence* 11 (2): 121–33.

Bryant, R. 2013. *Empty Seats: Addressing the Problem of Unfair School Discipline for Boys of Color.* Washington DC: CLASP.

Burdge, H., Hyemingway, Z. T., and Licona, A. C. 2014. *Gender Nonconforming Youth: Discipline Disparities, School Push-Out, and the School-to-Prison Pipeline.* GSA Network and Crossroads Collaborative at the University of Arizona.

Burke, P. J. 1989. "Gender Identity, Sex, and School Performance," *Social Psychology Quarterly* 52 (2): 159–69.

Chaudhry, N., and Tucker, J. 2017. *Let Her Learn: Stopping School Pushout.* Washington, DC: National Women's Law Center.

Clark Blickenstaff, J. 2005. "Women and Science Careers: Leaky Pipeline or Gender Filter?" *Gender and Education* 17 (4): 369–86.

Chemaly, S. 2014. "Why Is the Math Gender Gap So Much Worse in the US Than in Other Countries?" *Huffington Post.* https://www.huffingtonpost.com/soraya-chemaly/math-gender-gap_b_5268866.html.

Contractor, D., and Staats, C. 2014. "Interventions to Address Racialized Discipline Disparities and School 'Push Out.'" Kirwan Institute. http://kirwaninstitute.osu.edu/wp-content/uploads/2014/05/ki-interventions.pdf.

Crenshaw, K. (with Ocen, P., and Nanda, J.) 2015. *Black Girls Matter: Pushed Out, Overpoliced, and Underprotected.* New York: Center for Intersectionality and Social Policy Studies, Columbia University.

Cvencek, D., Meltzoff, A. N., and Greenwald, A. G. 2011. "Math-Gender Stereotypes in Elementary School Children," *Child Development* 82 (3): 766–79.

Damarin, S. 2008. "Toward Thinking Feminism and Mathematics Together," *Signs: Journal of Women in Culture and Society* 34 (1): 101–23.

De Welde, K., Laursen, S., and Thiry, H. 2007. *Women in Science, Technology, Engineering and Math (STEM).* https://www.uc.edu/content/dam/uc/win/docs/stem_fact_sheet.pdf.

Dockterman, E. 2014. "Google Invests $50 Million to Close the Tech Gender Gap," *Time,* June 19.

Dyer, S. K. 2004. *Under the Microscope: A Decade of Gender Equity Projects in the Sciences.* Washington, DC: American Association of University Women Educational Foundation.

Eads, M. 2015. *Gender Norms and Science, Technology, Engineering, and Math (STEM): Evaluation of a Model Pilot Intervention.* Health Management Associates Community Strategies (HMACS) for TrueChild.

Emdin, C. 2016. "Why Black Men Quit Teaching," *New York Times,* August 28, https://www.nytimes.com/2016/08/28/opinion/sunday/why-black-men-quit-teaching.html.

Ernest, P. 2007. "Questioning the Gender Problem in Mathematics," *Philosophy of Mathematics Education Journal* 20:1–11.

Fennema, E. 2000. "Gender and Mathematics: What Is Known and What Do I Wish Was Known," in *Fifth Annual Forum of the National Institute for Science Education* (pp. 22–23).

Ferguson, A. A. 2010. *Bad Boys: Public Schools in the Making of Black Masculinity*. Ann Arbor: University of Michigan Press.

Forham, S., and Ogbu, J. U. 1986. "Black Students' School Success: Copying with the "Burden of 'Acting White,'" *The Urban Review* 18 (3): 176.

Frieze, I. H., Whitley, B. E., Hanusa, B. H., and McHugh, M. C. 1982. "Assessing the Theoretical Models for Sex Differences in Causal Attributions for Success and Failure," *Sex Roles* 8 (4): 333–43.

Garcia, L. 2009. "'Now Why Do You Want to Know about That?' Heteronormativity, Sexism, and Racism in the Sexual (Mis) education of Latina Youth," *Gender and Society* 23 (4): 520–41.

George, Y. S., Neale, D. S., Van Horne, V., and Malcolm, S. M. 2001. "In Pursuit of a Diverse Science, Technology, Engineering, and Mathematics Workforce." Washington, DC: American Association for the Advancement of Science.

Gilliam, W. S., Maupin, A. N., Reyes, C. R., Accavitti, M., and Shic, F. 2016. *Do Early Educators' Implicit Biases Regarding Sex and Race Relate to Behavior Expectations and Recommendations of Preschool Expulsions and Suspensions*. Research Study Brief. New Haven: Yale Child Study Center, Yale University.

Gregory, J. F. 1995. "The Crime of Punishment: Racial and Gender Disparities in the Use of Corporal Punishment in US Public Schools," *Journal of Negro Education* 64 (4): 454–62.

Hannon, L., DeFina, R., and Bruch, S. 2013. "The Relationship between Skin Tone and School Suspension for African Americans," *Race and Social Problems* 5 (4): 281–95.

Harris, S. M. 1995. "Psychosocial Development and Black Male Masculinity: Implications for Counseling Economically Disadvantaged African American Male Adolescents," *Journal of Counseling and Development* 73 (3): 279–87.

Heitzeg, N. 2009. "Education or Incarceration: Zero Tolerance Policies and the School to Prison Pipeline," *Forum on Public Policy: A Journal of the Oxford Round Table* 5 (2): 1–21.

———. 2014. "Criminalizing Education: Zero Tolerance Policies, Police in the Hallways, and the School to Prison Pipeline," in Nocella, A. J., Parmar, P., and Stovall, D., eds., *From Education to Incarceration: Dismantling the School-to-Prison Pipeline*, 11–36. New York: Peter Lang.

Isom, D. A. 2007. "Performance, Resistance, Caring: Racialized Gender Identity in African American Boys," *The Urban Review* 39 (4): 405–23.

Johnson, T., Boyden, J. E., and Pittz, W. J. 2001. *Racial Profiling and Punishment in US Public Schools: How Zero Tolerance Policies and High Stakes Testing Subvert Academic Excellence and Racial Equity*. Research Report [and] Executive Summary. Oakland, CA: ERASE Initiative.

Jones, M. G., Howe, A., and Rua, M. J. 2000. "Gender Differences in Students' Experiences, Interests, and Attitudes toward Science and Scientists," *Science Education* 84 (2): 180–92.

Kinney, D. A. 1993. "From Nerds to Normals: The Recovery of Identity Among Adolescents from Middle School to High School," *Sociology of Education* 66 (1): 21–40.

Laura, C. T. 2011. "Reflections on the Racial Web of Discipline," *Monthly Review* 63 (3): 87.

Leaper, C., and Brown, C. S. 2008. "Perceived Experiences with Sexism Among Adolescent Girls," *Child Development* 79 (3): 685–704.

Lench, B. "Sports Drop Rate for Girls Six Times Rate for Boys," *Momsteam: The Trusted Source for Sports Parents*. http://www.momsteam.com/successful-parenting/youth-sports-parenting-basics/parenting-girls/sports-dropout-rate-for-girls-six.

Majors, R., and Billson, J. M. 1992. *Cool Pose: The Dilemmas of Black Manhood in America.* New York: Touchstone.

Martin, K. A. 1998. "Becoming a Gendered Body: Practices of Preschools," *American Sociological Review* 63:494–511.

McBride, N. R. 2016. "Singing, Sissies, and Sexual Identity: How LGBTQ Choral Directors Negotiate Gender Discourse," *Music Educators Journal* 102 (4): 36–40.

Meyer, E. J. 2008. "Gendered Harassment in Secondary Schools: Understanding Teachers'(Non)interventions," *Gender and Education* 20 (6): 555–70.

Miller, C. C. 2014. "Technology's Man Problem," *New York Times*, April 5.

Mizener, C. 1993. "Attitudes of Children Toward Singing and Choir Participation and Assessed Singing Skill," *Journal of Research in Music Education* 41 (3): 233–45.

Morris, E. W. 2005. "'Tuck in That Shirt!' Race, Class, Gender, and Discipline in an Urban School," *Sociological Perspectives* 48 (1): 25–48.

———. 2007. "'Ladies' or 'Loudies'"? Perceptions and Experiences of Black Girls in Classrooms," *Youth and Society* 38 (4): 490–515.

Morris, M., 2016. *Pushout: The Criminalization of Black Girls in Schools.* New York: The New Press.

Murphy, A. S., Acosta, M. A., and Kennedy-Lewis, B. L. 2013. "'I'm Not Running Around with My Pants Sagging, So How Am I Not Acting Like a Lady?': Intersections of Race and Gender in the Experiences of Female Middle School Troublemakers," *The Urban Review* 45 (5): 586–610.

National Education Association (NEA) Statement on the School-to-Prison Pipeline. 2016. https://www.google.com/url?sa=tandrct=jandq=andesrc=sandsource=webandcd=2andcad=rjaanduact=8andved=2ahukewil-ffjkk7dahwvd98kheozdxgqfjabegqicracandurl=https%3a%2f%2fra.nea.org%2fwp-content%2fuploads%2f2016%2f07%2fnea_policy_statement_on_discipline_and_the_school_to_prison_pipeline_2016.pdfandusg=aovvaw07nrlwmzdkfpn0tpisctyi.

Noguchi, S., and Mangaliman, J. 2008. "Smart vs. Cool: Culture, Race and Ethnicity in Silicon Valley Schools," *Mercury News*, San Jose, August 14. https://www.mercurynews.com/2008/04/05/smart-vs-cool-culture-race-and-ethnicity- in -silicon-valley-schools/.

Parsons, J. E., Meece, J. L., Adler, T. F., and Kaczala, C. M. 1982. "Sex Differences in Attributions and Learned Helplessness," *Sex Roles* 8 (4): 421–32.

Rensaa, R. J. 2006. "The Image of a Mathematician," *Philosophy of Mathematics Education Journal* 19: 1–18.

Riegle-Crumb, C., and King, B. 2010. "Questioning a White Male Advantage in STEM: Examining Disparities in College Major by Gender and Race/Ethnicity," *Educational Researcher* 39 (9): 656–64.

Rocque, M., and Paternoster, R. 2011. "Understanding the Antecedents of The 'School-To-Jail' Link: The Relationship Between Race and School Discipline," *The Journal of Criminal Law and Criminology* 101 (2): 633–65.

Rumberger, R. W., and Lim, S. A. 2008. "Why Students Drop Out of School: A Review of 25 Years of Research," *California Dropout Research Project* 15: 1–3.

Santos, D., Ursini, S., Ramirez, M. P., and Sanchez, G. 2006. "Mathematics Achievement: Sex Differences vs. Gender Differences," *Proceedings of the 30th Conference of the International Group for the Psychology of Mathematics Education* 5: 41–48.

Schmalz, D. L., and Kerstetter, D. L. 2006. "Girlie Girls and Manly Men: Children's Stigma Consciousness of Gender in Sports and Physical Activities," *Journal of Leisure Research* 38 (4): 536–57.

Schrock, D., and Schwalbe, M. 2009. "Men, Masculinity, and Manhood Acts," *Annual Review of Sociology* 35: 277–95.

Scott, H. 2008. *Masculinities and Music: Engaging Men and Boys in Making Music.* Newcastle upon Tyne, UK: Cambridge Scholars Publishing.

Shapiro, C. A., and Sax, L. J. 2011. "Major Selection and Persistence for Women in STEM," *New Directions for Institutional Research* 152: 5–18.

Skiba, R. J., Michael, R. S., Nardo, A. C., and Peterson, R. L. 2002. "The Color of Discipline: Sources of Racial and Gender Disproportionality in School Punishment," *The Urban Review* 34 (4): 317–42.

Skiba, R., and Rausch, M. K. 2004. *The Relationship Between Achievement, Discipline, and Race: An Analysis of Factors Predicting ISTEP Scores.* Children Left Behind Policy Briefs. Supplementary Analysis 2-D. Center for Evaluation and Education Policy, Indiana University.

Smith, T. E. 1992. "Gender Differences in the Scientific Achievement of Adolescents: Effects of Age and Parental Separation," *Social Forces* 71 (2): 469–84.

Snapp, S. D., Hoenig, J. M., Fields, A., and Russell, S. T. 2015. "Messy, Butch, and Queer: LGBTQ Youth and the School-to-Prison Pipeline," *Journal of Adolescent Research* 30 (1): 57–82.

Sonnert, G., and Holton, G. J. 1995. *Who Succeeds in Science? The Gender Dimension.* New Brunswick, NJ: Rutgers University Press.

Stets, J. E., and Burke, P. J. 2000. "Femininity/Masculinity," in Borgatta, E. F., and Montgomery, R. J. V., eds., *Encyclopedia of Sociology*, revised edition, 997–1005. New York: Macmillan.

Stevenson, H. W., Lee, S. Y., and Stigler, J. W. 1986. "Mathematics Achievement of Chinese, Japanese, and American Children," *Science* 231 (4739): 693–99.

Tam, P. 2018. "How Silicon Valley Came to Be a Land of 'Bros,'" *New York Times*, February 5.

Thompson, E. M., Sinclari, K. O., Wilchins, R., and Russell, S. 2013. "'It's How You Look or What You Like': Gender Harassment at School and Its Association with Student Adjustment," in Brooks, R., McCormack, M., and Bhopal, K., eds., *Contemporary Debates in the Sociology of Education*, 149–67. London: Palgrave Macmillan.

Townsend, T. G., Thomas, A. J., Neilands, T. B., and Jackson, T. R. 2010. "I'm No Jezebel; I Am Young, Gifted, and Black: Identity, Sexuality, and Black Girls," *Psychology of Women Quarterly* 34 (3): 273–85.

Versey, H. S. 2014. "Centering Perspectives on Black Women, Hair Politics, and Physical Activity," *American Journal of Public Health* 104 (5): 810–15.

Wilcox S., Richter, D. L., Henderson, K. A., Greaney, M. L., Ainsworth, B. E. 2002. "Perceptions of Physical Activity and Personal Barriers and Enablers in African American Women," *Ethnicity and Disease* 12 (3): 353–62.

Williams, J. G. 2011. *Male Participation and Male Recruitment Issues in Middle and High School Chorus.* Boston: Boston University Press.

Wiseman, R. 2009. *Queen Bees and Wannabes: Helping Your Daughter Survive Cliques, Gossip, Boyfriends, and the New Realities of Girl World.* New York: Harmony.

Wyer, M. 2003. "Intending to Stay: Images of Scientists, Attitudes toward Women, and Gender as Influences on Persistence among Science and Engineering Majors," *Journal of Women and Minorities in Science and Engineering* 9 (1): 1–16.

Yang, K. W. 2009. "Focus on Policy: Discipline or Punish? Some Suggestions for School Policy and Teacher Practice," *Language Arts* 87 (1): 49–61.

Zecharia, A., Cosgrave, E., Thomas, L., and Jones, R. 2014. *Through Both Eyes: The Case for a Gender Lens in STEM*. London: Sciencegrrl.

Zucker, K. J. 2005. "Measurement of Psychosexual Differentiation," *Archives of Sexual Behavior* 34 (4): 375–88.

6

Health & Wellness

It is well-known that men tend to have lower health outcomes than women. The statistics are as dreary as they are familiar: men are 1.5 times more likely to die from
heart disease, cancer, and respiratory disease, and on average die seven years earlier
than women. While women lead in a few major illnesses (breast cancer, osteoporosis,
etc.) men have higher rates of death for all fifteen leading causes of mortality. Even
when men and women suffer the same diseases, men are more likely to die of them
than women of the same age and diagnosis.

Men also suffer much higher rates of accidental injury, the third leading cause of
death among men worldwide (as well as a major cause of disability). Men also suffer
more from stress and stress-related illnesses like high blood pressure, heart disease,
diabetes, and heart attack. Although maintaining masculinity tends to be highly
stressful (so-called "Masculine Gender Role Stress"), men are less likely to think of
themselves *as* stressed, less likely take steps to reduce stress, and less likely to think
they need help dealing with it.

Whatever the cause, men are more likely to die earlier than their female peers.
As Ronald Levant, former president of the American Psychological Association has
explained, "Masculine gender socialization is hazardous for men's health, posing a
double whammy of poorer health behaviors and lower use of health care" (quoted
in Murray-Law 2011, 58). (He might have also added more risk-taking and higher
rates of chronic stress.) One key to impacts like these is understanding how manhood ideals shift during men's health lifecycle.

Men's Lifecycle

As Evans et al. (2011) point out, in youth, young men's lower health outcomes
are tied to social imperatives to demonstrate manliness through public displays of
risk-taking, athleticism, and strength. Young men are three times more likely to die
from death-by-accident than young women, four times more likely to die from suicide, and only half as likely to seek healthcare. When young men do try to commit

suicide, they are more likely to use violent and irreversible means (e.g., handguns) and succeed in their first attempt. When they seek medical care, it is twice as likely to be in an emergency room.

In the mid-life years, lower health outcomes are often related to work. Middle-aged men demonstrate manhood by overworking, being high-achieving and aggressive, surmounting obstacles, and showing they can be stoic in the face of hardship. Men who experience stress and depression are unlikely to report it—either through lack of awareness or simply by being in denial—and unlikely to seek help.

Mid-life crises, depression, and suicide are particular problems at this age, with men up to four times more likely to commit suicide than women. As Evans notes, the gender blindness among healthcare provides contributes to this, with depression-screening instruments slanted toward traditionally feminine symptoms of depression like sadness and self-judgment, rather than the anger, numbing, or substance abuse common among depressed males.

In old age, illness and aging may threaten their ability to sustain their ideals of vitality, strength, and virility. This can be especially true for men who retire, losing the combined benefits conferred by careers, professional status, and daily work as their evidence of masculinity and worth. Both factors can result in higher levels of stress, low self-worth, and depression—all factors linked to lower mortality outcomes. Men's illness or disability, in and of itself, can reduce men's social status, shifting their power relations with women and other men, and pushing them to great lengths to hide their deficits.

Across men's entire lifecycle, manhood ideals encourage toughness, risk-taking, denying stress or depression, hiding pain, and avoiding dependence. Men and boys are about one-quarter percent less likely to have visited a doctor, about one-quarter percent more likely to be hospitalized for avoidable pneumonia, and about twice as likely to have amputations because of avoidable diabetic complications.

The common limiting factor here isn't money or insurance (unlike with women), it's masculinity. Men—particularly young males—will avoid seeking help until their bodies are in crisis from treatable and in some cases even preventable illnesses because codes of manhood dictate that they ignore pain, avoid admitting weakness, and never ask for help.

This is the insight behind the "Real Men Wear Gowns" campaign, developed by the Department of Health and Human Services and adopted by many cities, including Atlanta, Knoxville, and the District of Columbia.

As Lipsky, Cannon, and Lutfiyya (2014) note, manhood ideas make "males more likely than females to engage in thirty risky health behaviors, including smoking, drinking to excess, eating a poor diet, and living a sedentary lifestyle" (140).

It is worth noting that some new studies are finding that manhood ideals can also confer benefits, particularly among African American men who see themselves as capable and cool-headed, and who are thus more likely to seek help to maintain their health. If African American men can do this, it may provide important hints for funders, policy makers, and nonprofits to develop programming that would encourage their non-Black peers to do likewise.

Femininity & Health Seeking

While not as extensively studied, researchers have documented the effects of feminine norms on women's health. This is of particular importance in communities and ethnicities where traditions stress the importance of caretaking and the ideals of self-sacrifice.

This can lead women to prioritize taking care of others' health, including younger siblings and infirm elders, at the cost of delaying their own health needs. Similar to men and masculinity, this can include ignoring signals of pain or illness and postponing medical care for treatable complaints until their bodies are in crisis.

Such attitudes can be exacerbated by some racial and ethnic traditions that say that women should take care of problems on their own and avoid seeking help outside of the immediate family. For instance, the American Heart Association's "Go Red For Women / Go Red For Por Tu Corazon" campaign is aimed at encouraging Hispanic women to attend to symptoms of heart attack, and to seek medical help promptly and prioritize their own needs.

Latinas, the campaign website notes, may "take on the role of caregiver superwoman, catering to the needs of everyone but themselves. . . . Many Hispanic women . . . are more likely to take preventative action for their families . . . [while] completely ignoring their own health . . . and these acts of selflessness can become deadly" because women postpone addressing their (often milder) symptoms of an impending heart attack and wait until it's too late (AHA 2019, n.p.).

Similar impacts are found in African America communities, where Black women must cope with cultural expectations of being "superwomen" who are always strong and never show signs of weakness, sadness, or pain. As researcher Deborah Lekan, David Williams, and others have noted, this "superwoman" ideal makes it difficult to acknowledge mental health problems like depression, or to seek attention for their own symptomatology.

This is compounded by what has been called the Sojourner Syndrome—an intersectional approach to how the chronic effects of structural racism, microaggressions, sexism, and/or poverty intersect and become cumulative overtime. This can lead to a "weathering effect" in which the bodies' ability to resist disease breaks down, and Black women become progressively vulnerable to chronic stress-related conditions like high blood pressure, stroke, diabetes, and cardiovascular disease.

The Undertreatment of Women

Healthcare is a deeply gendered system, and studies have repeatedly found that norms and stereotypes about femininity and womanhood held by medical personnel adversely impact the care provided to women in ways that hospitals have been slow to recognize and address.

For instance, because of archaic stereotypes that women are more emotional, irrational, and dramatic (i.e., *hysteric*), providers are more likely to routinely dismiss women's health complaints as psychosomatic, the result of anxiety, emotion, or an overreaction to symptoms. A recent report by the website Think Progress described a patient with potentially life-threatening uterine fibroids. Yet four different health professionals told her that her symptoms were all in her head.

Female patients' pain is scandalously and systematically undertreated in the United States. A 2016 *National Pain Report* found that an astounding 90 percent of women with chronic pain reported that they felt that the health system discriminated against them.

Studies also show that women who complain of being undermedicated are more likely than male patients to be given sedatives (to return them to being quiet and submissive females) than medicated for their pain.

This kind of undertreatment, along with the normative imperatives that women should be deferential and passive, can be deadly. For example, women postpone seeing doctors when having a heart attack because they fear being dismissed as overreacting or as hypochondriacs. (In one study, over three-quarters of women reported avoiding seeing a doctor for fear they would be not be believed and/or be seen as overreacting to their symptoms.)

Women even receive different and less care than men in the same hospitals when presenting with the same conditions and symptoms. In one study, Gabrielle Chiaramonte (2007) found that doctors who evaluated two hypothetical patients with classic heart attack symptoms (a forty-seven-year-old man and a fifty-six-year-old woman) shifted their entire understanding of the case when they were told that the patient had experienced stress. Their evaluations diverged strictly along gender lines. Just 15 percent correctly diagnosed the woman, versus 56 percent for the man. Only 30 percent referred the woman to a cardiologist, versus 62 percent for the man. Just 13 percent recommended heart medication for the woman, versus 47 percent for the man.

Overall, women are much more likely to be misdiagnosed with mental conditions they don't have, and are consistently given less time and attention by medical staff than if they were males. Perhaps because of this, when women do have heart attacks, they are twice as likely to die as men the same age.

Summing up the problem, Maya Dusenbery, executive director at the blog *Feministing*, explains, "We don't trust women to be the experts on their own bodies, or to be reliable narrators of their own lives" (quoted in Culp-Ressler 2015, n.p.).

Disordered Eating

While men and boys certainly have disordered eating, such disorders overwhelmingly occur among women and girls—in some studies more than three-quarters of them. This alone should make us likely to believe that norms of femininity and womanhood are central to understanding or developing such illnesses.

Eating disorders like binge eating and obesity often originate in adolescence. In her pioneering book, *Fat Is a Feminist Issue* (1978), psychotherapist Susie Orbach argued that some girls overeat as a direct (if sometimes unconscious) response to the sudden onset of intense male sexual attention that all too often accompanies girls' puberty. As girls' bodies begin to change, with breasts, hips, and buttocks becoming more prominent, males stare, make sexualized comments, invade girls' space, or commit unwanted touching.

All of this can be as terrifying for young girls as it is unwelcome. Orbach argued that girls respond by seeking fat as "armor": a shell that can simultaneously hide their bodies from the male gaze, de-emphasize newly sexualized body features, and furnish them with a protective layer.

Other researchers have studied anorexia and undereating, and its ties to cultural pressures on girls to be thin. The slender ideal presented by many popular role models for girls will be unachievable for many of them. This is even more true of online images, which are often heavily Photoshopped. The pervasiveness of online media today makes such idealized images hard to avoid or ignore.

Two-thirds of elementary school girls are "happy the way I am," but by high school that figure drops to about one-third. Girls who rigidly internalize such beauty ideals are especially vulnerable to chronic stress because of their bodyweight, even when it is entirely normal. Some studies find that it is not the ideals themselves, nor the attempts to meet them that is most at issue, but rather that girls experience severe stress when failing to obtain them.

While disordered eating used to start in "tween" and teen years; doctors now see patients as young as five and six. By third grade, studies find a majority of girls are dieting, with three-quarters already saying they weigh too much. By age ten, three-quarters of girls have already been on a diet. About half of thirteen-year-old girls have issues with their bodies, and by age seventeen, about over three-quarters do.

Complicating matters, adolescent girls often police one another's size and thinness. And Shakeshaft et al.'s study, "Boys Call Me Cow" (1997), documented how middle-school girls would describe male students mooing at them as they passed, or making similar rude remarks and/or noises because they considered the girls unattractive and/or heavyset. Some girls report dieting simply to avoid being teased or taunted. Clinicians have long noted that girls they treat for disordered eating also often have strong beliefs in traditional feminine ideals of beauty, thinness, and dependence. For example, some studies have found that bulimic women are more likely to be unassertive, dependent, and have low self-esteem.

Anorexic eating has also been linked to high-achieving girls who feel under constant pressure to do well, have packed schedules, and who end up feeling their lives are no longer under their own control. Some gravitate toward anorexia to provide an illusory sense of control over their own lives and bodies. One researcher noted that anorexia and bulimia were becoming the "disorder of choice" among young high-achieving Jewish women and girls.

Dieting and disordered eating is now so commonplace among girls that we must ask whether it still counts as an aberration. As Phares, Steinberg, and Thompson (2004) note, a case could be made that such attitudes are no longer abnormal, but that dieting, body-image dissatisfaction, and constant weight surveillance now constitute the normative experiences for the majority of tween and teenage girls, and thus have become integral to their understanding of the aesthetics of their bodies and the demands of feminine desirability.

Distressing as this thought may be, fortunately some girls show remarkable resilience in rejecting these demands, studies show. Studies consistently find that teenage Black girls have more success than their White peers in tuning out media stereotypes and thinness images. This seems to be because African American models and actresses remain the exception, and girls do not see mainstream images of White women as aimed at them or relevant to them. Their resistance may be bolstered by the fact that in many parts of the Black community, more curvy female bodies are seen as both feminine and desirable.

Black girls' resistance would appear to offer a template for policy makers, healthcare professionals, and nonprofits to create more effective ways to combat disordered eating and the epidemic of distorted feminine body ideals.

Substance Abuse

Readers of a certain age will remember the ubiquitous, hypermasculine ads of the 1960s to the 1990s that inevitably featured a rugged, chiseled cowboy getting a smoke at the end of another hard day on the range. These "Marlboro Man" ads took an undistinguished company with a one-percent market share named Philip Morris and a brand long considered a "women's cigarette" marketed for mildness, and made it into the top-selling cigarette brand in the United States. While the campaign initially tested images of construction workers, weightlifters, and mechanics, it was the strong, silent, rustic Western cowhand that became their ad campaign's sole, iconic focus.

Less than a decade later, as manufacturers sought to entice younger and younger buyers into smoking, R. J. Reynolds launched "Joe Camel"—a cartoon character clad in sunglasses and black leather (with a suspiciously phallic muzzle) who played pool, hung out with fast cars and women, and generally marketed a "cool" and virile manhood to insecure teenage boys.

Morris' Virginia Slims campaign—"You've come a long way, baby"—attempted to market its cigarette in the image of a youthful, svelte, feminist, and independent woman. It was launched around the same time as the Marlboro Man ads, but it didn't achieve the same level of success. The Marlboro ads were effective with both men *and* women, often more so than brands that specifically targeted and addressed femininity in women.

Beer advertising is similar, using the same lifestyle marketing to sell alcohol consumption as an act of strong, untroubled, risk-taking, heterosexual masculinity—to insecure young men. Binge-drinking, which has become a growing problem on college campuses, is also strongly influenced by young men's desire to display public masculinity by "manning up" and getting drunk. Conversely, being unable or unwilling to consume and hold down vast quantities of alcohol is considered a sign of weakness, femininity, or gayness.

Unlike smoking, the appeal of youthful heavy drinking paradoxically combines both the display of manly self-control by "holding your liquor" and appearing sober, with a manly disregard for social mores and conventions of total public intoxication (i.e., getting *smashed*, *wasted*, *shit-faced*, etc.). Needless to say, this attraction extends to other substances, including unmarketed and illicit heavier drugs, which have the added "outlaw" appeal of being illegal, thus further demonstrating control, social independence, and risk-taking.

It has long been a secret hiding in plain sight that cigarette and alcohol abuse are grounded in male anxiety to project masculinity. Substance abuse is youthful, rebellious, hip, even sexy—a means of publicly displaying defiance of authority, of health risk, and of conventional mores.

Despite this, funders' and policy makers' public-education campaigns have tended to focus almost entirely on messages telling young people that "smoking kills" or commanding them "don't drive drunk"—which simply amps up the outlaw value and coolness factor.

Perhaps even worse, those messages about acting responsibly and staying healthy are largely irrelevant to the target audience: a fifteen-year-old who tempted to try his first cigarette or chug a six-pack is unlikely to be overly worried about health consequences. Fear-based public education campaigns showing adults dying from lung cancer who are older than he can ever imagine being are unlikely to have maximal impact on a teenager who feels invulnerable and knows that he will live forever.

Similarly, it has long been known that a major factor behind drunk driving is young men's need to measure manhood by alcohol intake and display manliness by appearing to function while drunk. Yet anti-drunk-driving programs and education campaigns continue to ignore the role of manhood, and focus on the risks of having accidents or being caught by police.

In summary, we're still failing to address underlying attitudes about gender that drive substance abuse among young males, even though such attitudes are so well-known and recognized that they have been the foundation for cigarette and alcohol advertising campaigns for more than half a century.

LGBTQ Healthcare Seeking

When it comes to healthcare systems, we've mostly focused on *normative* gender attitudes and their impact. But prejudices and biases around *gender nonconformity* also play important roles, particularly with LGBTQ patients.

According to the National Center for Transgender Equality (NCTE), between one-fifth and one-quarter of transgender patients report being turned away by healthcare providers who refused to provide treatment.

Transgender and gender nonconforming patients who seek and receive care often find they are treated by medical staff who conduct themselves in ways that are disrespectful or judgmental, including insisting that the patient be referred to by their birth sex and/or their birth name (known in the trans community as "dead-naming"). This can be true even for transpeople who have fully transitioned, and who have government issued IDs for their correct sex, name, gender. This happens even at well-known hospitals in major urban centers (as your gentle author can personally attest).

This lack of basic cultural competence is exacerbated by the fact that trans patients are likely to find few medical personnel who have any specific competency or sensitivity training in their needs (this is also true of gay, lesbian, and bisexual patients).

Medical personnel may routinely assume that all sexually active transwomen must be attracted to males, and vice versa for transmen, even though by some estimates one-quarter or more of transpeople identify as gay, lesbian, or bisexual. They may assume that transwomen and transmen do not need pelvic examinations, or that transmen do not need or want contraceptive care. Medical personnel may also communicate that they are not comfortable with or actively disapprove of LGBTQ patients, often because they are visibly different, or in some way fail to conform to the caregivers' expectations of masculinity in males and femininity in females. This animus need not rise to the level of open bias or discrimination, but often takes the form of microaggressions—brief, routine interactions which communicate disparagement. Microaggressions can include questions or statements that reference common stereotypes: "But you look like a *real woman!*" or subtly disfavor a person: "When did you first become a lesbian?" They can also include more subtle nonverbal signaling that communicates disfavor, such as extended sighs, avoiding eye contact, looking at the floor during conversation, head-shaking, and pursing the lips—all the little things we do consciously and unconsciously to communicate that we're uncomfortable or displeased.

One of the things that makes microaggressions so hard to eliminate is that they occur even in people who believe themselves to be sensitive and tolerant.

If you're a gender nonconforming or transperson with a health issue, all these factors make you more likely to delay asking for medical help until you really need it. According to NCTE, up to half of all transpeople delay or avoid preventative care.

Similar problems can afflict those patients who are intersex or identify as non-binary. For intersex adults, few doctors are trained in their healthcare (which may include any of a wide number of "Disorders of Sexual Development"). As noted earlier, for intersex infants, the standard of care remains inflicting surgery that makes their genitals better resemble "normal" male and female, even in the absence of other health issues, even though scores of adults have come forward to testify how traumatizing and damaging the procedure can be.

As for nonbinary patients, too little is known about them and their healthcare experiences, and as with so many areas about gender, more studies are needed. Hospitals are spaces with fairly rigid gendered distinctions for male and female, and as more patients come forward as nonbinary this will pose a greater challenge in everything from forms of address (*Sir*, *Madam*, *Mr.*, *Miss*) to pronouns, to deciding who can occupy shared hospital rooms.

Systems Change

As the mistreatment of LGBTQ individuals and the undertreatment female ones show, combating gender norms' impact means addressing not only the patient-side of health, but also the systems themselves—hospitals departments, even local community-health centers.

TrueChild has already begun prototyping model curricula and toolkits for use by providers, along with Gender Self-Surveys (to help them become more aware of their own gender biases), and Gender Climate Surveys (to help identify gendered practices and policies across organizations). But this is truly a drop in the bucket compared to the need for health systems to interrogate their own gender assumptions and how they impede care delivery.

And those needs don't stop with patient care. Normative ideas about gender affect everything from who does what hospital tasks and whose opinion carries weight in department meetings to who is on boards of directors and who gets to make hospital rules.

As with education, healthcare is a highly gendered system, one whose gender biases are increasingly well understood even as they go largely unaddressed by those who fund and direct them.

Stories from the Frontlines: BLOOM

As noted above, young Black women and girls face unique challenges connected with their race and gender. Yet few health programs for them address feminine norms in African American communities.

With help from The Heinz Endowments and a very dedicated St. John's University researcher named Dr. Scyatta Wallace, TrueChild created a model curriculum called BLOOM (Black girls Living Out Our Meaning). BLOOM's seven exercises address the concept of gender and femininity, the narrow ways young women of color are portrayed in media and society, body-image issues and eating, dealing with stress and personal caretaking, sexual and reproductive health, partner violence, and celebrating the special strengths and resilience of young Black girls.

BLOOM is uniquely designed not to replace existing programs, but to be easily integrated into them, whether school-based or after-school. Each exercise features

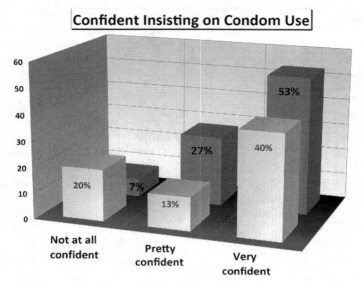

Figure 6.1 Pre-Post Measures for BLOOM Curriculum.

a core activity for girls, accompanied by optional discussion questions that can be tailored to their specific interests. It is supplemented by a unique Trauma Informed Guide, designed specifically for use with low-income girls of color.

BLOOM was piloted by a quartet of local partnering groups that included the Urban League and YWCA of Pittsburgh, and they got very encouraging results. Participants attitudes around things like partner violence, condom negotiation, and body image all improved, as two of the outcome graphs above in figure 6.1 illustrate. We hope to do additional pilots with larger groups, producing longer-term data.

Perhaps as importantly, we have begun prototyping similar model curricula and toolkits that could be used by entire healthcare systems as well as for small community-health centers.

References & Selected Reading

AHA (American Heart Association). 2019. "Heart Disease in Hispanic Women," *Go Red for Women*, website. https://www.goredforwomen.org/en/about-heart-disease-in-women/facts/heart-disease-in-hispanic-women.

American Psychological Association. 2009. *Stress and Gender.*

Bay-Cheng, L. Y., Zucker, A. N., Stewart, A. J., and Pomerleau, C. S. 2002. "Linking Femininity, Weight Concern, and Mental Health among Latina, Black, and White Women," *Psychology of Women Quarterly* 26 (1): 36–45.

Bunnell, D. 2016. "Addressing the Importance of Gender in Psychotherapy of Eating Disorders," *Eating Disorders Resource Catalogue.* https://www.edcatalogue.com/addressing-the-importance-of-gender-in-psychotherapy-of-eating-disorders/.

Byles, J. 2009. *Differences in Men and Women's Health: Chronic Disease and Disability/Ageing and Longevity.* https://www.uni-hohenheim.de/fileadmin/einrichtungen/hcecon/Dateien _und_Bilder/Dateien/Gender_und_Gesundheit/SS_10/02_Gender_differences.pdf.

Culp-Ressler, T. 2015. "When Gender Stereotypes Becomes a Serious Hazard to Women's Health," *Think Progress*, May 11. https://thinkprogress.org/when-gender-stereotypes-become-a-serious-hazard-to-womens-health-f1f130a5e79/.

Carter, R. T. 2007. "Racism and Psychological and Emotional Injury: Recognizing and Assessing Race-Based Traumatic Stress," *The Counseling Psychologist* 35 (1): 13–105.

Charmaz, K. 1995. "The Body, Identity, and Self," *The Sociological Quarterly* 36 (4): 657–80.

Chiaramonte, G. R. 2007. "Physicians' Gender Bias in the Diagnosis, Treatment, and Interpretation of Coronary Heart Disease Symptoms," PhD dissertation, Stony Brook University.

Courtenay, W. H. 2000. "Constructions of Masculinity and Their Influence on Men's Well-Being: A Theory of Gender and Health," *Social Science and Medicine* 50 (10): 1385–401.

Davison, K. K., Markey, C. N., and Birch, L. L. 2000. "Etiology of Body Dissatisfaction and Weight Concerns among 5-Year-Old Girls," *Appetite* 35 (2): 14351.

Dohnt, H. K., and Tiggemann, M. 2006. "Body Image Concerns in Young Girls: The Role of Peers and Media Prior to Adolescence," *Journal of Youth and Adolescence* 35 (2): 135.

Dusenbery, M. 2015. "Is Medicine's Gender Bias Killing Young Women?" *Pacific Standard*, March 23. https://psmag.com/social-justice/is-medicines-gender-bias-killing-young -women.

Elliott, S. 1991. "The Media Business: Advertising; Camel's Success and Controversy," *New York Times*, December 12. https://www.nytimes.com/1991/12/12/business/the-media-business-advertising-camel-s-success-and-controversy.html.

Ethics of Design. "Joe Camel." https://ethicsofdesign.wordpress.com/case-studies/bad-ethics /joe-camel/.

Evans, J., Frank, B., Oliffe, J. L., and Gregory, D. 2011. "Health, Illness, Men and Masculinities (HIMM): A Theoretical Framework for Understanding Men and Their Health," *Journal of Men's Health* 8 (1): 7–15.

Fenton, S. 2016. "How Sexist Stereotypes Mean Doctors Ignore Women's Pain," *Independent*, July 27. http://www.independent.co.uk/life-style/health-and-families/health-news/ how-sexist-stereotypes-mean-doctors-ignore-womens-pain-a7157931.html.

Fields, E. L., Bogart, L. M., Smith, K. C., Malebranche, D. J., Ellen, J., and Schuster, M. A. 2015. "'I Always Felt I Had to Prove My Manhood': Homosexuality, Masculinity, Gender Role Strain, and HIV Risk among Young Black Men Who Have Sex with Men," *American Journal of Public Health*, 105 (1): 122–31.

Fitzgibbon, M. L., Spring, B., Avellone, M. E., Blackman, L. R., Pingitore, R., and Stolley, M. R. 1998. "Correlates of Binge Eating in Hispanic, Black, and White Women," *International Journal of Eating Disorders* 24 (1): 43–52.

Griffith, D. M., Gunter, K., and Watkins, D. C. 2012. "Measuring Masculinity in Research on Men of Color: Findings and Future Directions," *American Journal of Public Health* 102 (S2): S187–S194.

Griffith, D. M., Ober Allen, J., and Gunter, K. 2011. "Social and Cultural Factors Influence African American Men's Medical Help Seeking," *Research on Social Work Practice* 21 (3): 337–47.

Hampton, R., Oliver, W., and Magarian, L. 2003. "Domestic Violence in the African American Community: An Analysis of Social and Structural Factors," *Violence Against Women* 9 (5): 533–57.

Hendy, H. M., Gustitus, C., and Leitzel-Schwalm, J. 2001. "Social Cognitive Predictors of Body Image in Preschool Children," *Sex Roles* 44 (9–10): 557–69.

Iwamoto, D. K., Cheng, A., Lee, C. S., Takamatsu, S., and Gordon, D. 2011. "'Man-ing' Up and Getting Drunk: The Role of Masculine Norms, Alcohol Intoxication and Alcohol-Related Problems among College Men," *Addictive Behaviors* 36 (9): 906–11.

James, S. A. 1994. "John Henryism and the Health of African Americans," *Culture, Medicine and Psychiatry* 18 (2): 163–82.

Jones, J., and Mosher, W. D. 2013. *Fathers' Involvement with Their Children: United States, 2006–2010*. US Department of Health and Human Services, Centers for Disease Control and Prevention, National Center for Health Statistics.

Kerrigan, D., Andrinopoulos, K., Johnson, R., Parham, P., Thomas, T., and Ellen, J. M. 2007. "Staying Strong: Gender Ideologies among African American Adolescents and the Implications for HIV/STI Prevention," *Journal of Sex Research* 44 (2): 172–80.

Lekan, D. 2009. "Sojourner Syndrome and Health Disparities in African American Women," *Advances in Nursing Science* 32 (4): 307–21.

Lindsey, M. A., Korr, W. S., Broitman, M., Bone, L., Green, A., and Leaf, P. J. 2006. "Help-Seeking Behaviors and Depression among African American Adolescent Boys," *Social Work* 51 (1): 49–58.

Lipsky, M. S., Cannon, M., and Lutfiyya, M. N. 2014. "Gender and Health Disparities: The Case of Male Gender," *Disease-A-Month* 60 (4): 138–44.

Martz, D. M., Handley, K. B., and Eisler, R. M. 1995. "The Relationship between Feminine Gender Role Stress, Body Image, and Eating Disorders," *Psychology of Women Quarterly* 19 (4): 493–508.

Matthews, D. D., Hammond, W. P., Nuru-Jeter, A., Cole-Lewis, Y., and Melvin, T. 2013. "Racial Discrimination and Depressive Symptoms among African American Men: The Mediating and Moderating Roles of Masculine Self-Reliance and John Henryism," *Psychology of Men and Masculinity* 14 (1): 35.

Murray-Law, B. 2011. "Why Do Men Die Earlier?" *American Psychological Association* 42 (6): 58. https://www.apa.org/monitor/2011/06/men-die.

O'Loughlin, R. E., Duberstein, P. R., Veazie, P. J., Bell, R. A., Rochlen, A. B., Fernandez Y Garcia, E., and Kravitz, R. L. 2011. "Role of the Gender-Linked Norm of Toughness in the Decision to Engage in Treatment for Depression," *Psychiatric Services* 62 (7): 740–46.

Orbach, S. 1978. *Fat Is a Feminist Issue*. New York: Paddington Press.

Phares, V. Steinberg, A. R., and Thompson, J. K. 2004. "Gender Differences in Peer and Parental Influences: Body Image Disturbance, Self-Worth, and Psychological Functioning in Preadolescent Children," *Journal of Youth and Adolescence* 33 (5): 421–29.

Ravenell, J. E., Johnson Jr. W. E., and Whitaker, E. E. 2006. "African American Men's Perceptions of Health: A Focus Group Study," *Journal of the National Medical Association* 98 (4): 544.

Reed, E., Prado, G., Matsumoto, A., and Amaro, H. 2010. "Alcohol and Drug Use and Related Consequences among Gay, Lesbian and Bisexual College Students: Role of Experiencing Violence, Feeling Safe on Campus, and Perceived Stress," *Addictive Behaviors* 35 (2): 168–71.

Shakeshaft, C. Mandel, L., Johnson, Y. M., Sawyer, J., Hergenrother. M. A., and Barber, E. 1997. "Boys Call Me Cow," *Educational Leadership: Schools as Safe Havens* 55 (2): 22–25.

Shirk, A. 2015. "The Real Marlboro Man," *The Atlantic*, February 17. https://www.theatlantic.com/business/archive/2015/02/the-real-marlboro-man/385447/.

Tallim, J. 2005. "Gender Messages in Alcohol Advertising," *Media Awareness Network*.

The Coalition on Men and Boys. 2009. *Man-Made: Men, Masculinities and Equality in Public Policy*. http://xyonline.net/sites/xyonline.net/files/COMAB, Man Made - Men, masculinities and equality in public policy 09.pdf.

The State of Obesity. 2007. *Special Report: Racial and Ethnic Disparities in Obesity*. https://stateofobesity.org/disparities/.

Wade, J. C., and Rochlen, A. B. 2013. "Introduction: Masculinity, Identity, and the Health and Well-Being of African American Men," *Psychology of Men and Masculinity* 14 (1): 1.

Williams, D. R. 2008. "Racial/Ethnic Variations in Women's Health: The Social Embeddedness of Health," *American Journal of Public Health* 98 (Supplement 1): S38–S47.

Williamson, S., and Delin, C. 2001. "Young Children's Figural Selections: Accuracy of Reporting and Body Size Dissatisfaction," *International Journal of Eating Disorders* 29 (1): 80–84.

Zaslow, J. 2009. "Girls and Dieting, Then and Now," *Wall Street Journal*, September 2. https://www.wsj.com/articles/sb10001424052970204731804574386822245731710.

7

Violence & Bullying

Intimate Partner Violence

Intimate partner violence (IPV) is deeply linked to gender inequality: men not only have greater physical power and are often more psychologically aggressive, but they usually can exercise more economic power—through higher and better-paying jobs and social resources, and through ties to other men in positions of strength.

Where they are acknowledged as heads of families, men exercise marital and family authority over everything from family investments to alimony payments. IPV need not involve actual physical assault. Psychological violence includes threats and intimidation, ridicule and humiliation, and producing ongoing anxiety, chronic depression, or posttraumatic stress in its victims.

It can include economic violence: if a woman is a full-time mother or is otherwise financially dependent, an abusive partner might threaten to throw her and the children out of the home, cut off financial support, or (if divorced), or delay child-support payments.

IPV can also include social violence, opportunities for which have been greatly amplified by the Internet. For example, "revenge porn," almost exclusively the province of jilted males, involves posting sexually explicit pictures of female ex-partners. It is so pervasive and psychologically damaging that some states have passed laws against it. Social violence can also utilize other avenues to attack an ex-partner's reputation and social standing, telling other members of the community that she is sexually "easy," a "gold digger," or mentally unbalanced.

Many young women see attracting an older, stronger, high-status male who can take care of them psychologically and financially as proof of feminine desirability. But older, stronger partners are also more likely to have economic and social resources far beyond those of these younger, less-mature partners, exacerbating the power imbalance and thus possibilities for abuse.

Generally, stronger belief in traditional masculinity has been linked to higher rates of partner violence. This is particularly true for what some researchers have termed "toxic masculinity"—a constellation of attitudes that include these beliefs:

- force is acceptable in an intimate relationship;
- men are justified in coercing sex from a reluctant partner;
- the man determines when and how sex occurs;
- violence is an acceptable response to a woman who challenges male authority; and
- control over and submission of a female partner is central to manhood.

The last item is often cited as particularly important to young men who believe that the proper response to girlfriend or wife who "showed me up" or "disrespected me" was to forcefully put in her subordinate place.

Studies show such attitudes are particularly common in low-income environments where money, jobs, and resources are scarce, and public control of a female partner may be one of the few avenues for men to demonstrate their masculinity publicly. In such circumstances an "unruly" female partner may be perceived as a direct threat to manly honor and status.

Studies have also shown that when a female partner in an abusive relationship gets a job, the odds of partner-violence increase—presumably because it may affront the man's role as chief breadwinner, as well as jeopardizing his control over his female partner.

In talking with convicted perpetrators, outdated stereotypes about womanhood can also be part of rationalizing violence. Perpetrators may justify their behavior by asserting that female partners "brought it on themselves" by not carrying out feminine responsibilities (e.g., household labor, cooking, child care, "taking care" of their man), being "demanding" (asking for personal or financial needs), and being emotional and "out of control." They may assert that they had a responsibility to control a partner who was "out of control" or "hysterical." They did something that needed to be done, and now *they* are the *true* victims.

Masculinity and ideals of power, violence, and dominance are so bound up in IPV that it remains one of the only areas where a significant core of funders and nonprofits have taken a strong gender transformative approach. It has helped that leading experts like Michael Kimmel of the Center for the Study of Men and Masculinity have researched and written about the connections between masculinity and violence for years. Also as noted earlier, organizations like A Call to Men, Becoming a Man, Futures Without Violence, Men As Peacemakers, Men Can Stop Rape, and Promundo have all developed unique initiatives that challenged ideals of violent, predatory, or homophobic masculinity. Moreover, they have done so in ways that avoid engaging young men simply as potential perpetrators, and instead as an integral part of the solution. (Important as partner-violence programs are, they are only a start. As one prominent Black funder put it succinctly, "It's important that anti-date-rape programs are springing up in campuses all over. But that does not exhaust the needs of young, college age men of color to interrogate traditional masculinity"—something equally true of their White peers.)

Women's Belief & IPV

Women in some subcultures may internalize similar belief systems to those of abusive partners. In studies, a significant number of young women in low-income communities agree that if a girl publicly "shows up" her boyfriend or openly disrespects him, he is justified in hitting her. Women who internalize traditional codes of submissive and obedient femininity may be even more accepting of partner violence (which can also be true in more repressive religious cultures).

Interestingly, studies have found that belief in narrow feminine ideals can also provide important protective benefits. Women in some Latinx subcultures have lower rates of IPV than with their White counterparts. One theory is that less-acculturated wives and/or those with stronger belief in more submissive womanhood ideals may be less likely to generate relationship friction with husbands that could spiral into physical abuse.

Power imbalances between men and women in communities of color have been exacerbated by the longstanding mass incarceration of Black and Latino men, leaving young women with fewer possible mates. This increases the bargaining power of the remaining eligible males, especially because Black women seldom date outside their race. The relative scarcity of males combined with the remaining males' power to dictate the terms of relationships may make some young Black women more likely to tolerate abuse.

IPV & Condom Negotiation

Partner violence has been found to strongly depress safer sex, because sustained negotiation can trigger violence against women. Many young women report that fear of retaliation or abuse is the main reason they don't discuss or insist upon condoms. Yet such commonsense observations still go unrecognized in data collection and analysis use, when health officials ask young women if they used a condom at last intercourse—as if this was entirely under their own control, and fear of retaliation was irrelevant.

The correct question might be if a young woman *attempted* to negotiate condom use with her partner, and if so, what was the result. This would recognize the power inequalities of condom negotiation in which sometimes a stronger and often more aggressive male partner must be convinced to take an action he doesn't like.

Infant & Maternal Health

IPV also impacts infant and maternal health. Studies show that between 4 to 8 percent of pregnant women in the United States are victims of partner violence. IPV is linked to a host of detrimental health outcomes among pregnant women, including higher rates of sexually transmitted disease, preterm delivery, and low infant birthweight. Other implications included higher rates of vaginal bleeding, severe nausea, vomiting, dehydration, and kidney infection or UTIs. Pregnant victims were also more likely to have cesarean sections than nonvictims. Age and race can also increase the vulnerability to partner violence and the likelihood of women experiencing it. Recent studies show that African American women, Native American women, and very young women are all at higher risk for IPV during pregnancy.

Homophobia & Sexual Harassment

Gendered Harassment

School sexual harassment encompasses a range of behaviors including sexualized name-calling, sexual jokes or obscene gestures, staring at or touching body parts, taking "up-skirt" smartphone pictures, and homophobic ridicule. Harassment changes with age and pubertal maturity. In later elementary and then middle school, name-calling is most common; by high school, unwanted sexual touching and forced sexual intimacy is.

"Sexual harassment" is an overloaded and often misleading term that both obscures and conflates very different types of events. First, it is often confused with (and totally distinct from) workplace *quid pro quo* sexual harassment, which occurs when a dominant colleague demands sexual favors from a subordinate in exchange for favors and/or advancement.

Second, it is probably inappropriate for describing elementary- and middle-school harassment, which may be framed in a sexualized manner, but is seldom physically sexual or actually about intercourse and sex. For reasons like these, some researchers have suggested reframing "sexualized bullying" by elementary- and middle-school students as "gender harassment." Moreover, removing sex from the terms might help enlarge the frame through which advocates view it to include male-on-male and trans- and-homophobic harassment, which are also both usually about gender.

Three Types of Students

Middle-school and high-school gender harassment overwhelmingly reenacts traditional norms of male entitlement, expressing dominance over weaker members of a group, often to promote masculine bonding among boys. Consider the following scenarios:

- On the way into class, a young man snaps the bra of a young woman in front of him; she blushes furiously and turns on him, but he walks away, saying to his friends, "Bitch."
- Seeing a boy trying out for the school play, one boy whispers *sotto voce* to boys sitting near him, "That's *so* gay!"
- A short-haired, assertive girl who plays on school sports teams finds that a Photoshopped image of her with a mustache, beard, and the word "Lezzie" across her forehead has been anonymously emailed to her classmates.
- Two boys discuss another student who identifies as trans and repeatedly refer to this student as "it"—in front of him.
- As a heavyset girl walks past a group of boys, one makes a loud mooing noise and the others burst out laughing.
- A young man walks behind a young woman and mimics her swaying walk; a student watching calls out, "Watch it—Roy is turning into a fag!"

Shakeshaft et al. (1997), who spent two years studying 1,000 New York City students and documented their findings in a study entitled "Boys Call Me Cow," noted that most of the school harassment they witnessed was directed at boys and girls who failed to conform to traditional gender norms. These included girls who were considered unattractive or who failed to dress stylishly, girls whose bodies were more developed than their peers, and boys who did not fit traditional stereotypic masculinity. The harassment of boys was most often because of how they acted; for girls it was because of how they looked.

"Fag Discourse"

C. J. Pascoe, who performed similar research on homophobic bullying during a year in the Denver schools, reported similar results in her landmark book, *Dude, You're a Fag* (2001). Abusers make important, if unconscious, distinctions about gender performance. As Pascoe explains, "[B]oys imitate presumed faggots and hurl the fag epithet so frequently at one another that I came to call it a 'fag discourse.' . . . Boys repeatedly differentiated fags from gay men . . . The term 'gay' functioned as a generic insult meaning 'stupid' or 'lame' . . . a fag was a failed, feminine man. They frantically lobbed the fag epithet at one another, in a sort of compulsive name calling ritual to ensure others saw them as masculine" (2007, n.p.).

Pascoe documented how the use of homophobic epithets in middle school is less about sexual orientation than about policing masculinity and punishing nonconformity to ideals of manhood. Put another way: at age twenty-one, calling someone "fag" is usually about sexual orientation; at age eleven it's about gender nonconformity.

I noted earlier that English has developed a distressingly elaborate vocabulary for stigmatizing gender nonconformity. Although some of its terms are used to punish unfemininity in females, the majority of them are for punishing unmanliness in boys, to which we seem to be much more sensitive. (After many of my gender workshops, at least one befuddled woman will come up and say something like, "My husband is a total feminist and really 'gets it,' but if our son picks up one of his sister's dolls for one second, he's out of his chair to take it away.")

Findings like Pascoe's and Shakeshaft's illustrate how two very different kinds of harassment hide under the common rubric of "homosexual bullying." The first is harassment of kids (mostly males) who are or are known or thought to be LGBTQ. The second, and much more frequent, is homophobic harassment of boys thought to be perfectly straight.

Since about 90 percent of boys report hearing or participating in such name-calling, and perhaps a similar 90 percent identify as straight, obviously the vast majority of Fag Discourse is straight-on-straight bullying. While certainly different from straight-on-gay harassment (which carries its own unique pain and stigma), straight-on-straight homophobia appears to be a primary weapon for policing masculinity and forcing other boys to *man up*.

Something this pervasive reasonably qualifies not as an aberration, but a norm—that is, a regular experience which most boys have, and through which they learn the contours and boundaries of masculinity and the punishments for stepping beyond them.

Fag Discourse mirrors Slut Discourse, which seeks to punish perceived lack of femininity in females considered fat, unstylish, unattractive, physically more developed, or too assertive through epithets like *bitch, whore, cow,* and *dyke*—as well as to penalize them for any sign of healthy female sexual agency. While boys are often targeted for perceived unmanliness, girls are targeted for not being feminine or attractive enough, or for having bodies that are "too" developed (again, policing women's sexuality and perceived sexual agency).

In addition, some studies have found that girls who are less assertive and more stereotypically and passively feminine are *also* more likely to be harassed. This can put middle-school girls in a no-win situation, hemmed in by gender-based hostility on both sides.

Making matters worse, gender harassment at school is neither an anomaly nor infrequent. Petersen and Hyde (2009) found that gender harassment begins as early as elementary school and increases in frequency every year until ninth grade. Shakeshaft's students described gender harassment as "more usual than unusual" and "a way of life."

The American Association of University Women's national survey Crossing the Line (2011) (to which TrueChild contributed) found that "sexual harassment is a part of everyday life in middle and high schools [with] nearly half of students experiencing it each year." Other researchers report that up to 80 percent of middle- and high-school girls are victims of gender harassment, with some recent studies (Lichty and Campbell 2012) finding rates for middle-schoolers as high as 96 percent. These numbers are certainly influenced by how the question is phrased, but even given that, they are astronomical. In addition, 80 to 90 percent of students report witnessing gendered harassment in the past year.

As one adult explained in Black Girls Matter, "Teachers have a culture of sweeping it under the rug. They will say 'Boys will be boys. . . . This is sexual awakening,' . . . Yet they know all the stuff that is happening . . . they talk about girls feeling shamed coming to school, like they can't concentrate because the boys are making lewd comments, constantly pressuring them to have sex with them, slapping their butts and bras."

Cyberbullying

Clearly, current school antiharassment programs are less effective than they need to be. Many such programs do a salutary job of conveying generic messages of the moral wrongness and hurtfulness of bullying ("This Is a No Name Calling Zone!", etc.) Yet they appear to do relatively little to address the specific attitudes and intolerances that drive gender-based bullying. Doing so has become increasingly important, as harassment and bullying continue to move from the classroom and the playground to the website and social media app.

Most school-based campaigns still depend on a combination of surveillance and punishment—encouraging educators to be watchful, intervene quickly, and punish perpetrators. With cyber-harassment this model simply won't work. First, it's largely anonymous, and even if it weren't, students may have rights that complicate suppressing online speech. It's also unclear if schools can punish students for activities outside of school hours and off school grounds.

Second, cyber-harassment is instantaneous and scales instantly, which makes really stopping it almost impossible. A sexualized image or homophobic email shared privately with a few friends can be posted on social media and shared by tens of thousands of strangers several time zones away within minutes. Online apps and websites are multiplying the venues and means for electronic harassment at an increasing rate: Twitter, Facebook, Snapchat, Musical.ly, Facebook Messenger, the lowly email and a hundred new apps all provide ways to harass others instantly and anonymously. Educators can't keep up.

Often cyberbullies are a decade ahead of the administrators trying to stop them, with the students having a marked advantage in technological savvy. The traditional regime of promoting "surveil and punish" does not transfer to cyberspace. We must begin to address the underlying gender animus that drives such bullying in the first place.

Everyday Social Interaction

So common and pervasive is gendered sexual harassment that it likely forms an important (if perverse and harmful) learning experience for most tween girls about what is expected of them as young women. It shows them the limits and social tolerance for antifeminine behavior or appearance, and (perhaps most importantly) it teaches them what is expected of young women in what is still a very patriarchal culture.

This is similar to an earlier point we touched on about Fag Discourse among boys and disordered eating. We seem to be in group denial about gender norms' effects on school-age children, and just how overwhelmingly pervasive they are. We refuse to see that behaviors that we publicly claim to deeply abhor—like sexualized harassment and homophobic bullying—are actually so completely common as to form a normative part of almost every child's experience of adolescence.

Certainly such harassment continues to be broadly tolerated in a way that other forms of assaultive activity—physical violence, racist epithets, or religious taunts—are not, and would never be tolerated today. Gendered harassment does not result from the unfortunate misbehavior of a few individual malefactors, who can be caught and punished. It is deeply woven into the "gender culture" of most schools—a part of everyday experience. Until we recognize this, we have little or no chance of stopping it.

Teachers know this. Studies consistently show that many teachers witness such harassment but fail to act. To begin with, they know that gender harassment is not an administrative priority. Second, it is so common that without institutional and collegial support, even well-intentioned teachers are overwhelmed and must constantly struggle with when to intervene and when to let gender harassment slide.

As one well-intentioned but beleaguered teacher put it, in a study by E. J. Meyer (2008):

> The kids are astute enough to see that when they use the word faggot they won't get sent to the office, and when they use a racial slur, they get sent to the office. It's a very quick connection to make. . . . I had one kid call another a faggot. I hauled him to the principal. I asked for a suspension, but the principal didn't want to suspend him. I spent the first couple months enforcing all of this (uniform policy, swearing, and name-calling) and there are some teachers that just never enforce it, and so you realize that out of twenty teachers, we have about five who do all the enforcing and you just can't anymore. You can't do it. (562)

It is especially distressing to consider that teachers feel overwhelmed by the sheer volume of gendered harassment they witness, when studies find that this represents only a small fraction of such incidents, perhaps as low as 10 or 15 percent. If an adult teacher feels overwhelmed with only one-in-ten incidents, what must it feel like for the students who endure them?

Homophobic Bullying & School Shootings

When a school tragedy strikes, Americans turn to the idea of the isolated loner, what might be called the "Lone Nut" theory. Perhaps this results from a reluctance to believe that anything pervasive in the fabric of American culture regularly gives rise to such killers. Vague terms like "teen violence," "suburban violence," and "school shooting" obscure the fact that something specific is going on around boys and violence. Thinking of each one as "random"—of each shooting as a singular and isolated anomaly—serves this narrative. After all, what could possibly tie together so many disparate acts of senseless violence?

In their landmark study, "Adolescent Masculinity, Homophobia, and Violence: Random School Shootings, 1982–2001" (2003), researchers Michael Kimmel and Matthew Mahler posed this question. Their findings are remarkable, even devastating for anyone who cares about education and youth safety.

Kimmel and Mahler first identified and investigated twenty-eight cases that occurred over a ten-year period, from 1982–2001. They found that the shooters were distinctly nonrandom. In fact, with just one exception, they are all totally similar: all were male; all but two (93 percent) were White; all but one (96 percent) occurred in rural communities; and about three-quarters (71 percent) occurred in "red states" that typically voted Republican with strong local masculinity and gun ownership cultures. (Later studies have confirmed that students in such rural "red state" communities consistently rate their schools as the most dangerous and likely to have shootings.)

Finally, almost all of the boys had stories of "being mercilessly and constantly teased, picked on, and threatened"; in effect, gay-baited, for "inadequate gender performance," and their violent assaults were efforts to retaliate against the threats to their manhood.

Moreover, as Kimmel (2003) notes, "strikingly, [they were attacked] not because they were gay . . . but because they were different from the other boys—shy, bookish, honor students, artistic, musical, theatrical, non-athletic, 'geekish' or weird" (1445). Just two of the many stories Kimmel documents will serve by way of example.

- Luke Woodham was a bookish and overweight sixteen-year-old in Pearl, MS. An honor student, he was part of a little group that studied Latin and read Nietzsche. Students teased him constantly for being overweight and a nerd, taunted him as "gay" or "fag." Even his mother called him fat, stupid, and lazy. Other boys bullied him routinely, and according to one fellow student, he "never fought back when other boys called him names." On October 1, 1997, Woodham stabbed his mother to death in her bed before he left for school. He then drove her car to school, carrying a rifle under his coat. He opened fire in the school's common area, killing two students and wounding seven others. After being subdued, he told the assistant principal "the world has wronged me." Later, in a psychiatric interview, he said, "I am not insane. I am angry . . . I am not spoiled or lazy; for murder is not weak and slow-witted; murder is gutsy and daring. I killed because people like me are mistreated every day. I am malicious because I am miserable." (1447)
- At Columbine High School, the site of the nation's most infamous school shooting, Evan Todd, a 255-pound defensive lineman on the Columbine football team and exemplar of the jock culture that Dylan Klebold and Eric

Harris found to be such an interminable torment explained: "Columbine is a clean, good place, except for those rejects," Todd said. "Sure we teased them. But what do you expect with kids who come to school with weird hairdos and horns on their hats? It's not just jocks; the whole school's disgusted with them. They're a bunch of homos. . . . If you want to get rid of someone, usually you tease 'em. So the whole school would call them homos." Ben Oakley, a soccer player, agreed. "[N]obody liked them," he said, "the majority of them were gay. So everyone would make fun of them." Athletes taunted them: "nice dress," they'd say. They would throw rocks and bottles at them from moving cars. The school newspaper had recently published a rumor that Harris and Klebold were lovers. . . . In the videotape made the night before the shootings, Harris says, "People constantly make fun of my face, my hair, my shirts." Klebold adds, "I'm going to kill you all. You've been giving us shit for years." (1447–48)

Some school officials even wink at such bullying as a part of the hazing that makes "boys into men" and teaches *overly sensitive* boys that they must man up and fight back—again, part of schools' "hidden curriculum" when it comes to gender.

Teenagers themselves get this. In their report, "Lethal Violence in Schools" (2001), Gaughan, Cerio, and Myers found that nearly 90 percent of students they interviewed believed that school shootings were about "a desire to get back at those who have hurt them . . . picking on them, making fun of them, or bullying them" (2). More than one in three (37 percent) students in Gaughan's study agreed that "there are kids at my school who I think might shoot someone" (2). Explained one, "If it's anyone, it'll be the kids that are ostracized, picked on, and constantly made fun of" (34).

Yet contemporary accounts and expert commentators continue to ignore the one single variable that cuts across all cases of school shootings and ties them together—masculinity.

Implicit racial bias also plays a part in this causative blindness. Kimmel and Mahler compared their data to the earlier wave of school shootings from the prior decade, between 1982–1991. Most were in urban inner-city schools, and, once again, all the shooters were boys, but this time they were boys of color wielding handguns (urban weaponry, as opposed to the arms common to rural America). Policy makers, experts, and media had no problem identifying a common cause then and there: the "inherent violence" of "inner-city" youth. However, as Kimmel notes, now that "the shooters have become White and suburban middle-class boys, the public has shifted the blame away from group characteristics to individual psychological problems, assuming that these boys were deviants who broke away from an otherwise genteel suburban culture" (1443).

A more honest and less racially biased approach might be to start investigating the "inherent violence" of rural and suburban, red state, White enclaves with high assault-weapon-to-home ratios. For instance, in Gaughan, Cerio, and Myers' study, about a quarter of students (24 percent) said they could "easily get a gun if I wanted to" and almost one in ten (8 percent) reported having thought about shooting a classmate (2).

As of this writing (2018), Kimmel and Mahler's study has been cited almost six hundred times. It is almost two decades old, and yet through shootings like the one at the Orlando night club, the Charleston church, Parkland, Sandy Hook, Virginia Tech, and others, their insights about the connection to toxic masculinity still feel relevant and on point. Kimmel has since expanded and updated his work, notably in a 2008 chapter titled, "Profiling School Shooters and Shooter's Schools: The Cultural Contacts of Aggrieved Entitlement and Restorative Masculinity" and the powerful 2010 study with Rachel Kalish titled, "Suicide by Mass Murder: Masculinity, Aggrieved Entitlement, and Rampage School Shootings" (2010).

Yet the myth of the "random" lone White shooter lives on, and remains as resilient as it is comforting. Like so much about gender norms, Kimmel's findings remain deeply compelling and well documented, yet utterly unable to inform policy, funding, or the national discourse.

Masculinity Threat & Police Violence against Communities of Color

According to FBI statistics, American police officers are involved in over four hundred "justifiable homicides" every year (reporting is voluntary, so the true number is higher). Yet from March, 2012 to March, 2013, police officers in England and Wales fired their weapons just three times. No one was killed. What could account for this difference?

According to *The Economist*, one key factor is that British constables still mostly work unarmed, while the United States has three hundred million guns in circulation in a country with a murder rate six times greater than that of Germany. And racial intolerance itself certainly contributes to the epidemic of fatal confrontations. Fortunately, new studies are pointing to entrenched attitudes of hypermasculinity that pervade many of America's police departments, prompting some to rethink their of use-of-force guidelines.

According to the *New York Times*, in 2015 US police chiefs visited Scotland to learn about local firearm-free policing. The result was a collision of institutional gender culture, at times sounding "like collective head-scratching . . . or therapy" (Baker 2015, n.p.). Even Scotland's elite response teams, who are fully armed, shot civilians just twice between 2005 and 2015.

US police are taught to be aggressive, to close in on suspects, to dominate and enforce submission. A perceived challenge to their authority is grounds for the use of force, including deadly force if the officer feels threatened—which, if they are closing in on a suspect whom they perceive is not obeying and is thus potentially violent, is practically inevitable. Officers who retreat are considered cowards, taunted, ridiculed, and ostracized for backing down.

Scottish constables are taught to slow things down, defuse, and retreat—what they call "tactical withdrawal." Their goal is not manly dominance, but rather to make sure everyone survives. As Prokos and Padavic's resonantly named study of police academy life, "There Oughtta Be a Law Against Bitches" (2002), noted, an officer in the United States who acted likewise would be publicly labeled a *pussy*.

American policing's keen focus on aggression, command presence, and enforcing instant submission creates other, less obvious imperatives to use deadly force, as Frank Cooper explains in his voluminously documented study, "Who's the Man? Masculinities Studies, Terry Stops, and Police Training" (2008).

Cooper explores situations in which dominance and aggression are neither necessary nor warranted, but enacted simply to bolster the officer's sense of manhood. Such contests are particularly issue in stop-and-frisk confrontations—known as "*Terry* stops" after the Supreme Court's *Terry v. Ohio* decision—in which officers disproportionately stop men of color, dominating and/or abusing those being stopped, and generally engaging in what Cooper calls a "masculinity contest." In fact, officers in many cities (NYPD is notorious for this) will arrest citizens simply for perceived discourtesy—the offense known as *Contempt of Cop*—because such disrespect challenges both to their manhood and command of the street.

Somewhat like boys challenged on a playground, police officers can never back down. This kind thinking is so embedded in our culture and our ideas of policing (not to mention being modeled and reinforced by a thousand cop shows) that it takes an example like those of the Scottish constables to see just how aberrant it is, and how rooted it is in primitive ideas about manhood and aggression.

As Prokos and Padavic note, "Hegemonic masculinity is the central defining concept in the culture of police work in the United States" (442). Strong belief in hegemonic masculinity is linked to higher levels of force against suspects, particularly those who are of color.

In addition, as Martinelli (2014) notes in "Revisiting the 21-Foot Rule," officers have long been trained that once an armed or aggressive suspect is within twenty-one feet, they are automatically at risk of grave bodily injury, and are justified in using deadly force. The rule has since been widely adopted and taught for decades in police academies throughout the United States, although the original study was never replicated, and turned out to be deeply flawed. Combined with masculinity imperatives that officers must advance, aggress, and dominate, the results are almost inevitably deadly.

Although the Twenty-One-Foot Rule has received almost no public attention, it is crucial in many unnecessarily deadly encounters. Here's the simple logic of Cooper's analysis:

1. An officer encounters a person they think *might* be a danger.
2. The hypermasculine norms of American law enforcement dictate that officers cannot simply observe from a safe distance and assess the situation, much less retreat and defuse it (even if that might secure their own and the suspect's safety) because they must dominate and control the encounter. The officer is thus forced to *close in on the suspect*.

3. Closing in takes the officer *within the twenty-one-foot radius*, automatically triggering the state wherein they are justified *by definition* in believing that they are in mortal danger and therefore can use deadly force at any time.

What is astonishing here is that it is the officer's *own actions*, not anything in the actions of the suspect or the actual and inherent danger of the situation, that create a situation of mortal danger. Were the normative attitudes in US police departments changed to allow officers to simply stand their ground at a distance and defuse a situation, or conduct "strategic withdrawals" and observe (assuming no civilians were at risk), this state of deadly peril might never have occurred.

Anti-Transgender Violence

Antitransgender violence today is well-known, and often murders of transgender people are covered in the mainstream press. But just a decade ago, it was little known or recognized. Victims were seldom covered in the mainstream press (or often dismissed in a few paragraphs deep in a newspaper, and with headlines like, "Man Found Murdered Wearing Women's Clothing") and even ignored by the gay press.

According to our data, if the FBI compiled statistics on transgender victims, it would have outstripped every category of hate crime except those based mainly on race. So how could such a tide of violence go so unnoticed? It was a working example of intersectionality, and how marginalized identities at the crossroads of many different kinds of oppression are often overlooked or rendered invisible to those in power.

The victims we found shared surprising similarities: they were overwhelmingly young, Black transwomen from low-income, urban communities. And living at the intersection of so many different forms of oppression—class, race, gender, age—their deaths simply were not on anyone's radar, there was no "frame" to hold such victims or integrate their murders part of the national discourse. So they remained largely invisible and their deaths often ignored.

We found that their killers shared surprising similarities as well. They were young, urban, and male; they often attacked in groups; they used profound violence (many victims were pummeled, stabbed, *and* shot) beyond that necessary to cause death; and because of police and public indifference, they mostly went free.

In 2007, GenderPAC developed the first formal national survey of fatal attacks against transgender and other gender nonconforming youth. "50 Under 30: Masculinity and the War on America's Youth," provided the first in-depth study of a silent epidemic of violence that had claimed the lives of more than fifty youth people age thirty and under from 1995 to 2005. Just two years later we documented so many additional murders that we reissued the report as "70 Under 30."

Stories from the Frontlines:
Anti-Transgender Violence Intervention

"50 Under 30" was adopted by the Hate Crimes Coalition on Capitol Hill, distributed to Members of Congress voting on The Matthew Shepard Act, and became a regular part of the annual hate crimes report put out by the National Coalition of Anti-Violence Programs. In that way it was effective, but nothing in the way of a programmatic application ever emerged.

Many very good "Trans 101" and "LGBTQ Tolerance" trainings have been developed to address school bullying among adolescents. But what "50 Under 30" documented was far from lunchroom bullying, and the assailants were not adolescents. In fact, we could find nothing specifically designed to combat hateful attitudes toward transwomen among the twenty- to thirty-year-old males who tend to be their fiercest assailants.

In 2011, in order to better understand the animus behind such assaults, True-Child and the DC Mayor's Office of LGBTQ Affairs and the Office of Human Rights conducted a series of focus groups and in-depth interviews. The District was chosen because it has experienced occasional surges in these kinds of attacks: over a ten-year period, it had more fatal attacks on transgender youth of color than any city in the country, as well as more than all but one or two states. The reasons for this remain unclear.

We were helped by Community Education Group (CEG)'s dedicated executive director, A. Toni Young, DC's legendary queer youth group SMYAL (Supporting and Mentoring Youth Advocates and Leaders), and renowned local transactivists Earlene Budd and Dr. Dana Beyer—as well as leading national advocacy groups like the Southern Poverty Law Center, the National Coalition of Anti-Violence Projects, and the National Center for Transgender Equality.

Our first step was to conduct focus groups at CEG to discover more about how transgender women are perceived, what is believed about them, and what attitudes might be driving such profound animus toward them. Four key points emerged consistently from those groups that seemed to be the mainsprings for hostility and violent attitudes:

1. Transgender women are really gay men being dishonest about what they are;
2. Rigid manhood ideals are drilled into young men from birth, they must fight each day to maintain them, and it is infuriating to see "gay men" publicly rejecting them;
3. Gay men and "transgenders" are always flirting to "test your manhood," so you have to respond violently; and
4. "Passing" by transgender women as "real women" is a fraud that seeks to deceive men into being wrongly attracted to them sexually.

Based on the formative research, we designed a one-hour model intervention with an accompanying toolkit and video that focused on these key message points.

Then, with young men recruited by the DC Department of Parks and Recreation, we tested it on several rounds of participants. The pre-post data from the third-party evaluation firm were encouraging, and likely made our intervention among the first evidence-based, anti-trans-violence programs available:

- 80 percent of participants agreed that: "If faced with a situation involving violence against transgender women, I would do something to stop it";
- 45 percent said the intervention made them think about transwomen differently; and
- 45 percent said the intervention changed their attitudes about violence against transwomen.

References & Selected Reading

Alston, A. T. 2017. *The Force of Manhood: The Consequences of Masculinity Threat on Police Officer Use of Force*, PhD dissertation, Portland State University.

American Association of University Women. 2011. *Crossing the Line: Sexual Harassment at School*.

Anderson, K. L., and Umberson, D. 2001. "Gendering Violence: Masculinity and Power in Men's Accounts of Domestic Violence," *Gender and Society* 15 (3): 358–80.

Baker, A. 2015. "US Police Leaders, Visiting Scotland, Get Lessons on Avoiding Deadly Force," *New York Times*, December 11.

Black, M. C., Basile, K. C., Breiding, M. J., Smith, S. G., Walters, M. L., Merrick, M. T., and Stevens, M. R. 2011. *The National Intimate Partner and Sexual Violence Survey: 2010 Summary Report*. Atlanta, GA: National Center for Injury Prevention and Control, Centers for Disease Control and Prevention.

Cooper, F. R. 2008. "Who's The Man: Masculinities Studies, Terry Stops, and Police Training," *Suffolk University Law School Faculty Publications*. Paper 57.

Crenshaw, K., Ocen, P., and Nanda, J. 2015. *Black Girls Matter: Pushed Out, Overpoliced, and Underprotected*. Center for Intersectionality and Social Policy Studies, Columbia University.

Cullen, D. 1999. "Inside the Columbine High Investigation," *Salon.com*. https://www.salon.com/1999/09/23/columbine_4/.

Felix, E. D., and McMahon, S. D. 2007. "The Role of Gender in Peer Victimization among Youth: A Study of Incidence, Interrelations, and Social Cognitive Correlates," *Journal of School Violence* 6 (3): 27–44.

Gaughan, E., Cerio, J. D., and Myers, R. A. 2001. *Lethal Violence in Schools*. New York: Alfred University.

Gibbs, N., Roche, T., and Goldstein, A. 1999. "The Columbine Tapes," *Time* 154 (25): 40–51.

GLSEN. 2012. *Playgrounds and Prejudice: Elementary School Climate in the United States* (A Survey of Teachers and Students)," conducted on behalf of GLSEN (the Gay, Lesbian, & Straight Education Network). https://www.glsen.org/sites/default/files/Playgrounds%20%26%20Prejudice.pdf.

Goff, P., Martin, K., and Gamson Smiedt, M. 2012. *The Consortium for Police Leadership in Equity, Protecting Equity: Report on the San Jose Police Department.* http://policingequity. org/wp-content/uploads/2016/07/Final-San-Jose-Report.circ_.pdf.

Hahn, H. 1971. "A Profile of Urban Police," *Law and Contemporary Problems* 36 (4): 449–66.

Hampton, R., Oliver, W., and Magarian, L. 2003. "Domestic Violence in the African American Community: An Analysis of Social and Structural Factors," *Violence Against Women* 9 (5): 533–57.

Jewkes, R. 2002. "Intimate Partner Violence: Causes and Prevention," *The Lancet* 359 (9315): 1423–29.

Jones, C. 2006. "Drawing Boundaries: Exploring the Relationship between Sexual Harassment, Gender and Bullying," in *Women's Studies International Forum* 29 (2): 147–58.

Kalish, R., and Kimmel, M. 2010. "Suicide by Mass Murder: Masculinity, Aggrieved Entitlement, and Rampage School Shootings," *Health Sociology Review* 19 (4): 451–64.

Kimmel, M. 2008. "Profiling School Shooters and Shooter's Schools: The Cultural Contacts of Aggrieved Entitlement and Restorative Masculinity," in Agger, B., and Luke, T. W., eds., *There Is a Gunman on Campus: Tragedy and Terror at Virginia Tech.* Lanham, MD: Rowman & Littlefield.

Kimmel, M. S., and Mahler, M. 2003. "Adolescent Masculinity, Homophobia, and Violence: Random School Shootings, 1982–2001," *American Behavioral Scientist* 46 (10): 1439–58.

Leaper, C., and Brown, C. S. 2008. "Perceived Experiences with Sexism among Adolescent Girls," *Child Development* 79 (3): 685–704.

Li, Q. 2007. "New Bottle but Old Wine: A Research of Cyberbullying in Schools," *Computers in Human Behavior* 23 (4): 1777–91.

Lichty, L. F., and Campbell, R. 2012. "Targets and Witnesses: Middle School Students' Sexual Harassment Experiences," *The Journal of Early Adolescence* 32 (3): 414–30.

Martinelli, R. 2014. "Revisiting The '21-Foot Rule,'" *Police: The Law Enforcement Magazine*, September 18.

McGinley, A. C. 2015. "Policing and the Clash of Masculinities," *Howard Law Journal* 59:221.

Meyer, E. J. 2008. "Gendered Harassment in Secondary Schools: Understanding Teachers' (Non)interventions," *Gender and Education* 20 (6): 555–70.

Moore, T. M., and Stuart, G. L. 2005. "A Review of the Literature on Masculinity and Partner Violence," *Psychology of Men and Masculinity* 6 (1): 46.

Nutt, A. 2016. "A Shocking Number of College Men Survey Admit Coercing a Partner into Sex," *Washington Post*, June 5.

Pascoe, C. J. 2001. *Dude, You're a Fag: Masculinity and Sexuality in High School.* Berkeley: University of California Press.

Pascoe, C. J. 2007. "'Dude, You're a Fag,'" *Inside Higher Ed* (op. ed.), https://www. insidehighered.com/views/2007/06/28/dude-youre-fag.

Petersen, J. L., and Hyde, J. S. 2009. "A Longitudinal Investigation of Peer Sexual Harassment Victimization in Adolescence," *Journal of Adolescence* 32 (5): 1173–88.

Poteat, V. P., Kimmel, M. S., and Wilchins, R. 2010. "The Moderating Effects of Support for Violence Beliefs on Masculine Norms, Aggression, and Homophobic Behavior During Adolescence," *Journal of Research on Adolescence* 21 (2): 434–37.

Prokos, A., and Padavic, I. 2002. "'There Oughtta Be a Law Against Bitches': Masculinity Lessons in Police Academy Training," *Gender, Work and Organization* 9 (4): 439–59.

Pulerwitz, J., Gortmaker, S. L., and Dejong, W. 2000. "Measuring Relationship Power in HIV/STD Research," *Sex Roles* 42 (7/8): 637–60.

Reidy, D. E., Shirk, S. D., Sloan, C. A., and Zeichner, A. 2009. "Men Who Aggress against Women: Effects of Feminine Gender Role Violation on Physical Aggression in Hypermasculine Men," *Psychology of Men and Masculinity* 10 (1): 1.

Rennison, C. M. 2001. *Intimate Partner Violence and Age of Victim, 1993–99.* US Department of Justice, Office of Justice Programs, Bureau of Justice Statistics.

Santana, M. C., Raj, A., Decker, M. R., La Marche, A., and Silverman, J. G. 2006. "Masculine Gender Roles Associated with Increased Sexual Risk and Intimate Partner Violence Perpetration among Young Adult Men," *Journal of Urban Health* 83 (4): 575–85.

Shakeshaft, C., Mandel, L., Johnson, Y. M., Sawyer, J., Hergenrother. M. A., and Barber, E. 1997. "Boys Call Me Cow," *Educational Leadership: Schools as Safe Havens* 55 (2): 22–25.

Sharps, P. W., Laughon, K., and Giangrande, S. K. 2007. "Intimate Partner Violence and the Childbearing Year: Maternal and Infant Health Consequences," *Trauma, Violence, and Abuse* 8 (2): 105–16.

Teitler, J. O. 2001. "Father Involvement, Child Health and Maternal Health Behavior," *Children and Youth Services Review* 23 (4–5): 403–25.

The Economist. 2014. "Don't Shoot," December 11. https://www.economist.com/news/unit ed-states/21636044-americas-police-kill-too-many-people-some-forces-are-showing-how-smarter-less.

Weidel, J. J., Provencio-Vasquez, E., Watson, S. D., and Gonzalez-Guarda, R. 2008. "Cultural Considerations for Intimate Partner Violence and HIV Risk in Hispanics," *Journal of The Association of Nurses in AIDS Care* 19 (4): 247–51.

West, C. 2009. "Still on the Auction Block: The (S)exploitation of Black Adolescent Girls in Rap(E) Music and Hip-Hop Culture," in Olfman, S., ed., *The Sexualization of Childhood,* 89–102. Westport, CT: Praeger Publishers.

West, C. M., and Rose, S. 2000. "Dating Aggression among Low-Income African American Youth: An Examination of Gender Differences and Antagonistic Beliefs," *Violence Against Women* 6 (5): 470–94.

White, A. L. 2000. "Understanding Peer Sexual Harassment among Older Male Adolescents," Master's thesis, University of British Columbia.

Williams, O. J., Oliver, W., and Pope, M. 2008. "Domestic Violence in the African American Community," *Journal of Aggression, Maltreatment and Trauma* 16 (3): 229–37.

Wood, J. T. 2004. "Monsters and Victims: Male Felons' Accounts of Intimate Partner Violence," *Journal of Social and Personal Relationships* 21 (5): 555–76.

III

GENDER NORMS &
YOUTH OF COLOR

The following chapters are drawn from white paper reports created by TrueChild and its strategic partners, and offer a deeper dive into at-risk populations, with an emphasis on connections with race and class.

8

Young Black Women & Health

This chapter is based on a report coauthored by Scyatta Wallace of the Janisaw Company with support provided by the Heinz Endowments. Beverly Greene, Beverly Guy-Sheftall, Tiffany Townsend, Carolyn West, and Carmen Lee, the Endowments' Communications Officer all provided input, advice, and guidance; Senior Officer Carmen Anderson provided her unique vision and guidance.

There is now an extensive body of research that examines both gender norms of masculinity and race. With Black girls, the effects of gender and race remain empirically understudied.

Scholars have thought about the impact of gender and race on Black women and girls for several decades. Many theoretical frameworks and scholarly writings have examined the issue (Cole 2009; Collins 1990; Giddings 1985; hooks 1981). However, the empirical research on race, gender norms, and Black girls is still in its infancy. There is a small but growing body of empirical research specifically devoted to Black girls and gender norms, one I hope will continue growing.

Fortunately, there is a wealth of study employing racially diverse, multiethnic samples that include Black girls in significant numbers. Given the limitations of the empirical research base, I focus on three problem areas:

- basic health and wellness;
- reproductive and sexual health, including teen pregnancy and STIs; and
- intimate relationships (including partner violence).

It is almost impossible to talk about race in America without also talking about class as well. The two are so intertwined it is almost impossible to separate them.

The impact of gender norms is no different. Many life disparities—obesity, early pregnancy/STIs and intimate partner violence—are strongly affected by class and socioeconomic status (SES).

Indeed, in underresourced communities, codes for masculinity and femininity are apt to be especially narrow, penalties for transgressing them particularly harsh, and opportunities for constructively displaying public manhood or womanhood few (Anderson 1999; Whitehead 1997). This means the impact of harmful gender norms on Black girls in these communities is magnified.

It is not that Black girls in affluent suburban communities do not experience similar problems with gender norms—studies show they do. Rather it is that in higher-income neighborhoods the impacts are buffered by living in an environment where girls enjoy more personal resources and social capital, and are exacerbated in impoverished environments where they lack them. Given the added risk of low-income status, this chapter focuses mostly on low-income Black girls. They were chosen not as an endpoint, but as a beginning to what is hoped will become a growing dialogue on the unique lives and challenges of Black women and girls.

It is also important to note that many such girls also experience multiple forms of trauma and other severe life stressors including poverty, homelessness, community violence, victimization, sexual/physical abuse, incarceration, and loss of loved ones to injury or illness (Ickovics et al. 2006).

Research has shown that Black girls can be more vulnerable than boys to adverse mental health consequences of such traumatic events (Graves et al. 2010). In addition, girls are two to three times more likely than boys to attempt suicide, and Black girls who experience trauma are more likely to display suicidal behaviors.

Harrington et al. (2010) found that Black girls tried to avoid the emotional distress associated with trauma-related memories through binge eating. Specifically, they found that exposure to trauma appears to influence how much Black girls internalized the cultural expectation of being emotionally tough ("strong black woman").

The expectation that Black girls be strong despite the trauma they experienced contributed to increased binge eating as a way to help them regulate the negative emotions they experienced. There are several other long-term effects of trauma, including anxiety, depression, hostility, risky sexual behavior, poor self-esteem, and increased substance use.

About Parents

It is well established that parent relationships are important for youth development. In particular, research has shown that supportive parent relationships (e.g., good communication, supervision, bonding) contribute to a positive self-esteem for female youth (Mandara and Murray 2000; McKinney, Donnelly, and Renk 2008). Most of these studies, however, focused on the mother's contributions. Father absence may have a negative influence on Black girls.

Given that African Americans are more likely to grow up in households where the father is not present, there has been a lot of conversation about the negative impact that father absence has on Black youth. However, there is limited research that has examined this issue as it relates to Black girls.

Cooper (2009) conducted a study examining the quality of relationships between Black girls and their fathers. The study found that Black girls who have better quality relationships with their fathers were more likely to have higher self-esteem. In addition, it found that Black girls with better quality relationships with their fathers were more likely to do well academically. The research of Mandara et al. (2005) found that father absence was associated with Black girls' understanding of and identification with gender norms. This study found that Black girls with fathers present were more likely to identify with higher levels of femininity and traditional female gender norms than girls from father-absent homes.

There are many disparities in health and well-being that disproportionately affect Black girls. Recent data shows:

- 30 percent of Black girls are considered obese;
- 6 percent of Black girls report having had sex before the age of thirteen;
- one in five Black girls have experienced intimate partner violence (IPV); and
- miscarriage is twice as frequent among Blacks than it is among white girls.

Basic Health & Wellness

Black girls have unique race and gendered experiences which result in multiple stresses that may weaken their immune system and expose them to higher rates of disease and lowered levels of health and well-being. Studies show this stress begins in childhood and continues into adulthood, and is affected by things like exposure to high rates of poverty, violence, and poor nutrition. The additive effect of these stresses can cause a "weathering effect," in which Black girls' bodies become physically and biologically vulnerable to disease and breakdown.

In addition to living in highly distressed neighborhoods, Black girls must also navigate racism and pressures to conform both to traditional feminine ideals of the larger culture and those specific to Black communities.

Black girls must learn how to navigate and cope with the inequities inherent in a traditional gender system that promotes males as strong and dominant and females as dependent and passive.

Black girls must also cope with culturally specific expectations of being emotionally strong "superwomen." For example, it can be culturally taboo for Black girls and women to publicly show signs of sadness or emotional pain (Williams 2008). This "superwoman" ideal makes it challenging for them to acknowledge depression or the need for assistance.

Feminine norms in the Black community prioritize the importance of caretaking and self-sacrifice. Thus girls and women are expected to prioritize taking care of family members and the larger community (Kerrigan et al. 2007), disregarding their own health, ignoring signals of pain or illness, and delaying medical treatment until they are in crisis (Lekan 2009).

The stress of being Black and female—the so-called "Sojourner Syndrome"—contributes to such women's disproportionately high rates of chronic health disorders like diabetes, high blood pressure, and heart disease. In addition, feminine ideals of being the primary caretaker, coupled with the cultural expectation for Black girls to be emotionally strong, may cause many to delay addressing their own health concerns and seeking treatment.

Being strong can be a positive attribute, and has helped many Black girls overcome important barriers. However, changing the discourse about the "superwoman" complex among parents, providers, and Black girls themselves could have a positive impact on their health and well-being. Programmatic efforts to redefine feminine strength as empowering Black females to also prioritize their own health and needs might be one way to reverse this trend.

Obesity

Black girls are disproportionately affected by the national obesity crisis that is linked to a host of chronic illnesses (e.g., diabetes, heart disease). Statistics show that 30 percent of Black girls twelve to nineteen years old are considered obese. This is compared to 18 percent of Hispanic and 15 percent of White girls. According to the Centers for Disease Control and Prevention (CDC), Black youth have the highest number of Type 1 diabetes cases associated with obesity of any group: 500 out of the 1,590 cases (CDC 2011; Mayer-Davis et al. 2009).

Black girls often internalize the cultural norm that "curvy" body types (i.e., high levels of body fat) are highly valued sexual traits for Black men. Also, strenuous physical exercise is often in direct conflict with hairstyling (Wilcox et al. 2002). The effects of both of these can be exacerbated by homemaking ideals that stress the importance of showing affection and care by making heavy, fried meals that emphasize fat, salt, and sugar.

Despite the high rates of obesity among Black girls, research has indicated they have higher levels of satisfaction with their bodies compared to White and Hispanic females (Akan and Grilo 1995; Mayville et al. 1999; Parker et al. 1995; Salazar et al. 2004; Story et al.1995).

This resiliency in feeling good about body weight has led many to assume that Black girls do not have issues with eating disorders. However, there is a growing body of evidence showing Black girls are more likely to suffer from bulimia and disordered eating patterns than girls from other racial groups (Striegel-Moore et al. 2000; Striegel-Moore et al. 2005; Tyler 2003).

Both types of eating disorders are related to being overweight and obese. Although environment, genetics, and cultural eating practices are associated with obesity, gender norms also play a role. There are many studies that have found that Black girls may overeat to compensate for and cope with the stressful demands of being female and of color (Baptiste-Roberts et al. 2006; Falconer and Neville 2000; Harris 1995; Harris and Kuba 1997; Parker et al. 1995; Patton 2006; Talleyrand 2010).

Infant Mortality

Black girls and women have very high rates of miscarriage and infant mortality. Miscarriage is twice as frequent among Blacks as it is among Whites (Chichester 2007; Kavanaugh and Hershberger 2005; Van 2001). Recent data shows that infant mortality is 12.1 per 1,000 live births among Blacks as compared to 5.5 per 1,000 live births among Whites (Price 2006).

Research has found that the stress Black girls experience associated with race and gender-based inequalities may negatively impact pregnancy and lead to pre-term and low-birth weights, which are risk factors for infant mortality (Barnes 2008; Hogue and Bremner 2005).

Black girls experience physical abuse from their romantic partners during pregnancy more than twice that of White girls (Barnes 2008). Physical abuse and poor relationships with men have also been identified in the research as having an impact on infant mortality.

As discussed, while there is a growing body of research suggesting that gender norms have a negative impact on Black girls' overall health, it is limited. More studies in this area, and the connections to infant mortality, are urgently needed.

Sexual & Reproductive Health

There are decades of research to show that sexual and reproductive health outcomes are worse for Black girls compared to girls from other racial groups. National studies have found that Black girls are more likely to have sex early (before age thirteen), and that the majority of these are from sexual abuse and/or statutory rape, which is associated with significant trauma that is often carried into adulthood.

In addition, Black girls are more likely to have multiple partners than women in other racial groups, and more likely to acquire an STI (including HIV). Gallup-Black and Weitzman (2004) found in their study that Black teens were 4.5 times more likely than White teens to get pregnant. They were also more likely to say that their peers found teen parenting acceptable.

Body Image

Skin color and appearance is an important issue for Black girls. Research shows that many girls experience a marked decline in their self-esteem during early adolescence (Pipher 1994). Because of the high value placed on beauty and image for women in our society, body image and appearance often becomes a big part in self-esteem for girls. Body image is a multifaceted concept regarding one's view of his/her body and its appearance.

Although previous research has found higher levels of body image satisfaction among Black girls, this is not to say there are no concerns related to body image. Research has found that skin color and Western physical features are particular concerns for many Black girls (Gordan 2008; Townsend et al. 2010). Specifically, some Black girls have a preference for physical characteristics that they believe will be judged more favorably (i.e., lighter skin, longer hair, fine hair texture, etc.), and this preference is related to negative outcomes (Wallace et al. 2011).

Cultural Expectations

Black girls suffer specific challenges because of feminine racial norms. Women of color are often perceived as exotic, hypersexual, and promiscuous. They feel pressure to conform to a standard of physical beauty—"good" hair and desirability—that is established not only by the dominant culture but also by young men of color.

Internalizing these normative beliefs and wanting to achieve this "gold standard" for womanhood creates an environment where Black girls are more likely to have early sex, have multiple partners, engage in unsafe sex, and acquire STIs—including HIV. National statistics from 2000 to 2008 show that the pregnancy rate for Black girls ages fifteen to seventeen was higher than for Hispanic or White girls, 73 per 1,000 compared to 70 per 1,000 and 22 per 1,000, respectively (Ventura et al. 2012).

In underresourced communities, having children is often considered proof of womanhood, single-parent maternal families are the norm, and motherhood offers one of the few acceptable routes out of school and into a respected social role. Sometimes having a baby may be the only way a young woman feels she can keep the relationship with her male partner.

In many Black communities, the lack of available male partners and the male-to-female ratio imbalances make relationship dynamics challenging. These imbalances are due to mass incarceration, high levels of mortality, and underemployment among young Black men.

In addition, Black women/girls are much less likely than women of other races to date outside of their race, which further exacerbates this imbalance (Banks 2012). The lack of available mates has been linked to more sexual risk-taking, STI/HIV infection and partner abuse among Black girls (Adimora and Schoenbach 2005; Brown et al. 2012), presumably because fewer male partners means those men that are left have more power to dictate the terms of relationship, and women believe they have limited alternatives.

Media Influences

Media images of Black femininity only reinforce the negative impact of racial gender norms. Young people spend up to seven hours with media daily, with Black youth spending thirteen hours each day (Brown 2002).

While there has been some recent progress (i.e., Marvel's *Black Panther* movie), TV, movies, and videos still tend to offer few affirming images for Black girls in terms of relationships, power, or sexuality. Black girls are still too often presented as devoid of personality or agency, and valued for their bodies or their relationship to males.

This sexualization of girls in the media creates an atmosphere where womanhood is equated with sex and a woman's physical body. Media viewers are fed images that a women's worth is highly valued based on the sexual pleasure they can provide men. This is coupled with the fact that sexual health content in the media is rare (Hust, Brown, and L'Engle 2008; Kunkel et al. 2003).

As mentioned, the media has a negative impact on the sexual and reproductive health of Black girls. One solution might be building online media partnerships that empower Black girls to counteract the negative images and create their own, more positive images (Brown 2009).

There are few examples of healthy dating and sexual relationships where Black girls can model more positive behaviors. Therefore, it is not surprising that a host of studies has linked internalizing these negative media images to depression, poor self-esteem, and low sexual self-efficacy among young women generally, and to early and risky sexual behavior, and unplanned pregnancy among Black girls specifically (APA 2010; Peterson et al. 2007; Wingood et al. 2001; Stephens and Phillips 2003; Townsend et al. 2010).

Understanding the relationship dynamics among Black girls and their partners is a crucial area of study. More research is needed that examines how gender norms are practiced in intimate and sexual relationships, what protective factors may help Black girls exert power in their relationships, and what programmatic strategies—particularly around gender norms—can help teach them healthier relationships.

Intimate Relationships & Partner Violence

IPV and girlfriend abuse are serious problems for many young women, particularly Black girls, among whom the rates of IPV are higher than that of those of Hispanics or Whites (Catalano 2007). One large study found that IPV was reported by almost one-fifth (18 percent) of Black girls (Wingood et al. 2001).

Studies have found that those who have experienced IPV have a significantly higher likelihood of inconsistent condom use, are more likely to have a sexually transmitted infection, and are more likely to have nonmonogamous male partners. Much of this is due to girls' fear of the perceived consequences of negotiating condom use, talking with their partner about pregnancy prevention, and feeling limited control over their sexuality (Teitleman et al. 2008; Wingood et al. 2001)

Race, Gender, & IPV

Scholars have argued that IPV should be examined through the lens of intersectionality, taking both race and gender into account (Crenshaw 2005; West 2004). Studies have found Black girls in particular are prone to believe that men mistreat women, that anger and rage are natural facets of masculinity, and that physical abuse is the way men express love (Johnson et al. 2005; Miller 2008a).

Research has found that Black girls in underresourced communities often feel that violence against women is a justified response to something a woman has done, or to punish women for being disrespectful (Jones 2010; Miller 2008b).

Some studies (Johnson et al. 2005) have found that Black girls consistently agreed that girls "do things to boys to try to make them want to hit them." One participant observed: "It's understandable why men abuse women . . . some women do not know how to be quiet."

These types of beliefs are also connected to racially based stereotypes and expectations that Black men are naturally dominant, aggressive, and physical rather than intellectual, gentle, and reflective.

Sexual violence is a continuation of the sexualization of Black girls. These actions against women are rooted in power and control by men and grounded in narrow constructions of masculinity. The stereotype of Black girls as promiscuous and always sexually ready adds to the risk of sexual violence against these girls.

One in-depth interview study of thirty-five Black girls and forty Black boys (Miller 2008b) found that the Black girls reported being pressured or coerced into unwanted sex, and described actual or attempted sexual assaults, as well as gang rapes.

In addition, nearly one in three of the girls had experienced multiple sexual victimizations, and nearly half of the young men in the study reported having "run trains" on girls (i.e., three or more males taking turns having sex with the same female, consensually or not).

In some communities, hypersexualization is prioritized to attract young men, and some Black girls resort to adopting the "video vixen" or "gold digger" culture with its emphasis on subservience, availability, and sexual exchange for money/gifts.

Because of the limited number of eligible young men and the lack of visible two-parent families in many Black communities, having and holding onto a male partner can be seen as an important goal to some Black girls. This leaves them more likely to tolerate male infidelity and/or violence.

Despite the perception that Black girls are vocal, the literature shows that Black girls are less likely to be vocal in their intimate relationships (Miller 2008b). They often avoid speaking out or taking action in order to preserve a sense of womanhood and fulfill public expectations of a romantic relationship with a man.

Black girls who are coerced or assaulted often feel they must say and do nothing because of racial feminine norms that stress showing solidarity with Black men in the face of a dominant White majority culture.

Some researchers (West and Rose 2000) have found that, despite suffering aggression in their dating relationships, Black girls have a strong desire to be traditional caretakers, and for their boyfriends to behave as protectors. These attitudes are strongly grounded in feminine stereotypes, and expose such girls to high rates of IPV.

It has been argued that educating young men about the harms of normative masculinity to themselves and to women and working to foster greater empathy and egalitarian connections with young women may be a strategy to combat IPV against Black girls (Miller 2008a).

In addition, we found that giving young Black youth the opportunity for more cross-gender friendships with girls, as well as activities and similar social engagement, is also likely to decrease sexually coercive behaviors and help them master more equal and egalitarian relationships.

There is utility in working with policy makers to set better protections for victims of abuse, and advocating for more programs that assist Black girls who are at risk for and/or experiencing IPV.

Finally, research indicates that important efforts must be made to challenge harmful codes of femininity and womanhood that continue to make Black girls more vulnerable to partner violence, prevent them from seeking help or going to authorities, and keep them going back to abusive partners.

References & Selected Reading

Adimora, A., and Schoenbach, V. 2005. "Social Context, Sexual Networks, and Racial Disparities in Rates of Sexually Transmitted Infections," *The Journal of Infectious Diseases* 191:S115–22.

Akan, G., and Grilo, C. 1995. "Sociocultural Influences on Eating Attitudes and Behaviors, Body Image, and Psychological Functioning: A Comparison of African American, Asian American, and Caucasian College Women," *International Journal of Eating Disorders* 18:181–87.

Amaro, H. 1995. "Love, Sex, and Power: Considering Women's Realities in HIV Prevention," *American Psychologist* 50 (6): 437–47.

American Psychological Association, Task Force on the Sexualization of Girls. 2010. *Report of the APA Task Force on the Sexualization of Girls.* http://www.apa.org/pi/women/programs/girls/ report-full.pdf.

Anderson, E. 1999. *Code of the Streets: Decency, Violence, and the Moral Life of the Inner City.* New York: Norton.

Banks, R. R. 2012. *Is Marriage for White People?* New York: Penguin.

Baptiste-Roberts, K., Gary, T. L., Bone, L. R., Hill, M. N., and Brancati, F. L. 2006. "Perceived Body Image among African Americans with Type 2 Diabetes," *Patient Education and Counseling* 60: 194–200.

Barnes, G. L. 2008. "Perspectives of African American Women on Infant Mortality," *Social Work in Health Care* 47 (3): 293–305.

Brown, J. D. 2002. "Mass Media Influences on Sexuality," *The Journal of Sex Research* 39 (1): 42–45.

Brown, J. L., Sales, J. M., Diclemente, R. J., Latham Davis, T. P., and Rose, E. S. 2012. "Characteristics of African American Adolescent Females Who Perceive Their Current Boyfriends Have Concurrent Sexual Partners," *Journal of Adolescent Health* 50 (4): 377–82.

Brown, R. N. 2009. *Black Girlhood Celebration: Toward a Hip Hop Feminist Pedagogy.* New York: Peter Lang.

Catalano, S. M. 2007. *Intimate Partner Violence in the United States.* Washington, DC: Bureau of Justice Statistics. http://bjs.ojp.usdoj.gov/index.cfm?ty=pbdetailandiid=1000.

Centers for Disease Control and Prevention. 2011. *National Diabetes Fact Sheet: National Estimates and General Information on Diabetes and Pre-Diabetes in the United States, 2011.* Atlanta: US Department of Health and Human Services, Centers for Disease Control and Prevention.

Chichester, M. 2007. "Requesting Perinatal Autopsy: Multicultural Considerations," *MCN: The American Journal of Maternal/Child Nursing* 32 (2): 81–86.

Cohen, C. J., Celestine-Michener, J., Holmes, C., Merseth, J. L., and Ralph, L. 2010. *Reports and Findings from the Black Youth Project.* http://research.blackyouthproject.com/survey/findings/.

Cole, E. R. 2009. "Intersectionality and Research in Psychology," *American Psychologist* 64 (3): 170–80.

Collins, P. H. 1991 [1990]. *Black Feminist Thought: Knowledge, Consciousness and the Politics of Empowerment.* New York: Routledge.

Constantine, G. M. 2001. "Addressing, Racial, Ethnic, Gender and Social Class Issues in Counselor Training and Practice," in Pope-Davis, D. B., and Coleman, H. L. K. eds., *The Intersection of Race, Class and Gender in Multicultural Counseling*, 341–50. Thousand Oaks, CA: Sage.

Cooper, S. M. 2009. "Associations between Father–Daughter Relationship Quality and the Academic Engagement of African American Adolescent Girls: Self-Esteem as a Mediator?" *Journal of Black Psychology* 35 (4): 495–516. Doi:10.1177/0095798409339185.

Crenshaw, K. 2005. "Mapping the Margins: Intersectionality, Identity Politics, and Violence Against Women of Color," in Kennedy Bergen, R. L., Renzetti, C. M., and Edleson, J. L., eds., *Violence Against Women: Classic Papers*, 282–313. Auckland, New Zealand: Pearson Education New Zealand.

Dominguez, T. P. 2010. "Adverse Birth Outcomes in African American Women: The Social Context of Persistent Reproductive Disadvantage," *Social Work in Public Health* 26 (1): 3–16.

Falconer, J. W., and Neville, H. A. 2000. "African American College Women's Body Image: An Examination of Body Mass, African Self-Consciousness, and Skin Color Satisfaction," *Psychology of Women Quarterly* 24: 236–43.

Gallup-Black, A., and Weitzman, B. C. 2004. "Teen Pregnancy and Urban Youth: Competing Truths, Complacency and Perceptions of the Problem," *Journal of Adolescent Health* 34: 366–75.

Giddings, P. 1985. *When and Where I Enter: The Impact of Black Women on Race and Sex in America.* New York: Morrow.

Gordan, M. K. 2008. "Media Contributions to African American Girls' Focus on Beauty and Appearance: Exploring the Consequences of Sexual Objectification," *Psychology of Women Quarterly* 32: 245–56.

Graves, K. N., Kaslow, N. J., and Frabutt, J. M. 2010. "A Culturally Informed Approach to Trauma, Suicidal Behavior, and Overt Aggression in African American Adolescents," *Aggression and Violent Behavior* 15 (1): 36–41.

Hancock, A. 2007. "Intersectionality as a Normative and Empirical Paradigm," *Politics and Gender* 3: 248–54.

Harrington, E. F., Crowther, J. H., and Shipherd, J. C. 2010. Trauma, Binge Eating, and the "Strong Black Woman," *Journal of Consulting and Clinical Psychology* 78 (4): 469–79.

Harris, D. J., and Kuba, S. A. 1997. "Ethno-Cultural Identity and Eating Disorders in Women of Color," *Professional Psychology: Research and Practice* 28 (4): 341–47.

Harris, S. M. 1995. "Family, Self, and Sociocultural Contributions to Body-Image Attitudes of African American Women," *Psychology of Women Quarterly* 19: 129–45.

Hogue, C. J. R., and Bremner, J. D. 2005. "Stress Model for Research into Preterm Delivery among Black Women," *American Journal of Obstetrics and Gynecology* 192: S47–S55.

hooks, b. 1981. *Ain't I a Woman. Black Women and Feminism.* Boston: South End Press.

Hust, S. J. T., Brown, J. D., and L'Engle, K. L. 2008. "Boys Will Be Boys and Girls Better Be Prepared: An Analysis of the Rare Sexual Health Messages of Young Adolescent Media," *Mass Communication and Society* 11: 3–23.

Ickovics, J. R., Kershaw, T. S., Milan, S., Lewis, J. B., Meade, C. S., and Ethier, K. A. 2006. "Urban Teens: Trauma, Post-Traumatic Growth, and Emotional Distress among Female Adolescents," *Journal of Consulting and Clinical Psychology* 74 (5): 841–50.

Johnson, S. B., Frattaroli, S., Campbell, J., Wright, J., Pearson-Fields, A. S., and Cheng, T. L. 2005. "I Know What Love Means: Gender-Based Violence in the Lives of Urban Adolescents," *Journal of Women's Health* 14 (2): 172–79.

Jones, N. 2010. *Between Good and Ghetto: African American Girls and Inner-City Violence.* New Brunswick, NJ: Rutgers University Press.

Kavanaugh, K., and Hershberger, P. 2005. "Perinatal Loss in Low-Income African American Parents: The Lived Experience," *Journal of Obstetric, Gynecologic and Neonatal Nursing* 34 (5): 595–605.

Kerrigan, D., Andrinopoulos, K., Johnson, R., Parham, P., Thomas, T., and Ellen, J. M. 2007. "Staying Strong: Gender Ideologies among African American Adolescents and the Implications for HIV/STI Prevention," *Journal of Sex Research* 44 (2): 172–80.

Kunkel, D., Biely, E., Eyal, K., Cope-Farrar, K., Donner-Stein, E., and Fandrich, R. 2003. *Sex on TV 3: A Biennial Report of the Kaiser Family Foundation.* Menlo Park, CA: Kaiser Family Foundation.

Lekan, D. 2009. "Sojourner Syndrome and Health Disparities in African American Women," *Advances in Nursing Science* 32 (4): 307–21.

Mandara, J., and Murray, C. B. 2000. "The Effects of Parental Marital Status, Family Income, and Family Functioning on African American Adolescent Self-Esteem," *Journal of Family Psychology* 14: 475–49.

Mandara, J., Murray, C. B., and Joyner, T. N. 2005. "The Impact of Fathers' Absence on African American Adolescents' Gender Role Development," *Sex Roles* 53 (3/4): 207–20.

Mayer-Davis, E. J., Bell, R. A., Dabelea, D., D'Agostino, R., Imperatore, G., Lawrence, J. M., Liu, L., and Marcovina, S. 2009. "The Many Faces of Diabetes in American Youth: Type 1 and Type 2 Diabetes in Five Race and Ethnic Populations—The SEARCH for Diabetes in Youth Study," *Diabetes Care* 32 (Supplement 2): S99–101.

Mayville, S., Katz, R. C., Gipson, M. T., and Cabral, K. 1999. "Assessing the Prevalence of Body Dysmorphic Disorder in an Ethnically Diverse Group of Adolescents," *Journal of Child and Family Studies* 8 (3): 357–62.

McKinney, C., Donnelly, R., and Renk, K. 2008. "Perceived Parenting, Positive and Negative Perceptions of Parents, and Late Adolescent Emotional Adjustment," *Child and Adolescent Mental Health* 13 (2): 66–73.

Miller, J. 2008a. "Violence Against Urban African American Girls: Challenges for Feminist Advocacy," *Journal of Contemporary Criminal Justice* 24 (2): 148–62.

———. 2008b. *Getting Played: African American Girls, Urban Inequality and Gendered Violence.* New York: NYU Press.

Mullings, L. 2002. "The Sojourner Syndrome: Race, Class, and Gender in Health and Illness," *Voices* 6 (1): 32–36.

Parker, S., Nichter, M., Nicther, M., Vuckovic, N., Sims, C., and Rittenbaugh, C. 1995. "Body Image and Weight Concerns among African American and White Adolescent Females: Differences That Make a Difference," *Human Organization* 54: 103–13.

Peterson, S. H., Wingood, G. M., Diclemente, R. J., Harrington, K., and Davies, S. 2007. "Images of Sexual Stereotypes in Rap Videos and the Health of African American Female Adolescents," *Journal of Women's Health* 16 (8): 1157–64.

Pipher, M. 1994. *Reviving Ophelia: Saving the Selves of Adolescent Girls.* New York: Random House.

Price, S. K. 2006. "Prevalence and Correlates of Pregnancy Loss History in a National Sample of Children and Families," *Maternal Child Health Journal* 10: 489–500.

Salazar, L. F., Diclemente, R. J., Wingood, G. M., Crosby, R. A., Harrington, K., Davies, S., Hook, E. W., and Oh, M. K. 2004. "Self-Concept and Adolescents' Refusal of Unprotected Sex: A Test of Mediating Mechanisms among African American Girls," *Prevention Science* 5 (3): 137–49.

Stephens, D. P., and Phillips, L. D. 2003. "Freaks, Gold Diggers, Divas, and Dykes: The Socio-Historical Development of African American Female Adolescent Scripts," *Sexuality and Culture* 7: 3–47.

Story, M., French, S. A., Resnick, M. D., and Blum, R. W. 1995. "Ethnic/Racial and Socio-Economic Differences in Dieting Behaviors and Body Image Perceptions in Adolescents," *International Journal of Eating Disorders* 18: 173–79.

Striegel-Moore, R. H., Fairburn, C. G., Wilfley, D. E., Pike, K. M., Dohm, F., and Kraemer, H. C. 2005. "Toward an Understanding of Risk Factors for Binge-Eating Disorder in Black and White Women: A Community-Based Case-Control Study," *Psychological Medicine* 35: 907–17.

Striegel-Moore, R. H., Wilfley, D. E., Pike, K. M., Dohm, F., and Fairburn, C. G. 2000. "Recurrent Binge Eating in Black American Women," *Archives of Family Medicine* 9: 83–87.

Substance Abuse and Mental Health Services Administration. 2004. *Overview of Findings from the 2004 National Survey on Drug Use and Health.* Rockville, MD: Office of Applied Studies, NSDUH Series H–27, DHHS Publication No. SMA 05–4061.

Talleyrand, R. M. 2010. "Eating Disorders in African American Girls: Implications for Counselors," *Journal of Counseling and Development* 88: 319–24.

Thompson, M. S., and Keith, V. M. 2001. "The Blacker the Berry: Gender, Skin Tone, Self-Esteem, and Self-Efficacy," *Gender and Society* 15: 336–57.

Teitelman, A. M., Ratcliffe, S. J., Moreles-Aleman, M. M., Sullivan, C. M. 2008. "Sexual Relationship Power, Intimate Partner Violence, and Condom Use among Minority Urban Girls," *Journal of Interpersonal Violence* 27 (11): 1694–712.

Townsend, T. G., Thomas, A. J., Neilands, T. B., Jackson, T. R. 2010. "I'm No Jezebel, I'm Young, Gifted and Black: Identity, Sexuality and Black Girls," *Psychology of Women Quarterly* 34: 273–85.

Tyler, I. D. 2003. "A True Picture of Eating Disorders among African American Women: A Review of Literature," *ABNF Journal* 14 (3): 73–74.

Van, P. 2001. "Breaking the Silence of African American Women: Healing After Pregnancy Loss," *Health Care for Women International* 22: 229–43.

Ventura, S. J., Curtin, S. C., Abma, J. C., and Henshaw, S. K. 2012. "Estimated Pregnancy Rates and Rates of Pregnancy Outcomes for the United States, 1990–2008," *National Vital Statistics Reports*, 60 (7). Hyattsville, MD: National Center for Health Statistics. https ://pdfs.semanticscholar.org/4232/21871f7a7d4ba4b597034b6c3e0374d40f04.pdf?_ga=2. 59355117.1729471841.1544247705-1618903874.1544247705.

Wallace, S. A., Townsend, T., Glasgow, Y. M., Ojie, M. J. 2011. "Gold Diggers, Video Vixens and Jezebels: Stereotype Images and Substance Use among Urban African American Girls," *Journal of Women's Health* 20 (9): 1315–24.

West, C. M. 2004. "Black Women and Intimate Partner Violence: New Directions for Research," *Journal of Interpersonal Violence* 19: 1487–93.

West, C. M., and Rose, S. 2000. "Dating Aggression among Low Income African American Youth: An Examination of Gender Differences and Antagonistic Beliefs," *Violence Against Women* 6: 470–94.

Whitehead, T. L. 1997. "Urban Low Income Black Men, HIV/AIDS, and Gender Identity," *Medical Anthropology Quarterly* 11 (4): 411–47.

Wilcox, S., Richter, D. L., Henderson, K. A., Greaney, M. L., Ainsworth, B. E. 2002. "Perceptions of Physical Activity and Personal Barriers and Enablers in African American Women," *Ethnicity and Disease* 12 (3): 353–62.

Williams, T. 2008. *Black Pain: It Just Looks Like We Are Not Hurting*. New York: Scribner.

Wingood, G. M., and Diclemente, R. J. 1998. "Partner Influences and Gender-Related Factors Associated with Non-Condom Use among Young Adult African American Women," *American Journal of Community Psychology* 26: 29–51.

Wingood, G. M., Diclemente, R. J., McCree, D. H., Harrington, K., and Davies, S. L. 2001. "Dating Violence and the Sexual Health of Black Adolescent Females," *Pediatrics* 107 (5): E72.

9

Young Latinas & Feminine Norms

This chapter is based on a white paper and was prepared in partnership with Hispanics in Philanthropy (HIP). Micah Gilmer of Frontline Solutions, Gelila Getaneh, Rediet Teshome, and Cliff Leek contributed to the references, and Scyatta Wallace provided advice and guidance. A Spanish-language version of the original report—"Normas de género: Una clave para optimizar resultados en las jóvenes latinas"—is also available on TrueChild's website (truechild.org).

It is rare to find funding or programming for young Latinas that addresses gender norms. Few social justice foundations today would seek to create portfolios that were race-blind or class-blind, and fewer still would fund grantees that offered race-or class-blind programs, particularly in communities of color. That's because they know that addressing underlying structures of oppression like race and class makes efforts more effective. Yet most funders still don't consider gender an essential lens for their funding strategy, although—as international donors continue to prove—reconnecting race, class, and gender in a truly "intersectional" approach can dramatically improve efficacy, while adding little additional cost.

Girls in low-income communities may have the added stresses associated with poverty and/or immigration regimes. Codes for femininity and masculinity are apt to be especially narrow in such communities, and penalties for transgressing them harsher.

Given the added risk of low-income status, it is important to focus on young Latinas in impoverished environments, as well as on three areas where the impact of rigid feminine norms is broad and well accepted:

- basic health, including healthcare seeking and depression and suicide;
- reproductive and sexual health, teen pregnancy, and intimate partner violence (IPV); and
- education, including school pushout policies, economic security, and STEM.

Considering gender norms in funding for these areas could have an especially big impact in improving life outcomes and making funding more effective.

It's important to note that while we are concerned with issues facing young Latinas, it is important not to overlook the immense resources and resilience young Latinas bring to surmounting the challenges they face.

Latin@s, Latina/o, Latinx?

We use the terms "Latina" and "Latino" to refer to male and female individuals in the United States who identify as having Mexican, Central, or South American (e.g., Latin American) or Caribbean ancestry. We use "Latinx" to refer to all persons of Latin American or Caribbean ancestry. We use the terms primarily as a broad ethnic, rather than specifically racial, category, recognizing that Latinx include many races. We also use it in lieu of "Chicana/os" (for Mexican Americans) or "Hispanics" (which also includes those of European descent—primarily Spanish or Portuguese). We make an exception when a study specifies one of those terms.

As Tanisha Love Ramirez, Latino voices editor for the *Huffington Post* explains, Latinx is the "alternative to Latino, Latina, and even Latin@ . . . It's part of a 'linguistic revolution' that aims to move beyond gender binaries and . . . makes room for people who are trans, queer, agender, nonbinary, gender nonconforming, or gender fluid" (Ramirez and Blay 2016). Moreover, in Spanish, the masculinized versions of words like "Latino" are considered to be inclusive. But many Hispanic "queers" and other gender nonconforming people want to move away from the idea that the masculine can ever truly be universal—and Latinx helps do that. In addition, unlike Latin@s, which is popular for some of the same reasons, Latinx appears to be more pronounceable.

Latinx Identity

Latinx comprise the United States' largest single racial and ethnic minority, and are among its fastest-growing groups. Yet despite this, significantly less is known about Latinx youth than their White peers. This is especially true in the area of gender norms and their intersection with race, class, and ethnicity.

In addition, estimates show that about 41 percent of Latinx are under the age of twenty-one. This demographic is set to grow at dramatic rates, thus addressing issues involving them is especially urgent.

Hispanic cultures have their own distinct forms of masculine and feminine norms. *Machismo*—originating mainly in Iberian cultures—stresses male pride and domination, sexual potency, and benevolent sexism toward and idealization of females.

Marianismo, a term for the feminine version of machismo, is connected to religious veneration of the Virgin Mary and tends to stress obedience to males, moral purity, motherhood, and self-denial. Such *machista* codes of femininity are common in many traditional Hispanic cultures, but are far from universal. Both machismo and marianismo are intertwined in *familismo*—the valuing of family ties as central to life.

Although popular culture often uses machismo as a shorthand for hypermasculine and aggressive male chauvinism, historically machismo also encompasses virtues like chivalry toward the weak, honor, and the importance of being family protector and provider (attributes sometimes summed up as *caballerismo*).

As with many other ethnic groups, rigid and traditional cultural norms are reinforced by immediate family members, as well as extended family, teachers and educators, social media, clergy, and religious institutions.

Nothing in this chapter is unique to young Latinas; on the contrary, studies show that many of the same impacts are experienced by young White, Asian, Native American, or Black women who internalize rigid feminine norms and/or live in low-income environments.

The challenges faced by recently immigrated and/or undocumented women are profound, and because of this, they have rightfully received the most academic attention. However, this also has the effect of shaping how we understand all Latinas—even if particular findings are not quite as applicable to (for example) highly educated, high-income women whose families have been in the United States for generations.

What is unique is the continuing impact of structural racism and ethnic hostility towards Hispanic communities, and the interaction of immigration and acculturation with traditional Hispanic cultural values. This is what makes the study of young Latinas so challenging, and the need for funders to address the impact of cultural feminine norms so imperative.

One complication in studying young Latinas is that significant parts of the wider Hispanic community include Afro-Latinx such as Afro-Cubans and Afro-Brazilians. We had hoped to find studies to include about them and how they interact with gender norms. While they were doubtless present in many samples, we found few, if any, studies specifically devoted to them and gender roles or norms. This is definitely an absence for future research to explore.

Marianismo vs. Malichismo

If marianismo is one side of the Hispanic femininity coin, malichismo may be the other. The term comes from La Malinche, who translated for Hêrnan Cortês, who destroyed the Aztecs and colonized Mexico. La Malinche carried on an illicit

affair with him while betraying her people, and was eventually cast aside and given
to one of his men. Yet some Chicana feminists have adopted her as a symbol of "bad
girl" feminine power: the "fallen woman" who went her own way and owned her
own sexuality, defying all the ideals represented by the Virgin Mary and traditional
femininity, yet was also deeply victimized by patriarchal male society.

Acculturation & Intersectionality

About half of all Hispanic women in the United States were born in their countries of origin. For many Latinx families, which often include undocumented
members, issues of immigration are a crucial aspect of an intersectional analysis,
and can interact with barriers like racial discrimination and poverty to color
nearly every family decision: accessing healthcare, interacting with public-school
systems, labor force participation, and so on.

Even if it is not always specifically mentioned, both acculturation and the
challenges posed by sometimes-hostile immigration enforcement constituted
major variables in nearly every problem area on which our research touches.

LGBTQ Latinas

Gender-nonconforming Latinas and those who are LGBTQ also face lower life outcomes. At school, they are more likely to be harassed and bullied by peers, as well as
more likely to be suspended or expelled by teachers. At home, they may be rejected
by traditionally minded families who are unable to accept their sexual orientation or
gender identity (some studies find that 40 percent of homeless youth are LGBTQ).

Rates of depression, suicide, and substance abuse among LGBTQ youth generally are also higher than their straight peers. And as murders like that of seventeen-
year-old Gwen Amber Rose Araujo in California demonstrate, Latina and Black
transgender youth remain significantly more vulnerable to violent assault.

Nonetheless, the lives of many gay and trans Latinas show remarkable strength
and resistance to the challenges that face them. Too few studies focus on them,
and much more needs to be known. Funders would do well to invest in expanding
our knowledge about them.

Basic Wellness & Mental Health

Health-Seeking Behavior

Young Latinas are more likely to act on their families' health needs and ignore their
own. Some learn it is wrong for women to seek help outside their family or to prioritize their own health. Such attitudes exacerbate avoidance or delay of health seeking.

Traditional feminine norms that teach the importance of caretaking, self-sacrifice, and self-denial encourage girls to subordinate their own health and take care of younger siblings or infirm elders—meanwhile ignoring signals of pain and illness in their own bodies and delaying medical attention.

As the American Heart Association's "Go Red For Women / Go Red Por Tu Corazon" campaign puts it, "Hispanic women take on the role of caregiver superwoman, catering to the needs of everyone but themselves. . . . Many Hispanic women . . . are more likely to take preventative action for their families . . . [while] completely ignoring their own health, and these acts of selflessness can become deadly" (AHA 2019, n.p.).

Traditional feminine norms may lead some young women to feel it is inappropriate to share their needs with outsiders beyond the immediate family (beliefs that can be amplified if they fear government officials, including healthcare authorities). Studies show one important factor that sustains such attitudes is strong belief in familismo, although being strongly family-oriented can help Latinas in other ways (missing). Programmatic efforts to promote femininity that balance caretaking and self-sacrifice could help girls' getting medical care and long-term health.

Depression & Suicide

CDC statistics show that young Latinas have one of the highest rates of depression of all racial and ethnic groups. While many factors contribute to the likelihood of depression (including impoverished neighborhoods, the stress of acculturation, hostile immigration regimes), gender norms are a key factor.

Young Latinas must deal with pressures to conform to both narrow dominant culture and Hispanic community feminine ideals. As Céspedes and Huey (2008) explain, "Compared to boys, Latina adolescents reported greater differences in traditional gender role beliefs between themselves and their parents, and higher levels of depression" (168).

Girls just entering puberty who were born in the United States and live in small towns with recently immigrated and/or low-acculturation parents appear to be especially vulnerable. The result is profound family conflict over traditional machista ideals of passivity, obedience, and chastity just when puberty and acculturation are pushing girls into greater autonomy, self-expression, and sexual exploration.

Nuñez et al. (2016) found that belief in traditional gender norms was related to worse mental health, regardless of a young person's sex, level of acculturation, or country of origin.

Suicide is closely linked to depression, and according to the CDC, adolescent Latinas have one of the highest rates of attempted suicide of all groups: 15 percent attempt to take their own lives (compared with only 10 percent for White and 10 percent for African American girls). Twenty-six percent of Latina teens have considered suicide, with rates peeking during the adolescent years of fourteen to fifteen.

Zayas et al. (2005) theorize that in acculturating, girls experience intense guilt for transgressing highly gendered "[c]ultural family traditions [that] socialize Hispanic women to be passive, demure, and hyper-responsible for family obligations, unity, and harmony. . . . As the girl's developing sexuality and autonomy is expressed as a prolonged and intense family struggle, management of the girl's body (where she goes, with whom, what she wears, etc.) takes center stage. This conflict increasingly endangers the family's wholeness and the girl comes to feel that extinguishing this struggle through suicide is the only response" (279, 282).

This may help explain why suicide rates for Latinas born in the United States are higher than those recently emigrated, or than those remaining in their countries of origin. The likely reason is that US-born girls have an accelerated acculturation, which also generates much more conflict with their families. This would also help explain why suicide rates are higher for Latinas in small towns, where they are likely to be more dependent on their families than their urban sisters.

Reproductive Health & Partner Violence

Reproductive Health

What girls believe is considered feminine and womanly has enormous impact on their reproductive and sexual health. Studies show that young women who internalize traditional feminine ideals have lower outcomes in nearly every area: unplanned and planned pregnancy, HIV prevention and condom use, and sexual coercion and partner violence.

These ideals can be especially challenging for Latinas, who must also deal with popular cultural stereotypes of young Hispanic women as "fiery" and smoldering Latin "bombshells," wielding their youth and beauty to seduce males.

Traditional marianismo beliefs also play an important role in reproductive and sexual health. Latina teens are less likely to carry condoms, acquire sexual knowledge, or have the skills to negotiate safer sex than their White or Black peers. Young Latinas are also less likely than their peers to feel comfortable discussing sex with males, and more likely to defer to male sexual prerogatives.

Because of this, Latina teens have one of the lowest rates of condom use of any racial or ethnic group, contracting HIV at nearly four times the rate of Whites. And although teen pregnancy rates for young Latinas are at near historic lows, they are also almost 200 percent that of White teens. In addition, Latinas are 150 percent more likely than other girls to have an early pregnancy followed by a repeat pregnancy.

Overall, half (51 percent) of Latinas become pregnant before age twenty—twice the national average—and over half of these pregnancies (56 percent) are unplanned.

In low-income communities, having children may be seen as proof of woman-hood. They may also offer young Latinas one of the few socially acceptable routes out of school and into a respected social role in areas where decent jobs are scarce.

It is important to note that traditional marianismo beliefs provide important protective benefits to young Latinas as well—delaying the age of sexual initiation and increasing the chances of avoiding sexually risky behavior. Young Latinas tend to have better infant mortality outcomes than their peers, which some researchers believe is connected to traditional marianismo and familismo beliefs—part of what has been termed the "Latino Paradox."

This "Latino Paradox" noted by infant mortality researchers contradicts well-documented studies showing the (intuitively reasonable) finding that higher income, more education, and improved prenatal care are linked to lower infant mortality. Yet Mexican-born women remain surprising exceptions: despite generally lower incomes, less education, and less access to prenatal care, they still tend to have better infant health outcomes overall than their White peers, or even US-born Chicanas. While the causes are still not entirely clear, one thing that is clear is that the Latino Paradox and the experience of these mothers appear to have important health lessons for all pregnant women and their doctors.

Intimate Relationships & Partner Violence

Rigid feminine ideals that promote male dominance and female dependence might be thought to expose women to higher rates of abusive, domineering partners. Yet with young Latinas, that only tells half the story. With IPV, marianismo and traditional feminine norms both protect young Latinas and expose them to harm. Studies theorize that lower IPV rates may be tied to stronger belief in marianismo—making young women more submissive and deferential to male partners, and thus generating fewer occasions for violent disagreement or abuse. As this hypothesis would predict, studies find that recently immigrated Latinas—who tend to have stronger belief in traditional feminine norms—also tend to report lower rates of IPV than their US-born counterparts (another example of the "Latino Paradox"). At the same time, such beliefs may also make Latinas more likely to tolerate abuse or sexual coercion, and to report it at lower rates than their peers.

This is one area where IPV funding could improve outcomes by better addressing feminine ideals that encourage Latinas to tolerate abuse, to feel shame over expos-ing "family business" to outsiders, and to equate attracting an older, stronger, more dominant male partner as a validation of womanhood.

Encouragingly, many of the groups most focused on challenging rigid masculine norms—including Futures Without Violence, Becoming a Man (BAM), Promundo, Men Can Stop Rape, and Men As Peacemakers—are also those leading the struggle to reduce partner violence.

Education, Pushouts, & STPP

Education & Economic Security

Up to 98 percent of young Latinas report wanting to graduate high school. Yet a third of them admit to feeling that it's not likely—and they are right. One in five drop out before completing their education—nearly double African American girls (11 percent) and five times that of Whites (4 percent).

About one-third (36 percent) of young Latinas who drop out report the cause is a teen pregnancy—showing again the importance of funders addressing feminine norms in R&SH and how more effective teen pregnancy programs can have widespread effects.

To begin with, young Latinas in low-income communities often internalize harmful stereotypes that they are expected to be submissive underachievers destined for caretaking jobs. These are also attitudes they may find reflected back at them—consciously or unconsciously—by teachers, counselors, and peers.

Attitudes like these not only make young Latinas less likely to complete their educations, but once they leave school, feminine norms can continue to act like invisible guard rails, silently pushing them toward low-entry barrier, low-paying service jobs, often in fields like healthcare. As one researcher explains, young Latinas are too willing to sacrifice their own academic achievement for romance or marriage, in the belief that for a young woman, boyfriends and husbands should trump schoolwork and achievement. Even Latinas who do prioritize achievement and career can find themselves stigmatized for being selfish and "unfeminine" because "good girls" should prioritize their families, children, and men—not their own ambitions.

All these attitudes depress not just graduation rates, but overall economic empowerment. Economic justice funders need to also look more closely at "gender transformative" approaches that challenge rigid feminine norms if they are to create more effective programming for young Latinas.

School Pushout Policies

The policing of racial gendered norms through Zero Tolerance, Three Strikes, and other "school pushout" policies have tilted the playing field decisively against young Latinx and Black students, making it more likely than ever that they may be suspended or expelled.

Over the past decade, a wave of studies has established definitively that Latina and Black females and males are punished more often and more harshly than their White and Asian American peers, often for the same infractions.

Leading authorities on youth of color, like Kimberlé Crenshaw and author Monique Morris, have begun focusing philanthropic attention on how such disparate treatment is due to yet another example of the power of intersectional approaches that combine race, class, and gender. Black and Latina girls who are lively and boisterous are more likely to be perceived as unruly, disruptive, and simply "unfeminine." And Latina and Black girls are more likely to be disciplined for "defiant behavior" or "showing disrespect," which are more a matter of subjective teacher perception than actual rule-breaking.

Often teachers respond by trying to enforce more middle-class White notions of passive, obedient femininity, only making matters worse.

As a result, Latinx are 1.5 times more likely to be suspended and about 2 times more likely to be expelled than their White peers.

School pushout policies negatively affect young Latinas just entering adolescence, allowing them little margin for error when navigating the twin tasks of mastering acceptable feminine behavior and avoiding narrow school disciplinary regimes.

STEM (Science, Technology, Engineering, & Math)

Improving the STEM participation of young women of color will require programs and funding that integrate a strong, specific focus on feminine norms. Because as girls enter adolescence, they begin to perceive a conflict between being feminine and being good at science and math; in this conflict, STEM loses.

During the "gender intensification" years of grades 5 through 9, STEM interest begins a long decline, until by eighth grade, only half as many girls as boys are interested in STEM careers.

While funders have done important work addressing a host of external barriers like lack of role models, parental attitudes, stereotype threat, and implicit teacher bias, clearly an age-related trigger involving girls' own attitudes, femininity, and adolescence is involved—and underaddressed. The decline in STEM participation is more evident among young Latinas, who are equally likely as Whites to major in STEM, but significantly less likely to earn STEM degrees. For instance, in 2010, although Latinx made up 16 percent of the US population, they received only 8 percent of STEM degrees. Yet in what is increasingly a knowledge economy, STEM industries will account for a large share of tomorrow's jobs, especially those with higher salaries and fewer "Old Boy" networks that might exclude young women, or stand in the way of their promotion.

References & Selected Reading

AHA (American Heart Association). 2019. "Heart Disease in Hispanic Women," *Go Red for Women*, website. https://www.goredforwomen.org/en/about-heart-disease-in-women/facts/heart-disease-in-hispanic-women.

Afabel, A., and Brindis, C. 2007. "Acculturation and the Sexual and Reproductive Health of Latino Youth in the United States: A Literature Review," *Perspectives on Sexual and Reproductive Health* 38 (4): 208–19.

Amaro, H. 1995. "Love, Sex, and Power: Considering Women's Realities in HIV Prevention," *American Psychologist* 50 (6): 437.

Cano, M. A., and Castillo, L. G. 2010. "The Role of Enculturation and Acculturation on Latina College Student Distress," *Journal of Hispanic Higher Education* 9 (3): 221–31.

Castillo, L. G., Perez, F. V., Castillo, R., and Ghosheh, M. R. 2010. "Construction and Initial Validation of the Marianismo Beliefs Scale," *Counseling Psychology Quarterly* 23 (2): 163–75.

Céspedes, Y. M., and Huey Jr., S. G. 2008. "Depression in Latino Adolescents: A Cultural Discrepancy Perspective," *Cultural Diversity & Ethnic Minority Psychology* 14 (2): 168–72. https://doi.org/10.1037/1099-9809.14.2.168.

Centers for Disease Control and Prevention. 2015. *Youth Risk Behavior Surveillance System* (YRBSS). https://www.cdc.gov/healthyyouth/data/yrbs/.

Coffers, N. I. 2002. "The Influence of Marianismo on Psychoanalytic Work on Latinas: Transference and Countertransference Implications," *The Psychoanalytic Study of the Child* 57:435–51.

Cole, E. R. 2009. "Intersectionality and Research in Psychology," *American Psychologist* 64 (3): 170.

Crenshaw, K. 1989. "Demarginalizing the Intersection of Race and Sex: A Black Feminist Critique of Antidiscrimination Doctrine, Feminist Theory and Antiracist Politics," *University of Chicago Legal Forum* 140:139–67.

Crenshaw, K. 1991. "Mapping the Margins: Intersectionality, Identity Politics, and Violence Against Women of Color," *Stanford Law Review* 43 (6): 1241–99.

Diclemente R. J., Wingwood, G. M., Crosby, R. Sionean, C., Cobb, B. K., Harrington, K., Davies, S., Hook, E. W. III, and Oh, M. K. 2001. "Parental Monitoring: Association with Adolescents' Risk Behaviors," *Pediatrics* 107 (6): 1363–68.

Fennema, E., and Sherman, J. A. 1973. "Fennema-Sherman Mathematics Attitude Scales: Instruments Designed to Measure Attitudes Toward the Learning of Mathematics by Females and Males," *Research in Mathematics Education* 4:76–84.

Flannery, M. E. 2015. *Falling Through the Cracks: Latina Dropouts*. National Education Association.

Gandara, P. 2015. *Fulfilling America's Future: Latinas in the US*. The White House Initiative on Educational Excellence for Hispanics. https://sites.ed.gov/hispanic-initiative/files/2015/09/Fulfilling-Americas-Future-Latinas-in-the-U.S.-2015-Final-Report.pdf.

Hancock, A. M. 2007. "When Multiplication Doesn't Equal Quick Addition: Examining Intersectionality as a Research Paradigm," *Perspectives on Politics* 5 (1): 63.

Jezzini, A. T. 2013. "Acculturation, Marianismo Gender Role, and Ambivalent Sexism in Predicting Depression in Latinas," PhD dissertation.

Johnson, S., Frattaroli, S., Campbell, J., Wright, J., Pearson-Fields, A. S., and Cheng, T. L. 2005. "'I Know What Love Means.' Gender-Based Violence in the Lives of Urban Adolescents," *Journal of Women's Health* 14 (2): 172–79.

Lavrin, A. 2004. "Latin American Women's History: The National Project," in Smith, B. G., ed., *Women's History in Global Perspective*, 180–221. Champaign: University of Illinois Press.

National Science Foundation (NSF). 2003. *Back to School: Five Myths About Girls and Science*. National Research Center for Career and Technical Education Dissemination (Press Release). http://www.nrccte.org/.

National Women's Law Center and Mexican American Legal Defense and Educational Fund. 2009. *Listening to Latinas: Barriers to High School Graduation.* Washington, DC: NWLC&MALDEF. https://nwlc-ciw49tixgw5lbab.stackpathdns.com/wp-content/uploads/2009/08/Listening-to-Latinas-NWLC-MALDEF.pdf.

Nieman, Y. 2001. "Stereotypes about Chicanas and Chicanos: Implications for Counseling," *The Counseling Psychologist* 29 (1): 55–90.

Nuñez, A., González, P., Talavera, G. A., et al. 2016. "Machismo, Marianismo, and Negative Cognitive-Emotional Factors: Findings from the Hispanic Community Health Study/Study of Latinos Sociocultural Ancillary Study," *Journal of Latina/o Psychology* 4 (4): 202–17.

PEPFAR Gender Technical Working Group Gender Special Initiatives. 2012. http://www.aidstarone.com/focus_areas/gender/pepfar_gender_special_initiatives.

Perez, J. 2012. "The Influence of Latino/A Gender Roles and Culture on Student Achievement and Resistance," Master's thesis, University of North Carolina at Chapel Hill.

Planned Parenthood. *Reducing Teen Pregnancy.* 2013. https://www.plannedparenthood.org/files/6813/9611/7632/reducing_teen_pregnancy.pdf.

Ramirez, T. L., and Blay, Z. 2016. "Do You Identify as 'Latinx'?" *Huffington Post*, July 5.

Rivera-Marano, M. 2000. "The Creation of the Latina Values Scale: An Analysis of Marianismo's Effects on Latina Women Attending College," PhD dissertation, Rutgers University. *Dissertations Abstracts International* 61 (5-B): 1741.

Rocha-Sanchez, T., and Diaz-Loving, R. 2005. "Cultura De Genero: La Brecha Ideologica Entre Hombres Y Mujeres," *Anales De Psicologia* 21 (1): 42–49.

Teitelman A. M., Ratcliffe, S. J., Morales-Aleman, M. M., Sullivan, and Cris, M. 2008. "Sexual Relationship Power, Intimate Partner Violence, and Condom Use among Minority Urban Girls," *Journal of Interpersonal Violence* 23 (12): 1694–712.

TrueChild, 2011. *Gender Norms: A Key to Combating School Drop-Outs and Push-Out Policies in At-Risk Communities.* Washington, DC: TrueChild.

———. 2013. *Gender Norms: A Key to Combating School- and Cyber-Bullying and Homophobic Harassment among At-Risk Youth.* Washington, DC: TrueChild.

University of Michigan. N.d. *Issues in Latina Health: Teen Pregnancy.* http://umich.edu/~ac213/student_projects07/latinahealth/sexualhealth.html

US Agency for International Development. 2012. *Gender Analysis Overview: 2012.* http://transition.usaid.gov/our_work/crosscutting_programs/wid/gender/gender_analysis.html.

Ventura, S. J., Curtin, S. C., Abma, J. C., and Henshaw, S. K. 2012. "Estimated Pregnancy Rates and Rates of Pregnancy Outcomes for the United States, 1990–2008," *National Vital Statistics Reports* 60 (7).

Wingwood G. M., and Diclemente R. J. 1998. "Partner Influences and Gender-Related Factors Associated with Non-Condom Use among Young Adult American Women," *American Journal of Community Psychology* 26 (1): 29–51.

World Bank. 2015. *Gender Overview.* http://www.worldbank.org/en/topic/gender/overview - 2.

Zayas, L. H., Lester, R. J., Cabassa, L. J., and Fortuna, L. R. 2005. "Why Do So Many Latina Teens Attempt Suicide? A Conceptual Model for Research," *American Journal of Orthopsychiatry* 75 (2): 275–87.

10

Young Black Men & Masculinity

This chapter is excerpted from a white paper written for and distributed by the Association of Black Foundation Executives (ABFE). Micah Gilmer of Frontline Solutions was a coauthor. Loren Harris (who has led racial equity initiatives at the Ford, W. K. Kellogg, and Nathan Cummings Foundations) provided the Foreword. Keon L. Gilbert, Rashawn Ray, and Scyatta Wallace all provided input and ideas. Cliff Leek assembled the references, and Clare Howell provided proofreading and editing.

Why We Still Can't Wait—A Foreword by Loren Harris

Ignorance of each other is what has made unity impossible in the past. Therefore, we need enlightenment. We need more light about each other. Light creates understanding, understanding creates love, love creates patience, and patience creates unity.

—Malcolm X

America is at a critical crossroads. The nation faces the challenge of fulfilling its promise as an inclusive democracy for all, or continuing as a society crumbing from the weight of anachronistic beliefs and behaviors that concentrate power, wealth, and resources in the control of a few. The prospect of realizing a more just society continues to pivot on matters of social and economic equity. The contours of opportunity remain overly determined by socially constructed hierarchies of race, gender, and class. Intersecting identities—such as being Latino, heterosexual, and working class, or gay and Black—too often function as filters for privilege and disadvantage.

Vitriol and violence surrounding the equitable treatment of Black people by the nation's criminal justice system have elevated beyond the boiling point. Current pleas for racial equity in the criminal justice system and beyond are not new—indeed, it can be asserted that these concerns are as American as apple pie. But interrogating both race and gender is important in the struggle for the integrity of Black bodies. Indeed, the bodily integrity of Black people has historically been a point of social and economic tension. The contemporary contention that "Black Lives Matter" can be seen as part of a centuries-long call for justice rather than a twenty-first century flashpoint. From this perspective, demands for an end to the racially inequitable treatment of (and state-sanctioned violence toward) young men of color might be better understood as part of the unfinished business of challenging long-held mainstream notions of Black masculinity as unbridled, exotic, dangerous, and even predatory.

This social stew informs the development of norms of manhood that influence how young Black men understand and engage educational opportunity, labor force participation, and relationships with women and other men. Rigid masculine ideals limit conceptions of opportunity and expose many young men to stigmatization, abuse, and violence because they are neither attainable nor sustainable over time. Masculinity and gender impact nearly every facet of funders' and agency's interaction with young Black men, yet they are seldom held up like race and class.

This important work by TrueChild and Frontline Solutions contributes to our understanding the lives of young Black males. It is a timely echo of Robert Frost's timeless writing, *The Road Not Taken*, in which two roads diverge in a wood. The analysis presented in this chapter offers a less-traveled path that could help improve awareness and grow understanding of how race and gender norms operate in a hierarchy of privilege. It also suggests openings for deepening how we make sense of gender norms and masculinity as factors that could be leveraged to improve life outcomes among Black men. If we take Malcolm X's foretelling to heart, the opportunities highlighted here could lead to a less familiar path that holds great promise for the future of Black communities, and indeed the whole nation.

Introduction

It's not safe to be any kind of Black man in America, and widespread awareness of that fact is long overdue. Only a few years ago, "respectability politics" still held sway: the argument that persistent lower life outcomes among young Black men were the result of their failure to internalize middle-class White ideals of manliness, from having a regular job, to "acting right," and saying "thank you" and "yes, sir" on cue. If young men would only pull their pants up and give up "street manhood," things would all get better.

"Doing" middle-class White manhood does not inoculate Black men who are still prey to police injustice, vigilante assaults, and community-based violence.

Being respectable like James Blake, well-educated like Henry Louis Gates, or rich like Thabo Sefalosha is no protection. In the wake of this reality, next-generation civil rights organizations like #BlackLivesMatter and Dream Defenders are arguing forcefully for the full humanity of Black men and their right to embody manhood on their own terms, whether or not it conforms to middle-class White ideals.

The problem, they argue, is not urban Black manhood, but that no version of manhood can now be expected to protect them from ingrained attitudes of structural racism.

What is needed now is to work on two fronts simultaneously.

First, we need to have a true national conversation about manhood ideals and the fiction that more respectable versions of masculinity will somehow protect young Black men and boys from oppression.

Second, since the promise of "respectability politics" has been revealed as empty, we need to explore how buying into rigid codes of masculinity still leads to lower life outcomes among young men, especially young men of color.

As Loren Harris noted in the Ford Foundation's 2007 report, "Why We Can't Wait: A Case for Philanthropic Action: "Gender roles influence the way [young Black] men understand and engage educational opportunity, labor force participation, and relationships with women and other men . . . limiting conceptions of opportunity and success and exposing some to stigmatization, abuse and violence" (Littles, Bowers, and Gilmer 2007, 2).

In addressing the impact of harsh ideals of manhood, we need to bear in mind that these are not "street codes" of manhood peculiar to the Black community, but rather frontier codes of American manhood that have a long history. They include injunctions to not show feelings, to never back down, and to always meet force with force. These codes of masculinity inform the behavior police officers involved in unjustified shootings display every bit as much as they impact the choices of the young men in their crosshairs.

We also need to bear in mind that while decades of studies suggest that addressing rigid codes of masculinity can lead to better life outcomes in areas like education, health, or economic security, they cannot and will not protect our young men from racism or fulfill the now-empty vision of "respectability politics."

The Challenge

All your life you was raised to be what? A man. You see what I'm saying? So my train of thought is when I see another man is that either you need to be doing what I'm doing or you doing something a little better than what I'm doing.

—young man in TrueChild focus group

As the quote above illustrates, young Black men and boys face special challenges and barriers related to both their race and gender that can impact their health, achievement, and life outcomes. This is especially true for those in low-income communities, who have the added challenges associated with poverty.

Indeed, in underresourced communities, codes for masculinity and femininity are apt to be especially narrow, penalties for transgressing them particularly harsh, and opportunities for constructively displaying public manhood or womanhood few (Anderson 2000; Whitehead 1997). This means that the impact of harmful rigid masculine norms on young Black men in these communities is magnified.

It is not that young Black men in affluent suburban communities do not experience similar problems with codes of manhood—studies show they do. Rather, it is that in higher-income neighborhoods these impacts are buffered by the presence of additional personal resources and social capital. Given the added risk of low-income status, this chapter focuses mainly on young men in low-income communities. This group was chosen not as an endpoint, but as a beginning to what is hoped will become a growing dialogue on the unique lives and challenges faced by young Black men.

This chapter addresses on four problem areas where the empirical evidence is extensive and well-accepted:

- basic health and wellness;
- educational achievement and economic security;
- reproductive and sexual health; and
- intimate partner and male-on-male violence.

Nothing in this chapter is unique to young Black men. On the contrary, studies consistently find that many of the same impacts are experienced by young White, Latino, Asian-Pacific Islander, or Native American males who internalize rigid gender norms and live in low-income environments (Field and Caetano 2004; Sirin 2005). Many of them also experience similar levels of stress and even trauma.

What is unique is the continuing impact of structural racism, and the effects of state-sanctioned racial subjugation—even, at times, extermination—the special challenges of poverty, and the chronic life stresses that can combine to create particular vulnerabilities for young Black men and boys.

In this connection, we are also sensitive to the need to avoid adding to the already extensive "Crisis Literature" on young Black men, which focuses narrowly on the grim outcomes many of them face. In addition, as community initiatives like Black Male Engagement (BMe) keep pointing out, young Black men and boys bring immense resources and resilience to the life challenges they face (Jealous, Shorters, and Simmons 2015). Many young Black men gain strength and sustenance from both masculinity and their interaction with other Black men. The expanding popularity of mentoring, and the rites of passage programs that pair younger and older males are just one example, as are programs like the Campaign for Black Male Achievement and A Call to Men.

As Loren Harris' "Why We Can't Wait" explained: "Our concern with the state of Black males is [the hope that] we are simultaneously challenging narrow notions of gender roles, particularly masculinity . . . and identifying strategies that can help reduce poverty among families and communities" (Littles, Bowers, and Gilmer 2007, 2).

Understanding narrow codes of masculinity in the African American community requires considering their roots in structural racism, and in historical and cultural forces. Slavery, Jim Crow, and then covert discrimination and structural racism have all acted to deny Black males more familiar routes to public masculinity, including decent wage-paying jobs, opportunities to accrue status or personal power, and the traditional patriarchal role as head of family, disciplinarian, and primary breadwinner.

Faced with these barriers, young men constructed alternative forms of masculinity based on what was available in their everyday interactions, more suited to their narrower horizons, and not dependent on the dominant culture. These could include intimate encounters with women, getting the respect of other men, displaying an aloof swagger, disdain of authority, and suppression of emotion.

Collectively, these attitudes comprise what Majors and Billson (1992) termed the "cool pose" of urban Black males, a sometimes hypermasculine response to chronic stress, discrimination, and disempowerment. It has its own postures, language, walking styles, forms of greeting, and styles of clothing that establish participants as possessing an alternative and specifically African American "cool" manhood that is independent of traditional White male ideals—one which has been widely admired and often copied by middle-class White youth and artists (See Majors and Billson 1992, esp. ch. 6).

Basic Health & Wellness

Stress & Trauma

Young Black men have unique race and gendered experiences that result in multiple stresses that may weaken their immune system and expose them to higher rates of disease and lowered levels of health and well-being.

Studies show this stress begins in childhood and continues into adulthood, and is exacerbated by things like exposure to high rates of poverty, violence, and poor nutrition (Davis and Stevenson 2006; Engle and Black 2008).

Chronic exposure to racial discrimination also creates psychological "wear and tear" that can affect both mental and physical health (James 1994; Matthews et al. 2013; Williams and Mohammed 2009).

Young men must also navigate pressure to conform to traditional masculine ideals of the dominant culture as well as "frontier" codes of masculinity common to many low-income communities, both Black and White, which prioritize toughness and aggression (Carter 2003).

They must learn how to navigate and cope with the inequities inherent in a traditional gender system that always demands that males be strong, dominant, and aggressive—and that females be dependent and deferential. Some will also be exposed to psychological, physical, or sexual violence, along with the trauma that so often accompanies it.

Many young Black men and boys in low-income communities also experience multiple forms of trauma and other severe life stressors including homelessness, community violence, victimization, sexual/physical abuse, incarceration, and loss of loved ones to injury or illness (Ickovics et al. 2006). This can be especially true in low-income communities.

Racism—both overt hostility and harassment and the microaggressions and frictions of everyday interactions have been linked to trauma and injury. Despite this, little research has addressed the impact of posttraumatic stress and related symptoms on young Black men (Carter 2003; Rich 2009).

Long-term effects of trauma can include hyper-vigilance and hostility, irritability and anxiety, risky sexual behavior, and increased substance use (Herman 2015). Cultural expectations that young Black men remain emotionally tough and silent despite the trauma they may have experienced, and deal with the effects alone, can contribute to the symptoms.

Health-Seeking Behavior

Even when healthcare is needed, rigid codes of manhood dictate that young men should man up by "toughing out" pain, injury, and illness and avoid complaining or seeking help from others (Addis and Mahalik 2003; Ruxton 2009).

Health-promoting behavior is generally perceived as feminine (and health harming ones as manly). As a result, young men "will often risk their physical health and well-being rather than be associated with traits they or others may perceive as feminine" (Griffith, Gunter, and Watkins 2012, 2). As a result, young Black men will often avoid seeking medical help until their bodies are in crisis from treatable, and in some cases, even preventable, illnesses. In low-income communities, money for medical care is often scarce, and there may be other competing priorities that take precedence over attending to personal health issues (Ravenell, Whitaker, and Johnson 2008). Even when they do resolve to focus on maintaining health, studies find that John Henryism can lead Black men to be overly self-reliant, making their own determinations about what health issues they are having, and coming up with their own "solutions" (James 1994; Matthews et al. 2013).

"John Henryism" describes a style of coping with chronic, impossible stress— such as the daily insults and setbacks of racism—by putting forth superhuman effort. Black men often struggle with an array of stressors and the everyday microaggressions and frictions of racism but have few resources to support them. Some leading authorities believe its cultural basis lies in the struggle of freemen following the Civil War to adopt core common values of hard work, self-reliance, and resistance in the face of a hostile White culture.

In some ways, it may be seen as the masculine counterpart to cultural expectations that girls learn to be "strong Black women" and the resulting impact on women's health through the "Sojourner Syndrome." The chronic stress associated with John Henryism can also result in a "weathering" effect, one that lowers Black men's immune systems and leaves them vulnerable to chronic health problems such as hypertension, diabetes, substance abuse, depression, and heart disease as they age (James 1994; Matthews et al. 2013).

In the short run, however, John Henryism can actually benefit Black men's mental health, increasing their sense of mastery over discrimination and other chronic stressors, and decreasing depression and helplessness. Being strong and self-reliant can be very positive attributes, especially in a system that works to persistently diminish the potential and contributions of Black men.

And in limited circumstances, John Henryism can also help reduce rates of depression, helping men feel a sense of mastery over poverty, discrimination, and other chronic stressors.

However, over time, other coping strategies that are more social and less strictly self-reliant are necessary for long-term health. Over time, the high-effort coping typical of John Henryism has been linked to higher rates of hypertension, stroke, diabetes, heart disease, and lower mental health among African American males (James 1994).

Changing the discourse about Black men and masculinity among parents, providers, and Black men themselves could have a positive impact on their health and well-being. Programmatic efforts to redefine masculine strength as empowering Black men to reach out to and engage others or accept medical assistance when needed might have many beneficial effects.

Reproductive Health

Unplanned Fatherhood & HIV

Decades of research have found that sexual and reproductive health outcomes are lower for young Black men compared to males from other racial groups. For instance, studies have found that young Black males are more likely to have sex early (before age thirteen) and that by age nineteen they have had an average of eleven sexual partners—double that of non-White Hispanic males (Lemelle 2010).

Power inequities are inherent in the norms associated with intimate male–female relations as well as genuine physical difference. It is apparent in the terms often used by adolescents for sexually active males versus females, and in norms that demand men to be the aggressor during sex while women are silent about their relationship and/or sexual needs.

Studies show that belief in rigid codes of manhood are strongly linked to less-intimate relationships, more sexual partners (including commercial sex workers), earlier age of first sex, more sexual risk-taking, and lower levels of condom use (Amaro 1995; Pleck, Sonenstein, and Ku 1993). In addition, belief in traditional masculinity has been linked to stronger tendency to view pregnancy as validating manhood, and female responsibility for preventing conception (Amaro 1995; Pleck, Sonenstein, and Ku 1993). All these attitudes and behaviors are tied to higher rates of unplanned fatherhood and HIV and other STIs.

In some low-income communities, young men may also "adopt manipulative and exploitative attitudes with women" with the objective of "getting over" in a game of sexual conquest. In one survey, three-fifths of Black adolescents thought that deception was acceptable to get a girl to have sex (Wolfe 2003).

Partially in response, low-income male peer groups "emphasize sexual prowess as a mark of manhood, at times including babies as its evidence" (Anderson 1989, n.p.). This is exacerbated by the aversion among some many young men (Black or White) to condom use as "undermining their masculinity or virility" (Wolfe 2003, 848).

Media Effects

Both gay and straight young men also face special challenges to their reproductive health from distorted media portrayals of Black masculinity, which only reinforce the negative impact of racial gender norms (The Opportunity Agenda 2011). While young people generally spend up to seven hours or more with media daily, Black youth spend up to thirteen hours each day with media. Yet movies, TV, and videos offer few affirming images for young Black men in terms of relationships, intimacy, or sexuality. Black men are often presented as devoid of depth or love, and as of little importance beyond their aggression or prowess with women.

This is reflected in the limited roles most often available for young Black male actors as thugs, enforcers, or rap stars. Moreover, there are few examples of healthy dating or intimate relationships available, in which young Black men might model more positive behaviors. A host of studies has linked internalizing these negative images to lower life outcomes. This can be especially important during childhood and adolescence, when Black boys are more susceptible to media influence (Martin 2008). Moreover, Black audiences are especially attuned to media representations of themselves (The Opportunity Agenda 2011).

Understanding the relationship dynamics among young Black men and their partners is a crucial area of study. More research is needed that examines how gender norms are practiced in intimate and sexual relationships, what protective factors may help young Black men build more productive images of masculinity in relationships, and what programmatic strategies—particularly around gender norms—can help teach them healthier relationships.

Intimate Partner Violence & Male-on-Male Violence

Partner Violence: Male Attitudes

Intimate partner violence (IPV) and girlfriend abuse are serious problems for many young women, particularly for Black girls, among whom IPV rates are higher than that of those of Hispanics or Whites (Catalano 2008). One large study found that IPV was reported by 18 percent of Black girls (Wingood et al. 2001).

Blassingame (1972) and Levine (1977) have noted that slavery, and then institutional racism, combined with chronic unemployment have often fueled feelings of male anger and frustration that can sometimes be displaced onto female partners—what one researcher termed "frustrated masculinity syndrome" (Hampton, Oliver, and Magarian 2003).

Young men who internalize ideals of manhood as defined by aggression, dominance, and toughness are more likely to abuse female partners (Anderson 2000). They are more likely to believe that control of a female partner can be a crucial indicator of public manhood. Being defied or shown up by an "insubordinate" female partner, or otherwise having her publicly challenge his authority, can be seen as the height of unmanliness and justification for a violent response (Miller 2008). Rigid codes of manhood may also include male privileges of determining when and how sex occurs, and the use of sexual coercion when an intimate partner is unreceptive or insists on negotiating condom use.

Some studies of abuse perpetrators have found that they have a strong system of self-justification for abuse, often asserting that female partners "brought it on themselves" by not carrying out feminine responsibilities (e.g., household labor, cooking, child care, and "taking care" of their man). Such narratives can play heavily on crude stereotypes of women as dependent, emotionally impulsive, and irrational.

Partner Violence: Female Attitudes

Attitudes among young Black women can also play a part. Studies have found that Black women themselves are prone to agree that, naturally, men mistreat women, that anger and rage are integral to masculinity, and that abuse can be one way men express love (Johnson et al. 2005; Miller 2008; West and Rose 2000). Young Black women may have been taught that they should defer to Black men and grant them the respect they have long been denied, to avoid adding to their ongoing emasculation, and show communal solidarity (Johnson et al. 2005; West and Rose 2000).

Many women see attracting an older, more powerful man as an important proof of femininity. Such relationships can add to the power inequalities already inherent in most heterosexual relationships, in which men not only have greater physical power, but usually can exercise greater economic power through higher status and better-paying jobs, greater social resources, and through ties to other men in positions of strength.

Because of this, partner violence can also include an older, stronger male threatening or punishing a younger, less-mature partner with psychological, economic, or social abuse.

Media Stereotypes

Media also plays a role in IPV. Studies show that viewing stereotypic portrayals of Black women can increase the risks of victimization by their male partners (Gillum 2002). Young men may also internalize race and gender-based media stereotypes of "strong Black men" who are naturally aggressive and dominant, and consciously or unconsciously seek to embody them. It has been argued that educating young men about the harms of normative masculinity to themselves and to women and working to foster greater empathy and egalitarian connections with young women may be a strategy to combat IPV against Black girls (Miller 2008).

It appears likely that providing Black youth with opportunities for cross-gender friendships, activities, and engagement may help decrease coercive sexual behaviors and foster more egalitarian relationships.

Male-on-Male

Male-on-male violence is still a critical problem in urban environments, with homicide often the leading cause of death for young men. Race, class, and gender norms all contribute to the problem. In narrow street codes of manhood, honor and respect are hard-won, easy to lose, and thus must be constantly defended. Even the smallest threat can grow into something bigger. In such an environment, as a 2009 report by the Men and Boys Coalition explains, "demonstrating toughness and a willingness to use violence can become central elements of masculinity . . . both to maintain a reputation and provide an illusion of safety" (Ruxton 2009, 125).

Significantly, studies have found that stronger beliefs in traditional masculinity are strongly linked to more lethal assaults, like gun violence (Blome 2004), and that young men who committed these assaults frequently had internalized exaggerated notions of masculinity and the need to defend their manhood at all costs (Lopez and Emmer 2002).

Complicating matters, one in three Black males will have some involvement with the juvenile or criminal justice systems during their lifetimes (Mauer 2011). There is also a growing awareness of the ways that law enforcement systems often target young men of color, which increases their risk of eventual incarceration. Many of these men will be exposed to penal environments where harsh and rigid codes of prison manhood are the norm, and violence is integral to survival, before being returned to their communities.

LGBT Violence

Author Michael Kimmel (2004) has argued that homophobia is a central organizing principle of manhood, because homosexuality represents the "feminine role." Homophobic and transphobic attacks may be seen not as a rejection of sexuality per se, but rather a rejection of anything weak, unmanly, or feminine (62). In one study of such attacks, a participant explained, "All my life I've been brought up to be a man. You're going to accept responsibility, you're going to be independent, you're going to take care of your family. Anything gets in the way, you're going to handle your business. So now here's something that's contrary to what a man is, walking down the street" (Wilchins 2006).

Balancing the Picture

Despite such explanations, and despite popular culture's reflexive association of young Black men with aggression, the vast majority are not violent toward one another or toward others (Ruxton 2009). Indeed, "although there is much public concern currently about violence by and among young men, most are not involved, and the quieter contribution of the majority of young men to the safety and well-being of others is generally unacknowledged" (126).

As the Black Male Achievement Initiative has noted, it is important to balance the widespread narratives of aggression or violence by always pointing to the "positive narratives that build off the assets that exist, and celebrates and promotes" young Black men (CBMA 2015, n.p.).

Education

Masculinity & Education

Studies have found that young Black males frequently do as well or better than their White counterparts right up until the "gender intensification" years of ten to fourteen, when drop- and stop-out rates begin to climb, and grade point averages begin to drop. Both can be tied to masculine norms.

To begin with, the increasing desire among many adolescents to be seen as manly can put them at odds with any of the activities necessary for successful schoolwork. Being respectful of teachers, obeying adult authority figures, sitting quietly in class, and obediently turning in homework are a set of behaviors, which, taken together, are a fair prescription for ostracism, bullying, or harassment at schools in many communities.

The interconnected effects of race, class, and gender also play an important role. As researcher Shanette Harris notes, "Although adolescents boys in general disparage feminine qualities, the intensity of this disdain appears to have a greater impact upon African American male youth. Unlike their European American counterparts, African American male adolescents are more likely to deny, devalue, and actually forgo intellectual interests to avoid the ridicule and shame that arise from academic success" (Harris 1995, 281).

As a young man explained in one study, "Absolutely I felt pressure to conform to images of masculinity in adolescence. I felt bad that I was reading or studying hard when all my peers were playing sports. I also felt bad about getting good grades because my peers looked down on me" (Roberts-Douglass and Curtis-Boles 2013, 12).

School Discipline

Studies show that educators are often reflexively inclined to view lower-income African American and Latino boys as potential troublemakers or even future felons (Ferguson 2001). Their response is increased surveillance, stricter regulation, and harsh punishment (Gregory, Skiba, and Noguera 2010; Skiba et al. 2002; Skibe and Peterson 2000), including proactive efforts to separate difficult students from the school system.

Researcher Russell Skiba has conclusively demonstrated that urban Black and Latino middle-school males are punished more often, and more harshly, than their White and Asian American peers, even for the same infractions (Skiba et al. 2002).

Even urban masculine fashion plays a role. A study perceptively titled "Tuck in That Shirt!" documented how hallway displays of contemporary urban manhood among young Black men—lowered and baggy pants, untucked shirts—had a profound impact on teachers. Educators—White and Black—immediately perceived the boys as oppositional and threatening, responding with more focus on bodily discipline, regulation, and punishment (Morris 2005).

Because of this, Zero Tolerance, Three Strikes, and similar school "push-out" policies have tilted the playing field decisively against young men of color, making it more likely than ever that they will be suspended or even expelled. And once suspended, it is much more probable that young men will never return, or end up in juvenile detention or under the supervision of the justice system—part of the "School-to-Prison" pipeline (Christle, Jolivette, and Nelson 2005).

Indeed, Michelle Alexander (2010) has argued that legalized discrimination toward young Black felons exiting prisons and jails (denying the right to vote, public benefits, jury service, etc.) may amount to a New Jim Crow—in effect a nationwide caste system.

Rigid codes of urban masculinity can put young men directly at odds with school disciplinary regimes (which only increases their odds of ending up in the "School-to-Prison" pipeline). Young men tend to establish status and dominance hierarchies through many of the behaviors—public boisterousness, risk-taking, defying adult authority figures, lack of engagement in academics, and suffering punishment silently—most likely to attract the attention of school authorities or increase their contact with juvenile justice systems.

By imposing the maximum penalty of expulsion, Zero Tolerance and Three Strikes policies offer young boys just learning to "do" masculinity precious little margin for error in navigating the twin shoals of adolescent manliness and school disciplinary regimes.

Taken together, these findings point to two great systems in blind and often disastrous collision: an urban male "gender culture" that demands that adolescent boys master public displays of traditional masculinity, and school systems inclined to view precisely those displays as oppositional and threatening, a cause for constant surveillance and punishment, and markers of eventual failure and probable incarceration.

Too many funding priorities, programs, and policies aimed at improving the outcomes of young Black men completely ignore the impact of rigid codes of masculinity and the deep need many young men of any race have to live up to and embody communal expectations of manhood.

Just like the dream deferred described by Langston Hughes, a dialogue about young Black men that continues to be deferred will have significant negative consequences. An intersectional understanding of gender, race, and class should be standard in social and philanthropic work if we seek to truly have a long-standing impact on the life disparities among young Black men and boys. We truly still can no longer wait.

References & Selected Reading

Addis, M. E., and Mahalik, J. R. 2003. "Men, Masculinity, and the Contexts of Help Seeking," *American Psychologist* 58 (1): 5.

Alexander, M. 2010. *The New Jim Crow: Mass Incarceration in the Age of Colorblindness.* New York: The New Press.

Amaro, H. 1995. "Love, Sex, and Power: Considering Women's Realities in HIV Prevention," *American Psychologist* 50 (6): 437.

Anderson, E. 1989. "Sex Codes and Family Life Among Poor Inner-City Youths," *The Annals of the American Academy of Political and Social Science* 501 (1): 59–78.

———. 2000. *Code of the Street: Decency, Violence, and the Moral Life of the Inner City.* New York: Norton.

Berry, E. H., Shillington, A. M., Peak, T., and Hohman, M. M. 2000. "Multi-Ethnic Comparison of Risk and Protective Factors for Adolescent Pregnancy," *Child and Adolescent Social Work Journal* 17 (2): 79–96.

Blome, J. 2004. "The Making of a Man: Masculinity Ideology and Its Relationship to Sexual Activity, Violent Behavior, and Academic Underachievement among Economically Disadvantaged, African American, Adolescent Males." PhD diss. Graduate School of Arts and Sciences, Columbia University, New York.

Bowleg, L. 2008. "When Black+ Lesbian+ Woman≠ Black Lesbian Woman: The Methodological Challenges of Qualitative and Quantitative Intersectionality Research," *Sex Roles* 59 (5–6): 312–25.

Brown, J. D., and Witherspoon, E. M. 2002. "The Mass Media and American Adolescents' Health," *Journal of Adolescent Health* 31 (6): 153–70.

Carter, P. L. 2003. "'Black' Cultural Capital, Status Positioning, and Schooling Conflicts for Low-Income African American Youth," *Social Problems* 50 (1): 136–55.

Harris, S. M. 1995. "Psychosocial Development and Black Male Masculinity: Implications for Counseling Economically Disadvantaged African American Male Adolescents," *Journal of Counseling and Development* 73 (3): 279–87.

Catalano, S. 2008. *Intimate Partner Violence in the United States*. Washington, DC: Bureau of Justice Statistics, US Department of Justice.

CBMA. 2015. *CBMA Strategy and Core Beliefs*. http://blackmale-achievement.org/aboutus/corevaluesandplan.

Christle, C. A., Jolivette, K., and Nelson, C. M. 2005. "Breaking the School to Prison Pipeline: Identifying School Risk and Protective Factors for Youth Delinquency," *Exceptionality* 13 (2): 69–88.

Cohen, C. J. 2010. *Democracy Remixed: Black Youth and the Future of American Politics*. Oxford: Oxford University Press.

Cole, E. R. 2009. "Intersectionality and Research in Psychology," *American Psychologist* 64 (3): 170.

Collins, P. H. 2002. *Black Feminist Thought: Knowledge, Consciousness, and the Politics of Empowerment*. New York: Routledge.

Crenshaw, K. 1989. "Demarginalizing the Intersection of Race and Sex: A Black Feminist Critique of Antidiscrimination Doctrine, Feminist Theory and Antiracist Politics," *University of Chicago Legal Forum* 140:139.

———. 1991. "Mapping the Margins: Intersectionality, Identity Politics, and Violence Against Women of Color," *Stanford Law Review* 43 (6): 1241–99.

Davis, G. Y., and Stevenson, H. C. 2006. "Racial Socialization Experiences and Symptoms of Depression Among Black Youth," *Journal of Child and Family Studies* 15 (3): 293–307.

Diaz, R. M. 1998. *Latino Gay Men and HIV: Culture, Sexuality, and Risk Behavior*. New York: Routledge.

Engle, P. L., and Black, M. M. 2008. "The Effect of Poverty on Child Development and Educational Outcomes," *Annals of the New York Academy of Sciences* 1136 (1): 243–56.

Evans, G. D., and Fogarty, K. 1999. *The Hidden Benefits of Being an Involved Father*. University of Florida Cooperative Extension Service, Institute of Food and Agriculture Sciences, EDIS.

Ferguson, A. A. 2001. *Bad Boys: Public Schools in the Making of Black Masculinity*. Ann Arbor: University of Michigan Press.

Field, C. A., and Caetano, R. 2004. "Ethnic Differences in Intimate Partner Violence in the US General Population the Role of Alcohol Use and Socioeconomic Status," *Trauma, Violence, and Abuse* 5 (4): 303–17.

Gender Analysis Overview. 2012. http://transition.usaid.gov/our_ work/cross-cutting_programs/wid/gender/gender_analy- sis.html.

Gillum, T. L. 2002. "Exploring the Link Between Stereotypic Images and Intimate Partner Violence in the African American Community," *Violence Against Women* 8 (1): 64–86.

Gregory, A., Skiba, R. J., and Noguera, P. A. 2010. "The Achievement Gap and the Discipline Gap Two Sides of the Same Coin?" *Educational Researcher* 39 (1): 59–68.

Griffith, D. M., Gunter, K., and Watkins, D. C. 2012. "Measuring Masculinity in Research on Men of Color: Findings and Future Directions," *American Journal of Public Health* 102 (S2): S187–S194.

Hampton, R., Oliver, W., and Magarian, L. 2003. "Domestic Violence in the African American Community an Analysis of Social and Structural Factors," *Violence Against Women* 9 (5): 533–57.

Hancock, A.-M. 2007. "When Multiplication Doesn't Equal Quick Addition: Examining Intersectionality as a Research Paradigm," *Perspectives on Politics* 5 (1): 63–79.

Herman, Judith L. 2015. *Trauma and Recovery: The Aftermath of Violence—From Domestic Abuse to Political Terror*. New York: Basic Books.

James, S. A. 1994. "John Henryism and the Health of African Americans," *Culture, Medicine and Psychiatry* 18 (2): 163–82.

Jealous, B., Shorters, T., and Simmons, R. 2015. *Reach: 40 Black Men Speak on Living, Leading, and Succeeding*. New York: Atria Books.

Johnson, S. B., Frattaroli, S., Campbell, J., Wright, J., Pearson-Fields, A. S., and Cheng, T. L. 2005. "'I Know What Love Means.' Gender-Based Violence in the Lives of Urban Adolescents," *Journal of Women's Health* 14 (2): 172–79.

Jones, J., and Mosher, W. D. 2013. "Fathers' Involvement with Their Children: United States, 2006–2010," *National Health Statistics Reports* 71:1–22.

Kimmel, M. S. 2004. "Masculinity as Homophobia: Fear, Shame, and Silence in the Construction of Gender Identity," in Rothenber, P. S., ed., *Race, Class, and Gender in the United States: An Integrated Study*, 81–93. New York: Worth.

Lemelle, A. J. 2010. *Black Masculinity and Sexual Politics*. Abingdon, UK: Taylor & Francis.

Littles, M. J., Bowers, R., and Gilmer, M. 2007. *Why We Can't Wait: A Case for Philanthropic Action: Opportunities for Improving Life Outcomes for African American Males*. Ford Foundation.

Lopez, V. A., and Emmer, E. T. 2002. "Influences of Beliefs and Values on Male Adolescents' Decision to Commit Violent Offenses," *Psychology of Men and Masculinity* 3 (1): 28.

Majors, R. and Billson, J. M. 1992. *Cool Pose: The Dilemmas of Black Manhood in America*. New York: Touchstone, 1993.

Martin, A. C. 2008. "Television Media as a Potential Negative Factor in the Racial Identity Development of African American Youth," *Academic Psychiatry* 32 (4): 338.

Matthews, D. D., Hammond, W. P., Nuru-Jeter, A., Cole-Lewis, Y., and Melvin, T. 2013. "Racial Discrimination and Depressive Symptoms Among African American Men: The Mediating and Moderating Roles of Masculine Self-Reliance and John Henryism," *Psychology of Men & Masculinity* 14 (1): 35.

Mauer, M. 2011. "Addressing Racial Disparities in Incarceration," *The Prison Journal* 91 (3 Supplement): 87S–101S.

Miller, J. 2008. *Getting Played: African American Girls, Urban Inequality, and Gendered Violence*. New York: NYU Press.

Morris, E. W. 2005. "'Tuck in That Shirt!' Race, Class, Gender, and Discipline in an Urban School. Sociological Perspectives," 48 (1): 25–48.

Naasel, K. R. 2014. "It's a Myth That Black Fathers Are Absent," *New York Times*, March 12.

The Opportunity Agenda. 2011. *Media Representations and Impact on the Lives of Black Men and Boys.* http://racialequitytools.org/resourcefiles/Media-Impact-onLives-of-Black-Men-and-Boys-OppAgenda.pdf.

PEPFAR Gender Technical Working Group Gender Special Initiatives. 2012. http://www.aidstar-one.com/focus_areas/gender/ pepfar_gender_special_initiatives.

Pleck, J. H. 1996. *Individual, Family, and Community Factors Modifying Male Adolescents' Risk Behavior "Trajectory."* Washington, DC: Urban Institute.

Pleck, J. H., Sonenstein, F. L., and Ku, L. C. 1993. "Masculinity Ideology: Its Impact on Adolescent Males' Hetero-Sexual Relationships," *Journal of Social Issues* 49 (3): 11–29.

Priess, H. A., and Lindberg, S. M. 2014. "Gender Intensification," in *Encyclopedia of Adolescence*, 1135–42. New York: Springer.

Ravenell, J. E., Whitaker, E. E. and Johnson Jr., W. E. 2008. "According to Him: Barriers to Healthcare Among African American Men," *Journal of the National Medical Association* 100 (10): 1153.

Rich, John A. 2009. *Wrong Place, Wrong Time: Trauma and Violence in the Lives of Young Black Men.* Baltimore: Johns Hopkins University Press.

Roberts-Douglass, K., and Curtis-Boles, H. 2013. "Exploring Positive Masculinity Development in African American Men: A Retrospective Study," *Psychology of Men & Masculinity* 14 (1): 7.

Ruxton, S. 2009. *Man-Made: Men, Masculinities and Equality in Public Policy.* London: Men and Boys Coallition. https://www.menshealthforum.org.uk/man-made-men-masculinities-and-equality-public-policy.

Sirin, S. R. 2005. "Socioeconomic Status and Academic Achievement: A Meta-Analytic Review of Research," *Review of Educational Research* 75 (3): 417–53.

Skiba, R. J., Michael, R. S., Nardo, A. C., and Peterson, R. L. 2002. "The Color of Discipline: Sources of Racial and Gender Disproportionality in School Punishment," *The Urban Review* 34 (4): 317–42.

Skiba, R. J., and Peterson, R. L. 2000. "School Discipline at a Crossroads: From Zero Tolerance to Early Response," *Exceptional Children* 66 (3): 335–46.

Thompson, E., and Pleck, J. H. 1995. "Masculinity Ideologies: A Review of Research Instrumentation on Men and Masculinities," in Levant, R. F. and Pollack, W. S., eds., *A New Psychology of Men*, 129–63. New York: Basic Books.

Thompson, E. H., Pleck, J. H., and Ferrera, D. L. 1992. "Men and Masculinities: Scales for Masculinity Ideology and Masculinity-Related Constructs," *Sex Roles* 27 (11–12): 573–607.

Tolman, D. L. 2009. *Dilemmas of Desire: Teenage Girls Talk about Sexuality.* Cambridge, MA: Harvard University Press.

Tolman, D. L., and Porche, M. V. 2000. "The Adolescent Femininity Ideology Scale: Development and Validation of a New Measure for Girls," *Psychology of Women Quarterly* 24 (4): 365–76.

TrueChild. 2011. *Gender Norms: A Key to Combating School Drop-Outs and Push-Out Policies in At-Risk Communities.* Washington, DC: TrueChild.

———. 2013. *Gender Norms: A Key to Combating School- and Cyber-Bullying and Homophobic Harassment among At-Risk Youth.* Washington, DC: TrueChild.

———. 2014. *Gender Norms: A Key to Improving Health and Wellness among Black Women and Girls.* Washington, DC: TrueChild.

West, C. M. 2004. "Black Women and Intimate Partner Violence New Directions for Research," *Journal of Interpersonal Violence* 19 (12): 1487–93.

West, C. M., and Rose, S. 2000. "Dating Aggression Among Low-Income African American Youth: An Examination of Gender Differences and Antagonistic Beliefs," *Violence Against Women* 6 (5): 470–94.

Whitehead, T. L. 1997. "Urban Low-Income African American Men, HIV/AIDS, and Gender Identity," *Medical Anthropology Quarterly* 11 (4): 411–47.

Wilchins, R. 2006. *50 Under 30: Masculinity and the War on America's Youth.* Gender Public Advocacy Coalition. http://www.impartofdc.org/assets/__50-under-302.pdf.

Williams, D. R., and Mohammed, S. A. 2009. "Discrimination and Racial Disparities in Health: Evidence and Needed Research," *Journal of Behavioral Medicine* 32 (1): 20–47.

Wilson, B. D., Harper, G. W., Hidalgo M. A., Jamil, O. B., Torres, R. S., and Fernandez, M. I. 2010. "Negotiating Dominant Masculinity Ideology: Strategies Used by Gay, Bisexual and Questioning Male Adolescents," 45 (1–2): 169–85.

Wingood, G. M., DiClemente, R. J., McCree, D. H., Harrington K., and Davies, S. L. 2001. "Dating Violence and the Sexual Health of Black Adolescent Females," *Pediatrics* 107 (5): E72–E72.

Wolfe, W. A. 2003. "Overlooked Role of African American Males' Hypermasculinity in the Epidemic of Unintended Pregnancies and HIV/AIDS Cases with Young African American Women," *Journal of the National Medical Association* 95 (9): 846.

World Bank. 2015. *Gender Overview.* http://www.worldbank.org/en/topic/gender/overview-2.

11

Women & Girls in the Global South

This chapter is based on a white paper developed by TrueChild with The MATCH Fund, Global Fund for Women, and Prospera. It was intended as an effort to recenter femininity in the dialogue on women and girls, and as a possible guide to future collective action in the Global South. The paper grew out of over three dozen interviews with NGOs, funders, agencies, and researchers in the Global South. In part because there are still few, if any, academic studies on this topic, we chose to focus on thought-leaders on the ground doing work in these countries. Excerpts from their remarks are throughout the text, and extended quotes from some of their interviews are at the end.

The following individuals were interviewed and/or provided their insight and guidance: Gayatri Buragohain, executive director, Feminist Approach to Technology (FAT); Abigail Burgesson, special programmes manager, African Women's Development Fund; Dora C. K. Byamukama, executive director, LAW and Advocacy for Women in Uganda; Satvika Chalasani, technical specialist, UNFPA (United Nations Population Fund); Hope Chigudu, regional advisor, JASS; Cynthia Coredo, executive director, Boxgirls Kenya; Gannon Gillespie, chief of staff, Tostan; Nick Grono, CEO, Freedom Fund; Purity Kagwiria, executive director, Akili Dada; Musimbi Kanyoro, president and CEO, Global Fund for Women; Kathy LeMay, CEO, Raising Change; Beverly Mademba, public health specialist formerly with WASH United; Diana Mao , president, Nomi Network; Wariri Muhungi, manager of global programs, The MATCH International Women's Fund; Jay Mulucha, executive director, Fem Alliance (FEMA) Uganda; Mabel van Oranje, board chair, Girls Not Bride; Jane Sloane; Howard Taylor, former managing director, Girl Effect; and Blain Teketel, programme officer, East Africa, Oak Foundation.

"Walk as Dragons"

Norms are critical. It all comes down to beliefs and practices. So I am very glad that this issue of gender norms is finally being addressed. What people fail to realize is that it is often women who impose and perpetuate these harmful traditions and practices, like genital cutting or child marriage, out of a desire to preserve beliefs, practices, and norms that come from patriarchy but that they have inherited. Women believe that if things change for the next generation of girls, that will be taking something away from them or make them incomplete. We often hear: "This was here before our time and it's still the way things must be done today." So we will never change these things as long as we assume women are implementing, and not agents of this system. We need to bring together the women's groups doing this work; we need a high-level network and engagement of donors, advocates, and activists. We need an alliance. Because when we work as a movement, we get results.

—Abigail Burgesson, African Women's Development Fund

In Cambodia, the *Chbab* are traditional prose poems that are passed from generation to generation and contain deeply ingrained gender norms and codes for each sex.

The *Chbab Proh* teaches boys to "walk as dragons": to be mindful of careless passion and weakness, to be knowledgeable, hard-working, and proactive. It promotes manhood as a site of agency, independence, toughness, and action, one in which each man is his own master.

The *Chbab Srey* teaches girls that females are subordinate, and exist solely to serve males. ("Remember to serve your husband. Don't make him unsatisfied—you must serve him regularly.") It teaches that a "good woman" is silent, submissive, deferential, subservient. And such attitudes are deeply internalized; according to UNICEF, 42 percent of Cambodian girls believe that wife-beating is justified.

Not Only at the Hands of Men

We wanted to help girls break through harsh old taboos about menstruation, and one woman stood up and said: "This is not done to us by men—this is what we believe, this is our culture."

—Beverly Mademba, Public Health Specialist,
formerly with WASH United

The Chbab Srey is not only taught in schools, but has been passed down to girls by mothers, aunts, grandmothers, and female elders for over a thousand years.

There is a myriad of factors that condone and sustain the subordination of Cambodian women and girls. Those often cited include officials who look the other way, a broken civil society, continued cycles of poverty, and an entrenched patriarchal culture that keeps power and privilege in the hands of men.

While each of these is important, as the Chbab Srey shows, social inequality is not only propagated by men onto women in an uncomplicated, unidirectional flow. There are many spaces in the fabric of social inequality where the flow is also from mother to daughter or from aunt to niece.

As Beverly Mademba says, "We were talking with Maasai mothers and grand-mothers to address all taboos around menstrual health with their girls. One woman stood and said. 'This is not done to us by men, this is what we believe—this is our culture.'"

Explains Purity Kagwiria of Akila Dada, "These older women have power in areas where men do not. People tell us the men need to change—but in these areas, it's the women who need to change—they are sitting in positions of power and maintaining these practices."

In the past decade, there has been a profound questioning of gender, gender identities, and related discourses in a range of disciplines, including internation-ally. In particular, there has been a clear documentation and challenging of rigid masculine norms. As a result, networks, model curricula, websites, convenings, data collection, and reports now support an array of efforts offering men new ways of being in the world.

Yet in a cluster of related areas that include child marriage, sex trafficking, genital cutting, ritual fattening, menstrual health, and education deprivation, beliefs and attitudes about femininity among mothers, aunts, and female elders can be as impor-tant to understanding and creating lasting change. While a core of NGOs provides groundbreaking programs that challenge rigid feminine norms, such norms are still rarely discussed, and little in the way of a formal infrastructure has grown up to support this work.

Feminine Norms

Older women train girls in everything down to the smallest detail: how to be a woman and be feminine; how to dress, how to eat, and what to cook; their education; their language all the things a woman can and cannot say.

—Hope Chigidu, JASS

These girls are disciplined by older women to be submissive, obedient, not ask questions, talk back, raise their eyes, or make decisions. Girls are watched, monitored, and corrected every moment. This is imposed mainly by women who enforce these traditional female norms. The responsibility of training girls to be "good women" lies on the older women of the family. We have a Hindi saying that literally translates to: "Women are the biggest enemy of women."

—Gayatri Buragohain, Feminist Approach to Technology (FAT)

Effectively challenging inequality in low- and lower-middle-income countries (LMIC) will mean taking into account the beliefs and attitudes about femininity and womanhood held by wives, mothers, and female elders—what are often called "gender norms."

But "the issue of femininity and feminine norms is not talked about and not named," explains Hope Chigidu of JASS. "People need to name it. People need to get that feminine norms don't always support women. These beliefs and practices are passed from one generation to the next, and perhaps more importantly, in the 'closed networks' of many societies where girls have little agency or privacy," explains UNFPA's Satvika Chalasani. "There is no escape from the constant enforcement of these norms."

This is not, to be clear, a matter of "blaming the victim," as if women are voluntarily contributing to their daughters' oppression. On the contrary, as many contributors to this chapter declared, women themselves are deeply victimized by the same patriarchal practices and norms.

Perhaps what is needed is to reframe how we think about the entire system of power that flows between women and girls. The goal of this reframing would be to better identify new points of agency that might contribute to solutions. It would obviously include mothers, aunts, and grandmothers, who are integral to girls' lives, and it would focus on tools, resources, and support—never assigning blame. Women are also the solution.

As Tostan's Gannon Gillespie notes, "Often when someone focuses on how women contribute to a problem, they're accused of 'blaming the victim.' But it's important that our efforts around gender norms engage both men and women, and use a holistic frame that calls people to a common humanity."

A number of NGO leaders doing women's rights or feminist work stressed how older women are forced to become elements in patriarchal systems that enforce rigid norms. Yet they also point out that women themselves are deeply victimized by patriarchal practices, and often at their mercy. Mothers may teach daughters to be submissive because they fear otherwise their daughters will be assaulted by young men, or become unmarriageable, or even be outcast. In many cases, religious traditions demand that older women teach subservience and submission to girls. Even when mothers, aunts, and grandmothers push back against patriarchal norms, it can be counterproductive: the communal response is often just to increase efforts to control the girls.

When mothers, grandmothers, and aunts do perpetuate patriarchal norms, they may not be fully aware, because they have internalized the same longstanding communal practices that everyone else follows. This shows how whole communities can come to perpetuate harmful patriarchal traditions, even when it is males who reap almost all of their benefits.

In challenging patriarchal norms, it is important to avoid allocating fault, and instead focus on possible points of agency that can contribute to progress.

Transforming Gender

Even after the girl has been educated and empowered economically, we are losing out by not doing the foundational work of changing women's attitudes about womanhood. Foundations are funding programs, but not the attitude change that makes the programs effective.

—Dora C. K. Byamukama, Law and Advocacy for Women in Uganda

Boxing is just an entry point to have a wider conversation about gender and gender roles. We are changing the way communities' attitudes think about girlhood and femininity, and today we finally see these norms are changing.

—Cynthia Coredo, Boxgirls Kenya

It takes time, sometimes years, but attitudes about girls and gender do change.

—Purity Kagwiria, Akili Dada

Policies and programs that highlight, challenge, and ultimately try to change rigid gender norms and the inequities they cause are called "gender transformative," a term coined by noted gender authority Geeta Rao Gupta.

As Ellen Travers of Girls Not Brides observes, "We've realized that success as a partnership is not only about delaying the age of marriage to eighteen and beyond, but transforming the gender norms and stereotypes about the role of women and girls in families and communities worldwide. So now we are putting much more emphasis on promoting gender transformative approaches."

While many policies and programs address specific behaviors, gender transformative approaches seek to address underlying and sometimes unacknowledged belief systems and ingrained attitudes that drive and sustain harmful behaviors.

For many major international donor institutions, gender transformative approaches are becoming the new model for "best practice."

For example, CARE, International Planned Parenthood, UNFPA, and WHO have all launched "gender transformative" programs that challenge rigid gender norms and the inequities they cause, and found them effective.

USAID no longer funds new programs that lack a strong analysis of gender norms and inequalities, and PEPFAR—the President's Emergency Plan for AIDS Relief—has made transforming masculinity one of its top three priorities worldwide.

Invisible Guard Rails

We have found we have to build girls up by helping them break through these norms—then they are able to exercise their other rights.

—Satvika Chalasani, UNFPA

Rigid feminine norms not only help sustain specific problem behaviors like child marriage, sex and labor trafficking, or FGM, but over time, the constant enforcement of narrow womanhood ideals and the constant threat of punishment for transgressing them can have pervasive effects. Girls learn to do a lot of internalized self-censoring, and feminine norms can be like invisible guard rails that shape and narrow their every thought and behavior. This is one reason that doing gender transformative work with girls can also have such pervasive effects on girls that are inseparable from restoring and exercising their other human rights. As UNFPA's Chalasani explains, "When we challenge rigid feminine norms, girls begin recovering all the things they have lost: they start making eye contact, standing up straight, speaking up, and recovering their mobility by getting out of the house. "These may seem small things to Western eyes, but they enable girls to exercise all their other human rights. We have to build girls up, and then other rights come after."

"This includes reproductive rights—so girls stop believing women exist just for male pleasure. And economic rights—so girls stop believing sex is their only asset and appreciate that their labor has value. And education rights—so they stop thinking girls are innately inferior, but can learn just like boys." Her observations illustrate one more reason that gender transformative approaches can be so powerful.

Gender Nonconformity & LGBTQ

I have been attacked very many times because of who and what I am.

—Jay Mulucha, Fem Alliance (FEMA) Uganda

Enforcing rigid or traditional feminine norms also takes a toll on girls who are gay or transgender. In many cases, it is their gender nonconformity that brings gay or transgender people to the attention of their community.

Says Jay Mulucha, executive director of Fem Alliance (FEMA) Uganda, "Transgender and gender nonconforming people are the face of Uganda's gay community. Sexual orientation is not always publicly identifiable, but gender nonconformity is, so we are often attacked."

Much of the homophobia and transphobia in Africa is the residue of colonization, when the European colonial powers imported intolerant attitudes around gender and sexuality, and forced local cultures to adopt them. Prior to colonization, in many parts of the continent, ethnicities and communities had originally developed ways to peacefully integrate a variety of sexual orientations and gender identities.

But today, as Jay explains, "Lesbians and transmen are often forced into early marriage, or even raped to force them to conform to traditional ideas of femininity. This includes 'corrective rape' to 'correct' their gender or sexual orientation and enforce submissive femininity. And 'collective rape,' where society believes that the more people do it, the more the girl will begin to 'like' it."

It is important to point out that such attitudes and behaviors not only harm young women with different sexual orientations or gender identities, but also those who are not gay or transgender. Explains Jay, "This hate affects heteronormative women and girls too. In many parts of Uganda, the man is head of everything, the woman is supposed to be submissive and dependent. So when young women look for jobs, exercise power, or act independent, people say, 'She must want to become a man' or 'She must be a lesbian.' And they are ostracized and attacked.

In this way, prejudice towards LGBT people becomes yet another weapon used to police and regulate the behavior of all girls—always a threat to be leveled if they step outside traditional gender roles."

Making Change

The change on the ground happens when women are able to stand up and shake up some of these gender norms.

—Diana Mao, Nomi Network

While gender transformative work in LMICs today is well ahead of that in developed countries, most of it is devoted to men and masculinity. In deeply patriarchal cultures where girls cannot pick their own husband, expect to be his sole mate, or inherit property, transforming patriarchal notions of masculinity must be the top priority.

Indeed, because of groundbreaking work by leading groups like Promundo, Sonke Gender Justice, the White Ribbon Campaign, and EngenderHealth, a robust infrastructure of reports, data analysis, model curricula, NGO networks (like MenEngage), and regular convenings have grown up to support the work of transforming rigid masculine norms.

Yet, as this report has argued, transforming masculinity will not exhaust the structural forces oppressing young women, endangering their bodies, and deforming their lives.

While individual NGOs are doing innovative and groundbreaking work challenging rigid feminine norms, their achievements are all the more remarkable because an infrastructure that might support such progress is almost totally absent, or fragmentary at best.

For instance, when interviewing leading NGOs for this report, we asked each if they knew the others or were in contact. Almost inevitably they were not. None of them were aware of convenings, reports, model curricula, data collection, or NGO networks that might support building such connections among them, or the growth of a broader movement to transform feminine gender norms.

As LAW Uganda's Dora Byamukama puts it, "Funders and agencies are very focused on the men and boys, not the girls' beliefs and attitudes, but these are crucial too." As African Women's Development Fund's Abigail Burgesson declares: "We need to bring together the women's groups doing this work; we need a high-level network and engagement. We need an alliance. Because when we work as a movement, we get results."

A Final Note:
Westernized Discourse

By Wariri Muhungi of The MATCH International Women's Fund
and Musimbi Kanyoro of the Global Fund for Women

Gender is more than an individual story. The South African philosophy of "Ubuntu"—"I am because we are"—is central to addressing negative gender norms propagated by women against women. We want to highlight three concerns that frequently arise in our work with women and girls globally.

1. The dominance of Western feminist discourses limits women's liberation to individual freedoms.
2. Issues like body image are disconnected from issues like genital mutilation and child marriage.
3. Too little attention is paid to questions of power and privilege in how issues are framed and whose voice is heard.

We know that gender is a social construct, so to make transformative change we must focus on society and not just the individual. And today women from non-Western communities are providing new models that reflect this. Yet this is not always reflected in the Westernized discourses commonly used to frame gender. In addition, in discussing women's roles in propagating harmful gender norms, we must avoid focusing mainly on issues mostly familiar to non-Western women. Finally, we must recognize that there is no universal solution to rigid gender systems: like women's lives, feminine norms are expansive, layered, and complex.

For the safety and dignity of all women, trans, and gender nonconforming people, we must work together to ensure that our efforts do not unintentionally create "blind spots," where some experiences marginalized, and some voices silenced. We need not one conversation, but many—and ones that stem from context-specific approaches.

Recommendations

There are a number of recommendations that might promote greater focus on and support of the work around women and feminine norms. They might include the following:

For NGOs

1. Consider the impact that negative gender stereotypes and norms have on your programs, and adjust your goals and objectives accordingly.
2. Document lessons learned, best practices, challenges, and opportunities while dealing with gender norms within programs that seek to achieve gender equality objectives.
3. Seek the advice and consult with local, national, or regional feminist organizations or leaders, including women's funds, in the design, monitoring, and evaluation of programs.

For Donors & Funders

1. Support an initial convening that brings together key stakeholders from the NGO, policy, and funding communities to share ideas, build consensus, and plan future action on eliminating negative gender stereotypes and feminine norms. This could be reinforced and extended through regular yearly convenings at different locations in the Global South.
2. Support the development of a series of white paper reports focused on key issue areas to build out the knowledge and thought leadership in this area, as well as to stimulate dialogue and build agreement on a common understanding of problem scope.
3. Fund an online research clearinghouse of key articles and studies, documenting the impact of feminine norms and providing a common space for stakeholders to share resources, results, and ideas.
4. Fund an online global network of NGOs doing transformative work on feminine norms to facilitate collating information, developing best practice, and coordinating joint action.

Interviews with NGO Thought-Leaders

The following extended quotes are excerpted from interviews conducted with a select group of thought-leaders whose (NGOs) are doing unique work around gender norms work in the Global South.

An Interview with Hope Chigidu of JASS

The issue of femininity and feminine norms is not talked about and not named, but people need to name it. People get that feminine norms don't always support women. I was talking with a group of young women about femininity and the things that women do for men, like spending money you don't have, because they are told they must look good, or elongating the labia, because men want them to. And we were wondering why women do it. It's because we are told by older women from the time we are little that you have to get a man. In Zimbabwe, if you aren't married you are nothing. If you don't conform you are told, "No man will want to marry you," and then you feel like nothing.

And it's not just about you; it's about your mother and the shame that you will bring her. For instance, if you are not a virgin bride, the person who bears that shame is your mother. She is shamed before her husband, her family, and her community. She is the Bad Mother who didn't raise her children right. Her husband, her aunties, and her own mother will pester her: "What kind of mother are you?"

A girl can become unfeminine because of the work she does, or even because she speaks up. For instance, girls in Zimbabwe are told there are only two careers open to them: nursing and teaching. Aunties and mothers will tell them, "If you become an engineer, who will marry you? You will have a strong voice, and this will be difficult for your husband."

Part of this is enforcing femininity. Especially around men, girls are told, "If a man speaks twice you speak once" and "Keep water in your mouth, so when your husband speaks, you remain silent."

Older women are constantly telling young girls how to be feminine and become a woman, how to dress, what to eat, what to cook, what their education should be, and what to say. There are things they can't say as a woman. For instance, if you say something sexual around men, you are not seen as a woman. Women will say, "How can a woman use this kind of language?" Most of the condemnation comes from women. So women are constantly monitoring and policing the behavior and activities of the girls.

It's the auntie—the husband's sister—who assumes the role of enforcing patriarchy in the wife's family and making its young girls into women. The power of aunties in enforcing femininity is much stronger than grandmothers. We have a saying: grannies are soft, but aunties are harsh. Because the aunt stands in for the father; she is the representative of patriarchy. If the girl does something wrong in the marriage, the person they go to is the aunt. And this is enforced by policies and national frameworks so it becomes institutionalized and normalized.

It's about changing women, changing aunties, changing grandmothers—that's where real change will come from. It's woman-to-woman: this is where the conversation must start.

An Interview with Purity Kagwiria of Akili Dada

Girls go to school and get an education so they can have choices; however they are constantly asked, "Who are these girls going to marry?" They hear from parents and guardians, community members that they can only have three or four staple homemaking roles. We work to challenge these gendered societal and familial biases.

In challenging these gendered biases, we have girls identify a challenge in their community, plan and execute community-enablement projects. In the past, some projects were very gendered: cleaning hospitals or taking care of old people. We asked our girls, "Why is this the work of women?"; is this the only challenge in your community? Within a very short time, the girls started building bridges, libraries and planting trees. This gender deconstruction is very powerful because girls start questioning what women can or cannot do. We work with them over several years to help them think through preconceived attitudes about womanhood and femininity. These girls end up designing and implementing really exceptional projects that break social-cultural gender norms.

In changing attitudes, it's not just the attitudes of men that need to change; other gatekeepers such as older women, teachers, and parents who do not know any better are consistently telling girls what their value is through statements like "You're not good enough" or "You're only good for a man as his wife." So girls do sometimes grow up with a myopic view of their potential. When girls are empowered to know their rights, even become teachers to these elders, changing their perceptions of girls. It takes time, sometimes years, but there is strong evidence that attitudes towards girls and gender do change.

On female genital mutilation, we realized that when we go into communities, there is often resistance from older men and women who act as custodians of the practice defending it as traditional. We engage both men and women in continuous conversations to counter this norm.

My grandmother, who taught me that I could do or be anything, raised me. It wasn't until I was in college that I saw lots of gender-based discrimination that I realized how valuable and important this lesson was—to grow up valuing myself and wanting more out of life. I could stand the tests and pressures on many accounts because I didn't see gender as a barrier to what I could be or do. More girls need that.

An Interview with Cynthia Coredo of Boxgirls Kenya

Our founder started out coaching boys, and two girls asked him, "We wish we could box like the boys," and he answered, "You can . . . you can even be better than the boys." That was the origin of Boxgirls.

Sometimes we have had really strong pushback from the families. Forty to 50 percent of the girls are from single-parent families. Mothers (and some of the fathers, too) will tell our girls, "You must not learn how to box, that is not for girls," or "If you learn to box, you will lose your womanhood and be un-feminine, and who will want you?" They ask, "You are being unwomanly, so who will you be able to marry, now that you've learned to box?"

The beliefs and actions of mothers and aunts are so important. Mothers and aunts have these attitudes that to be a young woman, you must stay in the home, do cooking, do chores, take care of the younger children.

So we had to come up with a strategy with how to change the parents' attitudes. Now an important part of our Parent Orientation is to engage them and the women of this community. We tell them they can share the work with girls and boys, and help free up girls. We change parents' attitudes that girls should have the potential to be who they want to be, that girls should not be confined to just doing chores, that girls should be able to play and enjoy their childhoods. Because girls can become leaders and transform themselves and their communities.

Boxing is just an entry point to have a wider conversation about gender, gender roles, and harmful gender stereotypes about how girls and boys are brought up. So our curriculum helps girls understand gender norms and how they interact with our cultural traditions about what a woman can be or do, and what is expected of them. We also try to puncture the terrible silence around the abuse of girls. And we also teach boys nine to twelve years old about gender and gender roles.

Boxgirls is challenging how communities think about womanhood and attitudes about girlhood and femininity. Today we finally see these norms about girls and womanhood changing. Today we finally see mothers and even fathers coming in and supporting their girls' boxing. And now, some girls who have to care for siblings bringing them along, so we have younger girls seeing the boxing and wanting to get involved—as we begin engaging the next generation.

An Interview with Gayatri Buragohain of Feminist Approach to Technology (FAT)

This is the root of the problem: in India education and careers for girls are not a priority—even if the family can afford it—because of feminine gender norms that dictate that the ultimate goal of all girls is only marriage, cooking, cleaning, and being obedient wives and daughters-in-law, ones who do not ask questions, talk back, raise their eyes, or make their own decisions.

This is not imposed only by men, but also by women of all ages. They feel a communal duty to uphold traditional female practices and ensure every girl obeys these norms. Men's interference in this role of women within a family often means that the women responsible are not doing a good job. And because women are responsible for disciplining these girls, they are often the most dominating and controlling, constantly pounding these norms into girls: be a good girl, be a good woman. When a woman does not perform her duties as a trainer for younger women, she often has to face the repercussions.

These norms are propagated by women as much as by men that the girls interact with. The family's oldest woman expects her older daughters to make sure their younger siblings are trained to be obedient, submissive, and respectful. Girls get it on every side: parents, sisters, grandmothers, neighbors, even teachers. And because these villages or urban communities are very close-knit societies, these girls have no escape from being watched, monitored, and corrected all the time.

If they do anything outside the lines, the neighbors start pushing back. And if a girl does not submit to these norms, her family is outcast. It can be worse if they are newly married. At one time, India had a very high rate of beating and killings of newly married girls by the in-laws, quite often the mother-in-law or sister-in-law.

Our domestic violence law takes this into account and includes women-to-women violence in families within its purview.

The primary expectation that women are supposed to be child-bearers and caretakers is the main reason women are unable to break out of their subservience. And much of this takes place between women. We feel that this is also the root cause of women's inability to grow in STEM fields.

Traditionally, a woman's identity has always been based entirely on the men in her life and how they treat her: mainly her husband and her son. We have a saying in Hindi that literally translates to: Women are the biggest enemy of women.

An Interview with Dora C. K. Byamukama of Law & Advocacy for Women in Uganda

Gendered attitudes about girls and womanhood are crucial, but funders and agencies are very focused on men and boys, and not on the beliefs and attitudes about girls. Yet it's these entrenched gender norms that determine what girls can and cannot do, including mobility—because it's not considered appropriate for girls to go out alone—or working, because certain jobs like construction are considered unwomanly and only for men.

This is especially true in the adolescent years, which are formative for a girl becoming what she wants to be. But girls have little agency, and a girl who wants to go into engineering, math, or politics still faces enormous pushback. So we lose out because we are not doing the foundational work of changing women's attitudes about womanhood so these girls can reach their full potential.

Even when a girl has been educated and empowered economically, she must still be more concerned with how the community will perceive her as a woman than with her own life. She will have to deal with great pressure to conform from parents, family, and peers. And much of this oppression happens woman-to-woman.

For instance, to combat FGM we use what we call the Grandmother Approach. We help the grandmothers talk to their grandchildren about the practice, how the cultural approach to womanhood has changed, and how FGM is no longer necessary. Through this kind of woman-to-woman interaction, the mothers and their daughters no longer feel they are being left out of age-old secrets or rites of passage. The grandmothers—who are the main female elders in this process—reframe the rite of passage to change attitudes around womanhood and feminine norms.

In other areas, even though I've been doing this work for twenty years, I don't think there's been a lot of change for girls. For instance, if I walk by a construction site today, I still won't see any women. Even though there are plenty of them nearby, and they really need good-paying jobs to supplement their income, attitudes about womanhood and what is appropriate and feminine still hold them back. And this is true in other areas like politics, marriage, and education. Women are held back in all of these because of what is expected of them as women—not only the men, but what the women around them think.

This is why funders just providing jobs and funding is not enough. They are funding programs, but not the attitude change that would make the programs effective. We have passed the laws, but the laws won't work unless we change the attitudes of women and grandmothers, and the beliefs of young girls. We want to give girls all these rights, but to take advantage of them we must first empower them as women. This is work that we are doing, that doesn't involve men, but that shows the power of women-to-women approaches.

An Interview with Abigail Burgesson of African Women's Development Fund

Norms are critical: it all comes down to beliefs and practices. We need to make this a priority, so I am very glad that this issue of norms is finally coming forward.

People need to realize that it is often women who perpetuate these harmful traditions and practices, as well as men. I don't blame them. It's patriarchy that put them in place. But now it is women who impose and maintain them. They are the ones who perpetuate child marriage; they are the ones who perpetuate genital cutting. They believe they inherited these traditions about femininity, and so this is what they must do to the next generation.

These women think if things improve for the next generation of girls, that will be taking something away from them: They think, "This was here before our time and it's still the way things must be done today." So we will never change these things as long as we assume women are just acted upon, and not agents of this system themselves.

Because this is how patriarchy operates in our part of the world. When it comes to culture and traditional norms, you have women who have been made to believe in these systems of power and their position within them. So they feel they have to enforce these practices. Also in many cases, oppressive norms and traditional practices that oppress women are supported by laws and public policies which enable and enforce legalized discrimination against girls.

Today, a woman who does things that don't fit with what is expected of a "good woman"—who is not submissive, who wants her rights to be recognized, who wants to let her daughter get educated and choose who she can marry—she is still going to get a lot of pushback.

This is not about one tribe or one village: it is about all women in Ghana, about womanhood, and a woman's human rights. It even cuts across income and education categories, and plays out at the highest level among the educated elites. They should be our leaders, but we are not getting people at the highest levels who understand women's human rights. So as much as we think we are gaining ground, there are still very entrenched beliefs and practices and norms, and we need a strong movement to change this.

We need to bring together the women's groups doing this work; we need a high-level network and engagement. We need an alliance. Because when we work as a movement, we get results.

An Afterword

Four Issues Not Covered

In Part II I've tried to detail the impact of gender norms on specific issues areas, where the research base is broad and longstanding, with specific attention to basic health, intimate relationships, and education. But there are many areas where less research has been conducted than is clearly needed, but studies show that gender norms are both important and overlooked.

This afterword provides a brief overview of several areas that I did not address specifically in the chapters of this book. I hope my closing words here will encourage readers to explore the impact of gender norms more broadly, going forward. These areas include economic security, climate justice, juvenile justice, and teen suicide.

Economic Security

Femininity shapes and narrows the economic horizons of young women in two important ways: First, girls' economic actions are frequently based on their own internal beliefs and attitudes. Second, girls' economic horizons are shaped externally, through the attitudes of parents, teachers, and other gatekeepers, as well as those of their classmates and age peers (and eventually employers and coworkers).

We teach girls traditional feminine norms that are directly in conflict with their own economic empowerment. To begin with, many girls learn that society judges them on appearance and desirability. This is the basis of their social worth. By some estimates, up to 80 percent of the compliments girls will hear by the time they're out of their teens will turn on their appearance.

As the proud parent of a little girl, I was shocked by how everyone from close family members to complete strangers would compliment DJ on being a "pretty little princess." In fact, I can't ever recall anyone complimenting her on anything *else*.

To counter this, whenever someone told DJ how pretty she was, Gina or I would reflexively add, "She IS pretty . . . AND smart AND strong AND brave." By age ten, DJ started responding to this protective parent mode with exaggerated eye-rolls and *"Really* Mom?", so we had to rein that in.

A man who focuses on his career and makes his profession his life's work and achieves, is considered successful, particularly if he makes it to the top ranks. A woman who does likewise is more apt to be considered incomplete—a social failure—because she has not prioritized marriage and motherhood. She may face repeated pressure from family to marry, give up her work, marry, and "settle down." (This can be true even in middle- and high-income families.)

Feminine norms emphasize that importance of being "nice"—avoiding conflict, hiding strong negative emotions, and prioritizing the caretaking of others and other's feelings. These are not skills that a young woman would need to land an important job or compete head-to-head with others to build a career.

Gender bias among adults tends to push young women away from fast-growing, high-paying jobs in technology, and toward jobs in the service sector, which generally have lower pay and fewer professional opportunities.

Even young women who do make it into more traditionally masculine fields still find gender's *invisible guardrails* pushing them toward lower-paying areas. For instance, women who get into medicine are much more likely to become pediatricians, gynecologists, or veterinarians than (for example) cardio-thoracic surgeons or neurologists. Even in fields traditionally dominated by women, such as nursing, male nurses are typically paid more for the same work and promoted at a higher rate.

Across a host of important professions: corporate management, coding, sales, stockbroking, construction—young women will likely encounter towel-snapping, jock culture that denigrates social skills and places a premium on aggression and toughness.

A woman who *is* aggressive and tough will face a no-win situation. Weakness and vulnerability will be chalked up to her being female. If she is strong, determined, and aggressive, she is likely to be perceived as mannish, unfeminine, cold, and unfriendly. As a culture, we still have tremendous ambivalence, even anxiety, about women in authority wielding power. While many of us, as parents, strive to help our daughters believe that they can be whatever they want, the truth is that this does not yet really include being a strong, aggressive leader.

Climate Justice & Environmental Racism

It may seem strange to think about gender norms as part of climate change and environmental issues, but robust scholarship has slowly grown up around just such a view. As the title of one influential paper by researcher Geraldine Terry put it: "No climate justice without gender justice."

The main thrust of such studies is threefold: because of gender norms, men and women use their environment differently, react to environmental and conservation efforts differently, and tend to suffer differently from climate change. A fourth charge is that even though women are disproportionately affected, and often lead many successful efforts in this area, women are often absent from climate-change discourse and climate policy—both of which tend to still be dominated by men. Yet according to one recent study, in the United States, women comprise 90 percent of the membership of environmental groups. In the Global South, women are uniquely dependent on climate-related issues regarding soil, air, and water, and are overlooked, although their input is key to sustainable, eco-friendly initiatives.

For example, low-income women make up nearly three-quarters (80 percent) of Africa's agricultural sector. But environmental policies in LMICs (and the US) continue to be mostly gender-blind. In addition, some LMIC advocates complain that policies too often promote bold, large-scale, highly technological approaches to improvement that are top-down, rather than smaller, simpler, bottom-up changes tied directly to the realities of women on the ground in affected communities.

As always with highly complex issues, it pays to use an intersectional approach that integrates race and class as well.

The dumping of toxic chemicals, the fouling of air by factory pollution, and the slow poisoning of residents of Flint, Michigan by public water all disproportionately affect low-income communities of color. Reports from the EPA show that "environmental racism" is real, even if it's often overlooked in the national dialogue over the uneven impact of climate change.

It was common knowledge to anyone following Hurricane Katrina that the majority of the New Orleans residents who could not move out of its path of destruction were African American. What news stories didn't cover, and what went largely ignored in the national dialogue, was that many were young women with dependent children who were most likely to inhabit low-income housing and also least likely to be able to move freely or quickly. This parallels Crenshaw's (1989) observation about Black women being erased from the national dialogue on police violence.

Men in developed countries have typically been more likely to view the environment and nature as something to be dominated and exploited for mankind's use. They have been more resistant to environmental efforts. A recent article in *The Guardian* asks, "why do men recycle less than women?," and suggests that recycling requires one to be orderly, cleanly, and to care, which are perceived as highly feminized traits (Somerville 2018, n.p.). In fact, eco-friendliness is generally perceived as highly feminine, "do-good" behavior by both men and women.

In the United States, men tend to feel less guilty about environmentally destructive behavior, care less about animal rights, and eat more red meat (in itself tied to enormous waste of ecological resources). Disdain for social norms of caring about the environment, and indifference to crises like global warming, are sometimes used to demonstrate masculinity. Some truckers engage in "rolling coal"—modifying their diesel engines to maximize exhaust fumes and spew huge clouds of dark, black soot. This conspicuous pollution is used to show manly indifference to ecological concerns, while serving as a form of aggressive public protest against what has been called the "green-feminine stereotype."

As a recent article in *Scientific American* noted ("Men Resist Green Behavior as Unmanly"), women tend to litter less, recycle more, and live in ways that leave a smaller carbon footprint (Brough and Wilkie 2017). In LMICs, women tend to show more concern about land and water use, and are more conservative with how they use them. In addition, women—who are usually responsible for collecting families' water and fuel and doing much of the farming—are likely to use greater care with the resources of their immediate environment, and to be receptive to adopting new, eco-friendly and sustainable methods. In general, as MenEngage notes in its 2016 discussion paper, "Men, Masculitinties & Climate Change" quoting from educator and activitst Maria Alejandra Rodriguez Acha: "Addressing the root causes of the climate crisis also requires tackling social inequalities . . . [including] gender inequalities" (MenEngage Alliance 2016, 5). Sums up MenEngage succinctly, "patriarchy is harmful to our climate" (5).

Juvenile Justice

The twin forces of race and gender drive juvenile justice.

> —Kim Taylor-Thompson, "Girl Talk-Examining
> Racial & Gender Lines in Juvenile Justice"

Juvenile justice is a gender-specific system . . . it reflects and operates on assumptions about gender, and reflects masculine [and feminine] norms.

> —Nancy Dowd, "Boys, Masculinities, & Juvenile Justice"

As with other large social institutions like healthcare, education, and religion, juvenile justice is a gendered and gendering system—expecting, rewarding, and punishing specific kinds of masculinity in boys and femininity in girls. Moreover, it is frequently intolerant of or ill-equipped to deal with gender nonconformity. This can be true not only of the young people in detention, but also with those who staff such places, and everyone from detention and probation officers to therapists, court advocates, and teachers.

In rethinking the role of gender and particularly boys, one could hardly do better than Nancy Dowd's 2008 study, "Boys, Masculinity, and Juvenile Justice," excerpted here at length:

> We have constructed juvenile justice as a gender-specific system to manage, control and respond to boys. It reflects and operates upon assumptions about masculinities, and reflects masculinities' norms. Yet we rarely think about or discuss this system as a gendered system. Rather, we simply assume it. (117)

> We have generally not focused on gender at all, rendering gender invisible.
>   When we do focus on gender, we focus on girls and exclude boys . . . [even though] it is a system that presumptively is about boys. [. . .] If we do look at it from a masculinity perspective, what do we see? The harsh punishment characteristic of the current system reflects the view of boys as dangerous and inherently violent. Boys of color are

particularly dangerous, as are gay boys and lower class boys. So the hierarchy of masculinities is evident in those who come into the system and how they are treated.

The strong shift to more punitive outcomes, the shift to treating boys as if they were adult men, the view of boys as super-offenders particularly identified by race as hyper-masculine all reflect assumed masculinities and stereotypes of boys that fly in the face of data to the contrary. The strength of the cultural norm of masculinity overcomes empirical data. Moreover, the justification of harsh punishment as necessary in order to control boys silently sanctions the worst offenses within confinement, most notably prison rape, leaving them unchallenged and permitted as a part of punishment.

What masculinities analysis most strongly exposes is how we have constructed the juvenile justice system to essentialize and biologize boys' presence and propensity, denying that masculinities are socially constructed. (131–32)

The punishment or rehabilitation of boys, moreover, is not with the goal of making them better or different men with a different sense of masculinity. Rather, the system reinforces traditional notions of masculinity rather than challenging them, at the very time when those traditional notions are the focus of adolescent masculinities and contribute to the actions of boys. (133)

Gender norms help create very different patterns for boys and girls in many areas of juvenile justice. Boys are more likely to be sentenced for violent crimes, girls for status offenses concerned with curfew, truancy, running away, and especially sexual behaviors such as prostitution. Many girls in Juvenile Justice (JJ) systems have been sexually abused at home, and when they run away from it, they are punished for it with jail time. Frequently, the systems designed to respond to girls' offenses also are places where they are likely to be reabused. Some studies have found that as many as one-third of girls have been sexually abused as children, compared with less than 10 percent of boys. Sexual abuse is a strong predictor of recidivism, with girls who are sexually abused up to five times more likely to end up back in JJ systems.

When girls are sentenced for status offences, they are likely to be treated much more harshly than males, presumably because we expect a certain amount of "boys will be boys" acting out from males, but submissiveness in girls. Once out of the system, girls are more likely to have their parole violated and be returned to detention for minor technical violations that might be overlooked with boys.

Young male offenders are more likely to be viewed through a lens of predation, and given longer sentences; girls are more likely to be seen through a lens of victimhood, and get lighter sentences. Low-income African American boys in particular are likely to perceived as possible predators and sentenced accordingly. Exacerbating this effect, as noted earlier, young Black and Latino men are likely to be perceived by adults as about four-and-a-half years older than they actually are. Overall, young Black women remain dramatically overrepresented in JJ systems nationwide.

Many young people in JJ systems have been traumatized, and here differences based on gender norms emerge as well. Young women are more likely to have been sexually traumatized—and to be sexually abused (or become pregnant) while in JJ systems. Young men are more likely to have suffered violence-related trauma— such as being assaulted, or seeing someone die. While both sexes react to trauma with similar emotional distress, young women are more likely to report being depressed, to self-mutilate, and to react with guilt (perhaps thinking they somehow contributed to the victimization).

Young men are more likely to react to trauma with anger and shame—the latter possibly because being traumatized means being emotionally vulnerable, and vulnerability is unmanly (and in some harsh environments, even unsafe). As several JJ therapists have noted, boys tend to avoid therapy, avoid discussing trauma, and refuse to show or share feelings. This makes healing youthful offenders who are dealing with profound trauma doubly difficult.

Girls who do find themselves in JJ systems often find programs designed and administered for boys, where all the outcome data on what is most effective is based on data from boys. One study of hundreds of JJ programs around the United States found less than 2 percent were designed for girls. Staff are often not trained in the special needs of girls, on girls' often different pathways into detention, or their differing experiences in it.

Some more progressive JJ departments may do a good job of addressing gender in the context of nonconforming and LGBTQ youth regarding everything from body searches and pronouns to bathroom use and clothing standards. However, few seem to have developed any policies or programs that might help detention and probation officers as well as in-house therapists or educators address the impacts of rigid gender norms on the *other* 90 percent of youth, or to become more aware of their *own* gender biases.

Teen Suicide & Gender

Through support provided by the B. W. Bastian Foundation, TrueChild was asked to research the link between teen suicides, masculinity, and homophobic bullying in Salt Lake City. Utah has among the United States' highest rates of teen suicide. While many studies have focused on one of these issues, we could find few that had explored their intersection. So with the help from the Human Rights Education Center of Utah (HREC) and the Utah Pride Center, we conducted focus groups and interviews with gender nonconforming students who had been bullied.

Similarly, our students felt that their being harassed was closely linked to their gender presentation. They experienced gender-based bullying less as a series of discrete acts, and more like a ruthless, pervasive atmosphere of gender policing that everyone knows, but no one names. Explained one participant, "Bullying is bad and hurtful—but the widespread acceptance and tolerance of [gender] bullying makes people desperate and hopeless." Said another, "Bullying is very often thought about as something very visible, very tangible . . . you can deal with it, you can see it. In my experience, it's been an atmosphere of silence and erasure . . . it enables a lot of violence which might not be physical."

Surprisingly, a large part of the hopelessness and sometimes suicidal depression they reported came not from bullying itself, but from being misunderstood and erased by adult authority figures whom they turned to for help and support. As GLSEN's 2012 report "Playgrounds and Prejudice" noted, 13 percent of teachers have heard other teachers make homophobic remarks about students, and about three times that many overheard teachers make biased remarks specifically about gender nonconforming youth (34 percent for girls and 39 percent for boys, respectively). (See GLSEN 2012.)

Adults, the Utah students noted, just wanted to check a box. One student complained succinctly, "To them, everything is gay." This amplified their sense of being alone and unwanted, and essentially revictimized them. For our students, gender nonconformity was not the visible "symptom" of their being gay or transgender, but a primary basis for their identity.

In effect, the young people whom antibullying advocates are trying to help have simply outrun the paradigm being used to understand their problems.

Participants felt that educators, parents, and advocacy organizations are completely out of touch with how to talk with or help them. It was this impossibility of being seen or understood by anyone—even those in charge—combined with a pervasive, unrelenting atmosphere of gender hostility that wore them down over time, and made them desperate, and eventually, suicidal. It was this, and not any specific acts of bullying, that these students identified as the source of teen suicides in their community.

Explained one boy, "Protections for physical and other forms of abuse really only exist if the person who is supposed to protect you can understand your identity. In high school, I was bullied a lot for being perceived as feminine. I think the administrators at my school didn't necessarily see a problem with that. . . . 'Oh that will make him a man now.' So if they don't understand your identity, they can't help you."

Added another participant: "There is no training for teachers or coaches or counselors or administrators on how to even begin to deal with [differences in gender identity or sexual orientation], so I don't feel welcome in any of these spaces at school."

Summed up one student poignantly: "Youth that I know in our community who have committed suicide . . . these are not kids who were tossed down a flight of stairs. Certainly those things happen, but more often than not, these are kids who are very slowly picked apart by things like behind-the-back gossip, and like mass text messages to the entire high school. Things like that really get [to] people."

If we're going to advocate for these young people, if we're going to help them, we're going have to start by understanding them. That may mean moving out of our comfort zones, beyond the simple identity boxes by which many of us have navigated our lives (and for which some of us have paid fearsome prices), to meet them where they are. And they are living in a new world defined, mostly, by gender.

References & Selected Reading

Brough, A. R., and Wilkie, J. E. B. 2017. "Men Resist Green Behavior as Unmanly: A Surprising Reason for Resistance to Environmental Goods and Habits," *Scientific American*, December 26. https://www.scientificamerican.com/article/men-resist-green-behavior-as-unmanly/.

Crenshaw, K. 1989. "Demarginalizing the Intersection of Race and Sex: A Black Feminist Critique of Antidiscrimination Doctrine, Feminist Theory, and Antiracist Politics," *University of Chicago Legal Forum* (1): 139–67.

Dowd, N. 2008. "Boys, Masculinites, and Juvenile Justice," *Journal of Korean Law* 8: 115–34.

GLSEN 2012. *Playgrounds and Prejudice: Elementary School Climate in the United States* (A Survey of Teachers and Students)," conducted on behalf of GLSEN (the Gay, Lesbian, & Straight Education Network). https://www.glsen.org/sites/default/files/Playgrounds%20%26%20Prejudice.pdf.

MenEngage Alliance. 2016. "Men, Masculinites, and Climate Change: A Discussion Paper." Washington, DC: MenEngage Global Alliance. http://menengage.org/wp-content/uploads/2016/04/Men-Masculinities-and-Climate-Change-FINAL.pdf.

Somerville, M. 2018. "A Vexing Question: Why Do Men Recycle Less than Women?" *The Guardian*, October 5. https://www.theguardian.com/environment/2018/oct/05/real-men-dont-recycle-how-sexist-stereotypes-are-killing-the-planet.

Index

LGBTQ community (lesbians, gays, bisexuals, transgenders, questioning/queer): acronym history, 28–29; binary gender affecting others besides, xii; gender lens exclusion of, 17–18; in Global South, 49–50; health seeking behavior among, 101–3; Latinas, 146; overview of issues affecting, xiv–xv; percentages, 28; pushouts and, 86–87; STEM participation, 88, *89*; US spending on, 28
LGBTQQI+?, evolution of term, 28–29
LGBT violence, 34, 165
LMICs. *See* lower-middle-income countries
Lone Nut theory, 116–17
Love, Sex Power: Considering Women's Realities in HIV Prevention (Amaro), 3
lower-middle-income countries (LMICs), 44, 47, 175–76; environmental racism and, 189, 190; gender transformative approaches in, 177–79

Maasai mothers, 175
machismo, 145
machista, 145
Madonna, 32
Mahler, Matthew, 117–18, 119
Malcolm X, 155
male gaze, internalizing, 61
male-on-male violence, 164
Male Role Norms Scale (MRNS), 5, 6
males: health and lifecycle of, 95–97; sexual agency, social capital of, 63
malichismo, 145–46
La Malinche, 145–46
Man with No Name, 32
marianisimo, 145–46, 148, 149
"Marlboro Man" ads, 100
masculinity (masculine norms): arts and, 78–79; characteristics of, 31–32; cultural "differences" between femininity and, 21; "doing" middle-class White, 156–57; frontier codes of, 157; funding for research on, 12–13;

gay men and, 66–67; Google Scholar on low outcomes and, 6; hegemonic, 31; international NGOs focus on violence and, 49; juvenile justice and, 190–92; key outcomes of believing in, 6; men's lifecycle and, 95–97; MSM and, 66–67; police violence and, 119–21; sexual desire and, 60; substance abuse and, 100–101; toughness and, 83; toxic, 110; virility and, 64. *See also* Black boys, masculinity and
Masculinity Ideology, 5, 10
MATCH Fund, 173, 180
maternal health, IPV and, 112
math: Japan vs. US student success in, 76; Pre-Post Measures, FaST and, *89*
The Matthew Shepard Act, 122
media: daily hours spent with, 162; gender stereotypes in, 164
medical interventions, 26; transpeople not choosing, 68
Men As Peacemakers, 12–13, 110, 149
Men Can Stop Rape, 12–13, 110, 149
Mendoza, Leticia, 65–66
MenEngage network, 53
men who have sex with men (MSM), 66–67
meritocracies, 77
Meyer, E. J., 116
microaggressions, 102
military, 22
Morris, Monique, 84, 150
Motorola Solutions Foundation, 75, 88
MRNS. *See* Male Role Norms Scale
MSM. *See* men who have sex with men
Mulucha, Jay, 178, 179
murders, of trans-youth, 33–34
Murphy, Ann, 82–83
musical instruments, gendering of, 79
"Musicality, Essentialism, and the Closet in Queering the Pitch" (Brett), 79

National Alliance for Partnerships in Equity (NAPE), 88

About the Author

Riki Wilchins is an author, activist and gender theorist. Riki currently serves as Executive Director of TrueChild, a network of experts and researchers that helps funders, nonprofits and policymakers challenge rigid gender norms by connecting race, class and gender. Riki has been a leading advocate for gender rights and gender justice for over two decades, one of the founders of modern transgender political activism in the 1990s, and one of its first theorists and chroniclers. In 1995, Riki launched The Transexual [sic] Menace, the first national transgender street action group with chapters in forty-one cities. The following year she launched Gender-PAC, the first national political advocacy group devoted to the right to one's gender identity and expression. Riki was an early supporter in the launch of the intersex rights movement, as well as the movement for alternative sexualities. She is the author of five books on gender theory and politics: *Read My Lips: Sexual Subversion & the End of Gender*; *Queer Theory/Gender Theory: An Instant Primer*; *Burn the Binary! Selected Writings on the Politics of Trans, Genderqueer and Nonbinary*; *Trans/Gressive: How Transgender Activists Took on Gay Rights, Feminism, the Media and Congress . . . and Won!*; *Voices from Beyond the Sexual Binary* (with editors Claire Howell and Joan Nestle); and this volume. Riki's writing and research on gender norms have been published in popular periodicals like The Village Voice and Social Text, as well as peer reviewed publications like the *Journal of Homosexuality* and the *Journal of Research on Adolescence*, as well as dozens of anthologies. Riki has overseen training on gender norms for public agencies like the White House, the Centers for Disease Control, HHS Office of Adolescent Health, and HHS Office on Women's Health, and for philanthropic networks like the Association of Black Foundation Executives, Hispanics in Philanthropy, and Women's Funding Network. *The New York Times* has profiled Riki's work; in 2001 *Time* magazine selected them as one of "100 Civic Innovators for the 21st Century." Riki is currently working on a transgender murder mystery titled, "The Sound of Angels Falling."